Henry Cadman

Harry Druidale, Fisherman from Manxland to England

Henry Cadman

Harry Druidale, Fisherman from Manxland to England

ISBN/EAN: 9783337124021

Printed in Europe, USA, Canada, Australia, Japan

Cover: Foto ©ninafisch / pixelio.de

More available books at **www.hansebooks.com**

HARRY DRUIDALE

FISHERMAN

FROM

MANXLAND TO ENGLAND

BY

HENRY ÇADMAN

LATE PRESIDENT OF THE YORKSHIRE ANGLERS' ASSOCIATION, ETC.

WITH ILLUSTRATIONS

London
MACMILLAN AND CO., Limited
NEW YORK: THE MACMILLAN COMPANY
1898

All rights reserved

PREFACE

THE year in which the greater part of this book has been written forms an epoch in the annals of the United Kingdom of Great Britain and Ireland, the Diamond Jubilee of Her Most Gracious Majesty Queen Victoria.

Many of the members of Her Majesty's family have given their royal countenance to the sports of the people, and to none more than to the gentle craft. Her Majesty's granddaughter, Her Royal Highness the Duchess of Fife, has especially distinguished herself amongst the mighty salmon, no less than six fish having fallen to her rod in one day, I believe, on more than one occasion. It is gratifying to a humble angler to feel that the Royal Family sympathise so much with the sport so dear to him as to identify themselves with it.

The author has endeavoured to portray the sport of angling for the last twenty years, up to and including the year of the Diamond Jubilee, from the point of view of the angler whose sport has been in well-fished waters, not in the highly-preserved waters only open to the wealthy few; and this the indulgent reader must bear in mind, should he be inclined to be a little sarcastic on the sport recorded. The record, so far as it goes, is a faithful one, and shows what sport may be obtained by an angler of moderate ability at the date of the Diamond Jubilee in well-fished club waters. The comparative weight of trout captured in several well-known rivers should interest the north country angler.

The author has to a great extent trodden on ground which has not had a Thomas Todd Stoddart or Francis Francis to illustrate it. He hopes that the juvenile angler or would-be angler may derive some benefit from the chapters on the various modes of fishing for trout, which are inserted somewhat late in the book in order that the youthful reader may have his interest aroused by such light reading as the Druidale Fishing Excursion and Bivouac.

The author also hopes that anglers who contemplate becoming members of the Kilnsey Angling Club, or the Yorkshire Anglers' Association, may derive benefit from his experiences.

The illustrations are from photographs taken by Charles Herbert Cadman, an amateur photographer.

HARRY DRUIDALE.

HARROGATE, *November* 1897.

CONTENTS

CHAPTER I

FISHING

The contemplative man's recreation—The birds, their solicitude for their young—The chaffinch's nest—Izaak Walton—Two classes of anglers—Competition—Lures for trout—The dry fly—Christopher North, Stoddart, Henderson—The Shepherd and North—Some distinguished anglers—Fishing a fraud—Weeding out large trout—Sitting by the river . . . . . Pages 1-10

CHAPTER II

HOW DRUIDALE BECAME A FISHERMAN

Mona's streams—First trout—Tickling—Loobing—Worm-fishing—Mining pollution of Neb—The Neb as it was—Manx witches—Slieu Whallin—Tynwald Hill—Rhenass—Good baskets—Anglers' yarns—The seclusion of Mona's glens—Lead-water and trout's tails.
Pages 11-19

CHAPTER III

THE WHARFE, KILNSEY

Origin of club—Mr. J. R. Tennant—Journey to Kilnsey—Rylstone—Cracoe—Threshfield—Netherside Hall—Arrival at Kilnsey—Antiquity of Kilnsey—The club-room—Mr. Thompson—Mr. Gleadhall—Worm-fishing looked down upon—My first trout at Kilnsey—The farm-house—Nutting . . . . . Pages 20-26

CHAPTER IV

THE DRUIDALE FISHING EXCURSION AND BIVOUAC

A stable at Ouchan—Camping out—The donkey—Start for Druidale—The Sulby river—Fishing near Injabreck—A halt for lunch—Fine trout—The donkey and cart up the hill—Snaefell—Beinn-y-Phott—Arrival—The tent pitched—Dinner—A night alarm—Breakfast—The carrion-crows' nest—Mr. Brooke—Fishing—The hawk's nest—Beauty of Druidale—Charlie's fine trout—Execution of young crows—Cooking the dinner—A wonderful pudding—Donkey's milk—Visitors to the camp—Fly and worm fishing—Midges—Tobacco—A glut of trout—Distinguished visitors—Last dinner in camp—Home . . . . . Pages 27-44

CHAPTER V

THE MAID OF HADDON

The Peacock, Rowsley—The Wye—Derwent—Rowsley meadows—The green drake—Haddon Hall—The guide—Isaak Walton's milkmaid—The maiden's sarcasm—Haddon revisited—The maid's niece—Beauty of the Wye—The sparrow-hawk . . Pages 45-51

CHAPTER VI

WALES—CLWYD, ELWY, LLUGWY

Rhyl—Rhuddlan Castle—Clwyd—Elwy—Fair fishing—Bettws-y-Coed—Llugwy—Swallow Falls—Capel Curig—Lakes—Bull—Llanberis—Caernarvon—Clwyd again . . . Pages 52-56

CHAPTER VII

THE VALE OF EDEN

Beauty of scenery—Pennine range—Source of Eden—Abundance of trout fishing—Penrith Angling Association—Appleby—Temple Sowerby—Kirkby Thore—The man in possession . . . Pages 57-66

CHAPTER VIII

THE AIRE, SKIPTON

The angling club—Mr. Tennant, Mr. T. H. Dewhirst, Mr. W. Naylor—Fishing—The two old gentlemen—Bob at fault—The blue dun—Baskets of trout—Old Bob disgusted—Killing flies .   Pages 67-72

CHAPTER IX

THE IRT, CUMBERLAND—AFTER SEA-TROUT

Calder Bridge—The Calder—,The Ehen, Egremont—Holmrook—Snug quarters—Santon Bridge—Fishing at Irton Hall—Sea-trout—Arrival of friends—The Mite—The village blacksmith—His sport—Colonel Mawson—Departure—The local hands at it—Mr. Burns-Linder.

Pages 73-81

CHAPTER X

THE URE, ASKRIGG

Source of Ure—Waterfalls—Trout and grayling—Grayling fishing—Aysgarth—Falls in flood—Millgill Force—Fishing at Hawes—Wet weather—Poor sport   .   .   .   .   .   Pages 82-86

CHAPTER XI

FLY-FISHING FOR TROUT

Fly-making—Pritt's *North Country Flies*—List of flies—Gut—Hair—Fly cast—Casting-line—Reel—Hooks—Rods—Modes of fishing—Stewart.

Pages 87-99

CHAPTER XII

CREEPER AND STONE-FLY FISHING

Time at Kilnsey—The male—The female—Kind of rod—Tackle—Mode of fishing—Suitable weather and water—Uncertainty—Fishing in a gale.

Pages 100-104

CHAPTER XIII

WORM-FISHING FOR TROUT

The clear-water worm—Proper season—Where to fish—The flood worm—Where to fish . . . . . Pages 105-111

CHAPTER XIV

MINNOW-FISHING FOR TROUT

The rod—Ariel tackle—Best line—The clear-water minnow—Discoloured water—Where to fish—Time of day . . . . Pages 112-116

CHAPTER XV

THE KILNSEY ANGLING CLUB

Members fishing—Extent of waters—Description of waters—Ancient bridges—Kettlewell—Monks of Fountains—Buckden—Hawkswick—Arncliffe—Lytton Dale—Nature of bed—Size and captures of trout—Mr. Pritt—A cold bath—Pritt's humour—Flies   Pages 117-131

CHAPTER XVI

FLY-FISHING AT KILNSEY

Good sport—Flies—A walk on Sunday—Conistone Church—Good sport in Skirfare—Good sport in August—Flies . Pages 132-139

CHAPTER XVII

MAYFLY-FISHING AT KILNSEY

The fever—Catching the flies—Introduction to the May-fly—Mr. Reffitt—Sport—Uncertainty of sport—The cuss—Fishing in a gale.

Pages 140-148

CHAPTER XVIII

WORM-FISHING AT KILNSEY

Clear-water worm—Good sport—The mail—Worm in a flood—The Field Dub . Pages 149-153

CHAPTER XIX

MINNOW-FISHING AT KILNSEY

A minnow-water—Clear-water minnow—The Devon—Uncertainty of sport . . . Pages 154-157

CHAPTER XX

AN EVENING AT THE TENNANTS' ARMS, KILNSEY

Dinner—Drinks—Bemoaning state of weather—The imitation stone-fly—The brown dun—Duck and snipe—Enter Jerry—Good news—We "wet" the night—Sport at Kilnsey—Mr. Thompson—Mr. Gleadhall—Creels—Mr. Hawes—The Dale folk and gin—The Maid of Arncliffe—Isaak Walton—The stone-fly—The fly-minnow fisher—Club-room tales—Mr. Werfdale—Shooting—Migration of birds—A fresh arrival—Mr. Raneley—The bull and the mushrooms—The bull and the three anglers—The parson and the barmaid—The parson and the keeper—The vale terraces—Projected lake—An electric tramway up Whernside—Snowstorms—Mr. Ruskin and Aysgarth Falls—To bed.
Pages 158-182

CHAPTER XXI

THE TWEED

Stoddart—Education of Tweed trout—St. Boswells—First cast—Fishless—Purdy—Lord Brougham—Fair sport—Merton Hall—Lord Polwarth—Dryburgh—Drowning of an angler—A field-day on Tweedside . . Pages 183-191

CHAPTER XXII

THE BORDER ESK

The Esk and Liddel Association—Honour to poachers—Netherby Hall—Herling and sea-trout—Local opinion—Longtown—The Major's escape—Bad sport—Chub—Wilkin's Pool—Penton Lynns—The Esk in 1896—The Baronet and salmon fishing—The Major and his friend—Night fishing—Metal Bridge—Worm-fishing in Liddel—The landlady condoles—Scarcity of trout in lower Esk . . Pages 192-209

CHAPTER XXIII

THE YORKSHIRE ANGLERS' ASSOCIATION

Mr. Pritt—Formation of association—Mr. Pritt's speech—Monthly meetings—Tulip—The angling column—The "Looker-on"—Coot, coot—Use of large flies—The Eden, Langwathby—The Eamont—The Lowther—Frenchfield—Naming the dubs—The Aire, Airton—Eden Hall—Presentation to Mr. Pritt—His works . Pages 210-225

CHAPTER XXIV

THE EDEN, LANGWATHBY

Free water—Good sport in the Nunwick Hall water—The Boat Pool—The Willows—Sport in Eden—Temple Sowerby—Weight of Eden trout . . . . Pages 226-231

CHAPTER XXV

THE EAMONT

Brougham Bridge—The Lowther—Large fly-hooks—Good sport in early spring—Paley's Walk—Swarms of iron-blue—The March brown—Mr. Pritt and his friends—Lady anglers—Minnow and worm—Good sport—Fly-fishing in June—Mrs. Armstrong—Heavy slaughter—Eamont

Bridge—Brougham Hall—Lowther Castle—Thunderstorms—Weight of Eamont trout . . . . Pages 232-254

CHAPTER XXVI

SALMON FISHING IN THE EAMONT

October floods—Uncertainty of sport—First salmon—The Castle Stream—Red Scar Pool—A smash—Fishing at Udford—Robson's Rock—Frenchfield—Wood Pool—Mr. Bradshaw and his salmon.
Pages 255-264

CHAPTER XXVII

WALES—THE WNION, THE ARTRO, LYNN OGWEN

Dolgelly—Hot weather—The Wnion—Cold weather—The Artro—Snow—Cader Idris under snow—The Panorama—Lynn Ogwen—Poor sport.
Pages 265-271

CHAPTER XXVIII

THE NIDD

The Harrogate Angling Associations—Captain Greenwood's liberality.
Pages 272-275

CHAPTER XXIX

TROUT FISHING IN THE ISLE OF MAN—THE SULBY RIVER

Streams of Mona—Snaefell—Beinn-y-Phot—Description of the river—Lost among the mountains—Fishing—The farmers and the law—Sulby Bridge—A day with the fly—Sulby Glen Hotel—A jubilee day with the worm—Thol-ty-Wull and the Manx fairies . Pages 276-285

CHAPTER XXX

THE DOUGLAS RIVER

The Dhoo—Braddan Bridge—Union Mills—Two record days in the Dhoo—The Glass—Tromode—St. George's Bridge—Sea-trout—Mr. Arthur—East Baldwin Stream—West Baldwin Stream—Injabreck—Sport.
Pages 286-294

CHAPTER XXXI

THE RIVER NEB

Foxdale Mines—Description of the river—Quine's Mill—Glen Mooar—Glen Helen—Rhenass Waterfall—Good sport with fly and worm—Peel the mouth of a mining sewer . . . Pages 295-301

CHAPTER XXXII

THE LHEN AND OTHER STREAMS

Large trout—Mr. Bernard Brooke—Andreas Church—Charlie's sport—The eels—Miss Florence Brooke's advice—The spell—Mr. Kelly of Abbeyville—Largest trout—Silver Burn—Sir Walter Scott—Santon Burn—The Colby river—Glen Meay river—Glen Mooar—Glen Wyllin—Glen Dhoo—The Cornah river—Glen Roy—The Isle of Man Fresh-Water Fishery Act—Weight of trout in Mona.
Pages 302-317

CHAPTER XXXIII

THE DRY FLY

Mr. Dewar—Mr. Gedney—Walton and Cotton—Lord Lytton—Colonel Hawker—Conclusion . . . . Pages 318-321

LIST OF ILLUSTRATIONS

	PAGE
CONTEMPLATION . . .	*Frontispiece*
RIVER NEB AND SLIEU WHALLIN	. 12
KILNSEY . .	*to face* 20
DRUIDALE . . .	. 28
ENTRANCE TO APPLEBY CASTLE .	58
NETHERSIDE . .	118
CONISTONE BRIDGE .	121
BROKEN BROW	122
MEETING OF THE WATERS . .	126
THE FALLS, KILNSEY	. *to face* 132
SKIRFARE BRIDGE .	136
WASH DUB .	141
KETTLEWELL BECK . .	. 150
KETTLEWELL BECK .	155
"THEY PUT THEIR RODS THROUGH THE OPEN WINDOW"	159
HAWKSWICK BRIDGE . . .	165
A LITTLE FIVE-YEAR-OLD (PORT ST. MARY)	*to face* 198
EAMONT BRIDGE	211
FRENCHFIELD	221
WEIR POOL .	234
BROUGHAM CASTLE	237

Paley's Walk	. to face 239
Brougham Bridge	. . 240
The Island Stream .	. to face 245
Crown Hotel, Eamont Bridge .	. 249
Red Scar Stream	. . 253
Robson's Rock	. to face 256
Red Scar	258
The Hut	. 261
At Frenchfield, October 1897	. 264
Birstwith Weir, Nidd	. to face 272
The Road to Ellan Vannin	. . 277
Sulby Glen and Snaefell	. to face 280
Sulby Glen .	283
Glen Helen	. . 296
Port St. Mary .	. to face 305
Silver Burn	307
Silver Burn	309
Colby Glen .	. 311
Colby Falls	. 312

CHAPTER I

FISHING

You are to note that we anglers love one another: men of mild and sweet and peaceable spirits, as indeed most anglers are.—PISCATOR.

ANGLING is described by Izaak Walton as the contemplative man's recreation, and aptly so, for the angler is much alone, and the mind of man cannot long remain inactive; consequently he must think, and his mind is directed to think of the things he sees in the green meadows, or the wild uplands, and he will oft be inclined to think that the happiness of man in this world doth consist more in contemplation than in action.

The immediate object of angling, no doubt, is to capture fish, but after all, that is not the only object. Angling has a great advantage, it can be pursued when a man has become advanced in years. It may be compared to rowing in this respect, that a man may make the exercise either light or heavy. Angling appears to be particularly beneficial to persons who are compelled to pass most of their time indoors; they have the advantage and the pleasure of being able to pass a long day in the open air, and enjoy their pastime without undue fatigue. Their attention is naturally directed to the surroundings. They note the arrival of the spring migrants, the sandpiper, the wagtails, the swallows, swifts, and cuckoo among others of the feathered tribe. Their ears are charmed by the music of the sweet songsters, such as the thrush, blackbird, and the lark, the last named soaring up until he is a mere speck in the blue sky, and singing the while. Then how interesting the sandpiper is, as he flits over the river, with his piping note, and the lapwing, as he circles in his flight with plaintive cries; how he suddenly comes to the ground, and runs along with one wing trailing as if wounded. We then know that we are in the neighbourhood of a nest, and that the bird is endeavouring to lure us from it. As we approach a bend in the river, a startled heron rises with heavy flight and hastens off, and we now and then come on to a couple of wild ducks with their brood of ducklings.

How tame the ducks are at this season, so different to a month or two hence! Their tender care for their young is the reason; they will not forsake them, even for fear of man. This must raise a beautiful thought in the angler's breast, the natural affection of wild creatures for their young, quite as strong as that of the human parent. When a mere child an incident came under my notice.

At that time, as I was too young to climb a tree, I found a boy, who is mentioned in another chapter as Tommy, to climb for me. One day Tommy got me the nest of a chaffinch from a tree, and there were about four eggs in the nest. As I was carrying the nest the hen bird perched on my shoulder, and called "spink! spink!" so plaintively, that I begged Tommy to replace the nest in the tree, but he would not do so. Ever since that time I have felt a great regard for the chaffinch.

In the course of a day's fishing the angler often sees pretty bits of scenery which he would never see otherwise, such as grottos of ferns in out-of-the-way places, mosses of various hues, water dripping from rocks, and such like. The angler of the present day may be divided into two classes: (1) the man who fishes from a real love of the sport, and such a man is born, not made; or as our Father Izaak says, "Angling is somewhat like poetry, men are to be born so"; and (2) the man who fishes for the sake of emulation, or because it is considered the right thing to be a fisherman. An angler of the former class likes to fish alone, to land his own fish and carry his own basket, to be alone with nature, to be left to his own thoughts. The angler of the latter class wants an opponent, some one to fish against. His sole object is to beat the other man, and should he succeed in doing so, he crows over him, and should he not succeed, he is often morose. To my mind emulation in fishing is most objectionable. A true angler angles for his own pleasure, not for the sake of catching more than anybody else. When he has had fair sport he often reels up, when the fish are taking, because he has captured enough for one day. Then there are men who fish almost every day in the season, men who in effect make a business of it. These men fish from mere habit; they cannot really enjoy it. Fishing is given us for recreation, not as the sole object of life.

If sport is followed to repletion it must become stale, it looses the recreative charm; sport is made into a toil in the end. If a man is constantly intent on beating other men, an end of a day's fishing is often bitterness of spirit; if he fishes having no thoughts of competition, he is at peace with himself and with others, and he can act on the precept of our Father Izaak, that anglers should love one another. An angling contest is in my view very objectionable. Some men would fain measure sport by a monetary standard, as if money were everything, and the sport of angling of secondary importance; such men are not true lovers of the art, they are not by nature fitted for contemplation and quietness. They are anxious for the prize at the end of their day's fishing, and to be flattered for their day's performance; when the result is to a great extent accidental or fortuitous. A prize is offered for the largest trout: one man catches a trout one ounce heavier than the rest and he gets the prize; pray, wherein lies the merit of the performance? Having had our fling at the mercenary angler, we will proceed to address the honest angler on the subject of fishing for trout.

The commonly recognised lures for trout are the artificial fly, worm, and minnow. Creeper and stone-fly fishing are so restricted, as to the place and opportunity, that they need no mention here. When a youth decides to become an angler, he has to consider whether he will be what is styled an all-round trout-fisher, or what branch of the art he will take up. There are men who confine themselves to fly, others to worm, and a few to the minnow, when minnow-fishing is at all practicable.

In my estimation worm-fishing (including up-stream worm) is the easiest branch of the art, the next fly-fishing, and the most difficult to acquire, the art of fishing with the up-stream minnow in low clear water. My advice to the would-be angler is to acquire all three of the arts, and I will proceed to give my reasons. In the first place, fly-fishing is certainly the nicest and most pleasant branch of the art; our Father Izaak says: "Is it not an art to deceive a trout with an artificial fly?" During the months of April and May the trout take the fly better than worm or minnow, as a rule, and the trout captured with fly in those months are in better condition, and more palatable, than those captured with worm or minnow.

Fly is the favourite and the most nourishing food for trout in the spring months, and fly feeding fish get sooner into condition than the minnow or worm feeding fish do, and under reasonably favourable conditions satisfactory baskets of trout may be secured with the fly in March, April, and May, and well into June; but after June it is generally most difficult to have fair sport with the fly in the daytime, until about the middle of August, and that interregnum is the carnival of the worm and minnow fisher. But let him use these deadly lures with extreme moderation, unless he is one of the favoured few blessed with private waters, for nothing causes more friction in trout-fishing clubs than that man who is always plying the worm or minnow. In some cases special rules have to be framed to restrain this objectionable man in his practices. My advice is never to resort to worm or minnow when fair sport may be had with fly, and the angler will then be held in respect and esteem by his brothers of the angle. Even when trout are taking the up-stream worm well, it is a relief to vary the monotony of worm-fishing with the more artistic up-stream minnow, but it must be borne in mind that trout cannot be caught so quickly with the minnow as with the worm.

Then again with regard to the use of the worm, there are many streams in which worm-fishing only is practicable; and what after all is more pleasant or health-giving than to wander by some mountain stream, rod in hand, the only care a few hooks on gut and a bag of worms, no bother about flies, far away from the busy haunts of man, alone with nature, yanking out a few trout here and there and an occasional herring-sized fish, which looks a veritable monster by the side of the wee anes. To enjoy such sport the angler may hie to the pretty glens of Mona's Isle, and wander about to his heart's content, disturbed by no jealous keeper.

The reader may inquire about the mysteries of the dry fly, fishing with the dry fly being considered a distinct branch of the art of fishing; it may here be stated that this book is written from a north country point of view. The so-called wet fly will never, in the northern parts of the kingdom, be extinguished by the dry fly. There is no doubt that the time will come when the dry fly will be more practised in the north than it is now, but so long as men may fish with worm and minnow, the attractions of the dry fly will not be great. Where trout exceed a pound on the average, as in a few south country rivers, it is well worth while to spend much time in endeavouring to allure them with the dry fly, but when in the north country the rising trout is about six ounces or under, the angler cannot afford the time necessary, should he wish to obtain a fair basket of fish.

It is all very well for the man of leisure to amuse himself with endeavouring to catch small trout with the dry fly, but when the business man has escaped from his office or counting-house for about three days, and has travelled thirty or forty miles to the river-side, he naturally wishes to have some material sport, and not to spend his time in experimental dry-fly fishing. If he knows what he is about, he can obtain sport with the worm or minnow.

The Wharfe, with its numerous flats of shallow water, is a fair specimen of many north country streams, and I should like to make the acquaintance of the man who could in low water kill 10 lb. of trout with the dry fly in a day in a similar stream. Probably he might kill his three brace or so, as in the south country, but what a difference in weight!

In these days when a man is considered either a very good or very fortunate angler who can capture 10 lb. of trout in a day in ordinary club waters, it is refreshing to turn over the pages of such renowned anglers as Professor Wilson (Christopher North), Stoddart, and Henderson, and to speculate how they managed to make their immense hauls of trout, and what they might do in Yorkshire rivers at the present time. If Professor Wilson had kept an angling diary it would have been exceedingly interesting. We are fortunately indebted to Mrs. Gordon, his daughter, in her *Memoirs of Christopher North*, for some interesting information as to his fishing exploits. We are informed that between the 25th of July and the 26th of August 1815 he killed in the Highlands 170 dozen of trout; one day 19 dozen; in Loch Awe, in three days, 76 lb. weight—all with fly.

What delightful reading the inimitable *Noctes* are even at this date! what ambrosial nights they were with the flowing bowl, and the words of wisdom and of wit emanating from the soul of the immortal Christopher! I commend the 36th *Noctes* for the angler's refreshment, in which the Ettrick Shepherd credits himself, as the result of a day's amusement, with 4 or 5 dozen trout and a 20 lb. salmon, caught with the fly, and 2 dozen trout caught with the otter, mounted with 150 hooks; and he winds up with 25 pike and 25 eels caught on night lines.

Taking leave of the romantic Christopher we turn to the pages of Mr. William Henderson's most interesting work

(*My Life as an Angler*), and we find that Mr. Henderson, in June 1854, killed 27 lb. of trout in the Glen in four hours with worm; and assuming that the trout averaged a quarter of a pound each, as Mr. Henderson's narrative indicates, he killed trout at the rate of 27 an hour, and that in four successive days in June 1859, in twenty-seven hours' fishing, he killed 81 lb. of trout with the worm. Mr. Henderson also records some large captures with the fly. Taking leave of Mr. Henderson we commend to the reader the veteran Mr. Stoddart's *Angler's Rambles and Angler's Songs*, a most delightful book, for some wonderful captures of trout. He will read how Mr. John Wilson, the son of the Professor, killed 26 dozen trout in one day, and Mr. W. Macdonald, of Powderhall, killed in six hours in Teviot, in a part of the river which runs through a poaching district, 57 lb. of trout.

Well, I trow that a regular tiptop poacher would hardly beat this, so where, my brethren of the angle, is the line to be drawn between fair fishing and poaching? The distinction appears to consist only in the mode of capture. The honest angler is supposed to capture fish by delusive means, the poacher by force.

After reading the exploits of anglers in the *Noctes*, *An Angler's Rambles and Angler's Songs*, and *My Life as an Angler*, it is not to be wondered at that anglers are usually credited with exceedingly well-developed imaginations by the persons denominated scoffers, one of which class, no doubt, was Ben Jonson, who described an angler as a fool at one end of a rod, with a worm at the other. However, it is consolatory to feel that among the so-called fools there were and are many eminent men learned in the law and science, and divines, such as Sir J. W. Chitty, Sir Ford North, and the late Bishop of Wakefield, Sir Henry Manisty, Sir Humphry Davy, the Rev. Chas. Kingsley, Colonel Hawker, and many others. The pleasures of angling are exemplified when one thinks of the eagerness with which such eminent men rush off to endeavour to capture a few trout, and perchance a salmon; how such great cases as that of Bardell *versus* Pickwick sank into insignificance when my lord came to be engaged in the case of Judex *v.* Salmo fario—or more still, Judex *v.* Salmo salar.

What can be the great charm of fishing? Is it because the legitimate lures are steeped in fraud and concealment? The artificial fly is the perfection of fraud. The angler offers the trout a piquant fraud in the shape of a hook clothed with feathers and silk, whereby the poor trout is deceived. The worm-fisher conceals a hook with a worm. The minnow-fisher lures the trout with a minnow, apparently in difficulties as he wobbles down the stream. Fishing is undoubtedly a fine art, so is fraud. Can it be that the savage nature of man delights in fraud or violence, and is developed by the predatory instincts inherent in man?

De Quincey classed murder as one of the fine arts. Now the shooter, as compared with the angler, is an honourable man; he brings down his quarry *per vi et armis*. He would think it iniquitous to bait a hook for a pheasant. Who can gauge the heart of man? At the best, what constitutes sport is custom or habit. Why should it not be considered sport to catch fish by any possible means, according to the fancy of the fisherman? Why should a man who catches about 30 trout with worm or minnow be classed as a kind of poacher, while he who captures 50 with fly is congratulated as an honest angler?

"*Chacun à son goût*" should be the motto of the angler: live and let live. The minnow or worm fisher is entitled to as much consideration as the fly fisher. I write thus because I am aware that many persons, who confine themselves to the artificial fly, look down with contempt on anything which they do not themselves practise, and they appear to do so from a want of appreciation, a lack of sympathy with others.

I contend that worm and minnow fishing, practised to a reasonable extent, are beneficial to trout streams; thereby the overgrown trout, which have acquired the habit of feeding on their fellows, are weeded out, consequently the stock of fair-sized trout is kept up. It is generally admitted that overgrown trout are seldom caught with the fly. With regard to most rivers, it would be beneficial to extract therefrom all trout of a pound weight or upwards. There is quite as much reason for weeding out voracious trout as the pike. With regard to the edible qualities of trout, so far as my experience goes a trout under half a pound is more toothsome than one of more than that weight; there is, therefore, no object to be gained in endeavouring to increase the size of trout in most northern streams. When a trout has got to a certain size and age, like man, he begins to deteriorate. This chapter cannot be better concluded than in the words of our Father Izaak, as an introduction to the next chapter—"I have found it to be a real truth, that the very sitting by the river-side is not only the quietest and fittest place for contemplation, but will invite an angler to it."

CHAPTER II

HOW DRUIDALE BECAME A FISHERMAN

It is an easy thing to scoff at any art or recreation.—PISCATOR.

MEMORY carries me back to the time when, as a boy, I lived on the banks of the river Neb, one of the pure streams of Mona, dear little Ellan Vannin, with its green hills by the sea. From being a mere child it was my delight to wander on the banks of the river and watch the trout dart about; and I used to wonder whether I could ever succeed in catching them. I date my commencement as a fisherman from the following circumstance. When about seven years old, one fine summer day in the forties, in company with some other boys, I wandered along the bank of the river. A bathe was suggested and we all went in; I believe it was my first bathe. I was standing up to my knees in the water, afraid to dip my head, when a horrid boy threw me down and ducked me. This over, I felt brave. I spied something, which appeared to have life, in shallow water near the shelving shore. I approached cautiously, and with both hands chucked it on the shore; and oh, joy! it was a magnificent trout of two ounces—my first trout. Shortly afterwards I made the acquaintance of a boy called Tommy, who was an adept in tickling and loobing

(*Anglice* snickling) trout, and he initiated me into the mysteries of both those arts, and I soon became a proficient. The *modus operandi* of loobing was thus. An ash wand about twelve feet in length was procured, and a double horsehair noose or loob attached to the end.

A hot sunny day was chosen, when the trout lay basking

RIVER NEB AND SLIEU WHALLIN.

in the sun. A trout is espied lying against a stone; the point of the rod is gently lowered, and the noose drawn over the head of the trout to about the middle of the body, and then the trout is yanked out on to the bank. If veterans think the operation easy, try it; throwing the fly is nothing to it. It requires the very best of sight, and the nerves must be in excellent order, otherwise the operator may bob the point of the rod against the trout, and he is off like a flash to seek shelter under the bank. In those happy days there was no one to find fault; the streams were unpreserved, and were fished but little. There was then no daily service between Liverpool and the island; visitors did not flock to Mona's shores in the thousands they do now. All visitors were called by the boys, "Cotton Balls," "Manchester Weavers," in derision; in fact, the boys appeared to despise them, the why and the wherefore I cannot tell, but they were not above running after the cars and begging coppers.

I in due time discovered that loobing and tickling were not the best modes of catching trout; when somewhat over ten or eleven years of age I became initiated into the mystery of capturing trout with the worm in clear water. I well remember my first day with rod and line—and such a rod it was too, an ash wand about eleven feet long; a piece of thin wood ran through the rod near the foot, on which the line was wrapped and thence passed through a ring at the top. I sauntered down the river to a well-known dub called Quayle's Dub, which lay near the road to Kirkpatrick. The weather was hot and bright, and the water like crystal. I was on the low shore, and opposite there was a high bank; I threw my worm into water about five feet deep, and as it descended I saw a trout seize the worm; a mighty pull and the trout is lying jumping on the shore. This is repeated three times more and I have four trout. I was too much delighted to fish any more that day. I must get some one to share the joy of my sport, so I hastened home and displayed my spoils. From that time I became an enthusiast in fishing, and I began to look down on loobing and tickling as beneath me. The true sportsman soon begins to appreciate the difference between taking fish by force and luring them to their own destruction by false pretences, for is not what is called fair fishing a system of the grossest fraud? and does not fishing with the net and similar modes savour of honesty?

Shortly after my first success with the worm I commenced to catch trout by the dozen, and I always had the best sport when the weather was bright and hot and the water clear. One did not think of scoured worms in those days. The thing desired was to obtain plenty of them, which was sometimes no easy matter in dry weather. The Peel river, the Neb, was the usual scene of our operations; alas! the Neb, that once beautiful river, teeming with yellow trout, and the salmon and sea-trout in their season, the latter called by the Manx the white trout, but alas! what now—a lead-mine sewer; instead of water like crystal, the colour of milk; water instead of teeming with life being under the shadow of death; all the pools which formerly formed a refuge for the large trout and salmon being silted up with the deposits from the lead-washings; but so long as the dividends are good what do the Foxdale Mining Company care? But away with sad thoughts, let us think of the river when it was pure and I was young.

The river Neb falls into the sea at Peel. Commencing at Peel we will wander up the river, as we wandered forty years ago; I write in the past, not in the miserable present. In about half a mile we get to Glenfaba Mill, and in that length there are charming pools and runs famous for sea-trout in spring and autumn. The top pool of the length is the far-famed Ling Hole, overhung by steep sides, studded with trees, and supposed by the natives to have no bottom. Just above the Ling Hole, past the picturesque bridge which spans the river, is a fine pool where the water flows from the mill-wheel, famous for fine trout.

A few hundred yards above the mill the stream is dammed up to form a mill-dam, and in this dam are goodly fish which can be captured with the fly in a breeze; then for about two miles there is a succession of pools and streams to the junction of two streams which form the Neb proper. A short distance below the junction a small stream called Halsall's Glen joins the river. At this point there is a rather shallow pool in which, from the road above, which for some little distance runs parallel with the river, can be seen shoals of trout, such shoals indeed as live in one's memory, alas, only. A short distance above, a rustic bridge spans the river.

The stream on the right trends to Foxdale, about three miles, and passes under steep Slieu Whallin covered with gorse; and legend says that in the good old times of fairies, ghosts, and witches, when an old woman was suspected of witchcraft, she was closed up in a barrel and rolled from the top of the hill to the bottom, and if she were dead when she got to the bottom she was an honest woman, if not, she was a witch and duly burnt to death,—and this in view of Tynwald Hill, the Hill of Justice, whence the laws to this day are promulgated. The stream to the left trends up Glen Mooar, which is singularly beautiful, the sides of the valley being steep, and clothed partly with plantations, and partly with the gorse and bramble, wild roses and honeysuckle intermixed. The Glen owes a considerable portion of its beauty to a Mr. Threlfall, who emigrated from across the water and took up his abode at Cronkykilly, which he extensively planted. At the end of Glen Mooar the main stream diverges to the right, and Swiss Cottage, the summer residence of a Mr. Marsden, another emigrant, is reached, and a lovely valley with steep sides planted by Mr. Marsden is traversed to Rhenass Waterfall. Here again is a junction of two streams, the waterfall stream going to Little London. Above the waterfall some of the trout are remarkable for their beauty, reminding one of the colours of the rainbow.

We generally confined our operations to the main river, that is, below the junction which was free from trees and afforded free, open fishing. I did not make any record of my captures until my last year, 1856, when I was fifteen.

The following extract from my diary in that year may be interesting at the present time, as showing what the river was capable of in those happy days, when the river was pure, and the sandpipers flitted about with their cheery piping note, and the cattle drank out of the river; and it must be borne in mind that the tackle was of the most primitive description, common unstained gut, about three lengths to a cast, to which was attached one hook. I had not then heard the name of Mr. Stewart, and I did not know whether it was better to fish up or down, but, so far as my memory goes, I fished either way:—"16th February, 31 trout; 1st March, 20; 22nd March, 28; 28th May, 28; 15th July, 57; 20th August, 48."

I well remember the red-letter day when I captured 57 trout. The water was low and clear, and the weather bright and hot. I walked a mile or so down the river and fished up. I caught trout after trout until I had exhausted my stock of worms, and then endeavoured to find more worms; but they were harder to find than the trout were to catch, and I wound up early in the afternoon, more than satisfied, and hasted home to exhibit my spoils.

We sometimes met the Vicar of Peel's son when fishing, and always compared notes; the vicar's son used artificial fly only, and I always found that my worm-caught trout ran a better average than his. Mr. Quane of Ballaspet was a good hand with the fly during the earlier days of my fishing career, and many big baskets he took; he confined himself to fly, and one day he gave me a red spider and with it I caught two trout. I came to the conclusion that the fly was too slow for me, and I was not, at any rate at that time, prepared to admit that the art of worm-fishing in low and clear water was less difficult than fly-fishing or less sportsmanlike.

When I was about eleven years of age, I had my first experience of the weakness of some anglers, which produces the crop known as "anglers' yarns." I was wending my way home along the river-side, after catching only four trout. I met two anglers evidently from across the water; I was accosted thus:—"Have you caught any trout, my boy?" "Yes, but only four; they are not taking." "May we look at them?" The gentlemen gazed at my trout with longing eyes. "Will you sell them?" one of them said. I said I did not mind. So after some bargaining the trout were deposited in their capacious basket, and fourpence passed into a pocket which was generally void of money. "Now, my boy," one of the gentlemen said on parting, "you will meet two gentlemen fishing down the river; don't tell them you have sold us your trout." I promised them I would not. Presently I spied the two gentlemen alluded to, so to avoid awkward questions I cleared over a hedge out of sight. This reminds me of the story of a lady who asked her husband whether it was usual for anglers to cut off the fins and tails of fish after their capture.

How delighted we were when we caught a real whopper; one such caused a disaster more than once. I must premise that in those early days I had no idea of playing a trout, but fortunately our tackle was good enough for a two pounder. I cast into a stream at the head of a good pool, there was a tug, and I pulled without regard to my tackle or the strength of my rod. Just when I had hauled the fish on the verge of the gravel, the rod broke in two places. I rushed to the margin of the river, went down to the ground and embraced my prize in my arms, but at the expense of a ducking. That trout remains an unknown weight.

In addition to trout, there were many eels in the river. One day whilst I was walking by the river, I saw an eel seize a small trout and give it a shake. As I moved to the edge of the water, the eel dropped its prey, and I managed to get the trout out: it was dead.

In those days there was no railway in the island; the telegraph cable had not been laid. The old *King Orry* managed to do the passage from Liverpool to Douglas in about eight hours in fair weather. In a gale, it was a prolonged agony of twelve hours and upwards. The trout licence had not been invented, neither had the gun licence. The boys might roam about with a gun at their own sweet will, without molestation, and might bring to bag a woodcock or a snipe, if they could only hit it,—and the chances were in favour of the bird. The blackbirds and thrushes, though, often came to grief, as they afforded easy sitting shots; and the question as to whether to hit a bird perched on a tree or on the ground constituted the greater marksmanship, was a source of much discussion and never satisfactorily settled by the disputants.

Limited liability companies had not formed tea-gardens and dancing-platforms in the secluded glens, to the destruction of their natural beauty. The contemplative man was not disturbed in his reveries by the derisive shouts of those tourists who rejoice in being vulgar. The solitary angler was almost the only person who invaded the wooded glens, sacred to trout and woodcock. After all, there are still some places sacred to the angler and other real lovers of nature— the man who likes to be alone with nature—to which I propose to conduct the reader in subsequent chapters which treat of fishing in the Isle of Man.

I must, however, before I conclude this chapter, mention that the Rhenass, otherwise the Glen Helen river, is still unpolluted and abounds with trout. The Foxdale stream is, and is likely to remain a mining sewer for years, and thus it pollutes the whole of the main river Neb. About the year 1855, trout had become scarce in the Foxdale stream owing to the pollutions, and I frequently observed that portions of the tails of trout were wanting. They appeared as if they had gradually come off, no doubt owing to the poisonous state of the water; and as I never captured a trout minus the whole tail, I concluded that death put an end to their sufferings before the tailless stage was reached. At this stage I was torn from my first love, but soon learned to find other loves in fresh woods and pastures new (Amateur Angler), as will appear in the next chapter.

CHAPTER III

THE WHARFE, KILNSEY

I am, sir, a brother of the angle, and therefore an enemy to the otter.
—PISCATOR.

PREVIOUSLY to the year 1840, the Wharfe in the neighbourhood of Kilnsey was practically unpreserved, as the various tenants readily gave permission to fish. About that time some gentlemen in search of sport put up at the Tennants' Arms inn, and were very much pleased with the sport; indeed, so much so, that they resolved to endeavour to form an angling club, having Kilnsey for the headquarters. The late Rev. Mr. Berry of Chapel House, who was then the perpetual curate of Conistone-cum-Kilnsey, and an ardent angler, interested himself in the matter, and he may be designated as the founder of the Kilnsey Angling Club. The principal landowner, the late Mr. J. R. Tennant of Kildwick Hall, who was a true sportsman and a very generous gentleman, was approached, and he at once consented to the proposed club taking his portion of the river actually free of charge, and this liberality was continued so long as Mr. Tennant had control of the Tennant estate, which was happily for many years. The club was formed, and in a short time enjoyed the

fishing from Netherside, the mansion of Col. Nowell, to Starbotton on the Wharfe proper, to the pretty village of Arncliffe on the tributary called the Skirfare. The nature of the fishing and the scenery will be found described in a subsequent chapter. The principal object of this chapter is to show how I became a fly-fisher.

In the month of September 1858, I was invited by Mr. Lionel William Knowles, a member of the club, to accompany him as his friend to Kilnsey, each member having the right to take a friend whenever he pleased, with the restriction that a friend was not allowed to wade. We proceeded to Kilnsey on the 28th of September, driving in a carriage and pair from Skipton, the capital of Craven, a distance of about twelve miles. Mrs. Knowles and her sister, Miss Emily Antwiss, a nice young lady of seventeen summers, accompanied us, and as Mr. and Mrs. Knowles were very nice also, I was clearly in for a good time, whether I could captivate the very particular Wharfe trout or not. I was much impressed by the beautiful scenery on the way. On the right for some distance lay the steep moors forming part of the Bolton Abbey estate of the Duke of Devonshire, with extensive pine woods at their base ; then after about three miles, we pass on our right the residence of Captain Henderson, with its beautifully wooded grounds ; then through the pretty village of Rylstone, which calls to memory the poet Wordsworth in his " White Doe of Rylstone," with its church and embattled tower picturesquely standing on rising ground. To the left, just before we ascend a steep hill, a fish-pond with groups of old-fashioned houses clad with luxuriant ivy ; and near by, a rookery in the high trees. Then on past the village of Cracoe, with its two ancient little inns, and a few houses, with well-tended lawns and gardens. A little distance on the left, on the side of a hill, the residence of Colonel Maude, embosomed in trees. We are now in sight of Great Whernside (2314 feet) to our right front, and of Grassington lying on a slope at the foot of Grassington Moor. Then we come to the Catchall Inn, placed at the junction of the Kilnsey and Grassington roads. The road to the right leads to the pretty village of Lynton; our course is straight on.

We soon approach the dreadful hill which conducts us to the pretty village of Threshfield, with a tiny brook flowing by, lying in a hollow sheltered from the wind. In a short time we pass Netherside Hall, with its well-timbered grounds, perched high above the river below, faced on the opposite bank by extensive pine woods. As we proceed down the steep hill, a short distance past the Hall, we have a lovely view of the river in the deep valley below on our right, the meadows being studded here and there with the hawthorn with its red berries; on our left rising ground, studded with hawthorn and the hazel full of nuts which are now ripe, and culminating in a steep ridge, thickly planted, and in a hollow below, high up, and overlooking the valley, is the cosy-looking Chapel House, with Chapel Lodge below near the falls, where the river rushes over the limestone grit, and forms a series of cascades, terminating in deep pools hollowed out of the rock by the action of the water for ages; then about a mile on the left of the valley the village of Conistone, with the steep gorge behind trending in the direction of Conistone Moor 1500 feet or more above the valley; the little church on the north of the village.

Shortly I am deposited at the Tennants' Arms and introduced to several members of the club in the snug club-room, fitted up with racks for the rods, and embellished with a case of stuffed otters and two pictures, trout "Not long caught" and "A few of the Finny Tribe."

The tiny hamlet of Kilnsey is about 300 yards to the south of Kilnsey Crag. It appears to have been in days gone by a place of much more importance than at present. It may be inferred from Burton's *Monasticon* that there was a church there in the twelfth century, and Kilnsey was known to the Popes of Rome. "Edolphus de Kylnsay in A.D. 1174 gave a carrucate (*i.e.* two oxgangs) of land here. . . . Confirmed by Pope Adrian IV. in A.D. 1156" (Burton's *Monasticon*). There was a grange at Kilnsey. "Aliza de Rumeli gave forty loads of dead wood to Kilnsey Grange 1175," and the Monks of Fountains were endowed with a right of free warren. "In A.D. 1292, twenty Edward I., the king granted them to have free warren here." In those days Kilnsey was designated a town. The antiquarian will be much interested in the remains of the old Hall, which was probably the grange mentioned by Burton.

Mr. Knowles and party proceeded about half a mile farther up the valley to a farmhouse in which they had engaged rooms. Among the anglers assembled in the club-room there were Mr. Thompson, Mr. Aked, Mr. Halliwell, and Mr. Aaron. I soon discovered that Mr. Thompson was considered about the best all-round fisherman in the club. In the course of the evening Mr. Henry Gleadhall came in for a smoke and a chat. Mr. Gleadhall had taken up his abode at Kettlewell about three miles farther up the valley shortly after the formation of the club, and there he remained a fixture for some thirty years, devoting himself to the capture of trout and the making of flies, in which he was an adept. I must pay him this tribute in addition, that he was very generous to the poor in the district, and was of great service in promoting the interests of the club, of which he continued to be a member long after he became unable to follow his favourite pastime in consequence of the infirmities of age.

As may be well imagined, the conversation was about fish and fishing, and the endless subject of flies. The orange partridge appeared to be thought the most of. I informed the company that I had fished only in the Isle of Man, and only knew how to fish the worm. I soon discovered to my chagrin that worm-fishing was looked down upon, and that the only sportsmanlike mode of fishing was the fly in the estimation of that distinguished body, the Kilnsey Angling Club, to be a member of which was evidently considered as eminent as being created a peer of the realm. I was thenceforth impressed with the idea that I must fish with fly, and in addition make my own flies, if I wished to attain the dignity of the complete angler. I retired to roost feeling that I was not in it, and that there would be no use in endeavouring to win the admiration of the Kilnsey Angling Club by means of prowess with my favourite worm.

On the following day, the 29th of September, in company with Mr. Knowles, I fished the main river and scored 0, Mr. Knowles 2, so I consoled myself with the fact that the veteran only caught two more than I did. During the night rain fell and next day there was a muddy fresh, and in the morning Mr. Knowles caught 1 with worm and I 2. In the afternoon the water somewhat cleared, and the veteran caught 4 with fly and the tyro 0. My time had not yet come; on the morrow it came, a mixture of success and mortification. My tackle provider was my kind friend; he had provided me with some hair casts and flies dressed on hair, in an evil moment for me, a tyro. On the previous day I had learnt to throw a fly, and to-day there was a nice ale-coloured fly-water. We elected to try the Skirfare. I soon began to rise fish, then a big tug and a smash. That celebrated pool the Wash Dub, of which more hereafter, was the place of my greatest misfortunes. A monster of unknown weight took away the whole of a cast, and I cannot say how many more flies I lost on that eventful day. However, in the end I caught 3 trout and Mr. Knowles 28; Mr. Thompson caught some 15 lb. weight —some 40 fish or so—and other anglers did well. On the next day, Saturday, we again fished in the Skirfare, and my friend killed 15 and I 9. How proud I felt at the farmhouse when the ladies as usual turned out our baskets, and praised us for our success.

On Monday we changed our water; we walked some distance up Kettlewell Beck, of which more hereafter, and fished down in the approved north country fashion, and Mr. Knowles caught 16 and I 7. On Tuesday we fished in the main river, and Mr. Knowles caught 12 and I one. It must be borne in mind that Mr. Knowles waded and I did not, and the advantage of wading at Kilnsey, and especially in the main river, is very great. This was our last day's fishing. The morrow was to be the ladies' day; we arranged to go nutting, as some compensation for the days the ladies had suffered desertion, while the inferior sex were on slaughter bent. The weather was beautiful, and we climbed the hills at the back of Kilnsey's far-famed Crag, and plucked the hazel-nuts, and much enjoyed the pureness of the atmosphere in that elevated region. I had been very remiss in my attendance in the club-room, as I only spent my first evening in it. The quiet attractions at the farmhouse were too powerful.

As the shades of night fell we of the farmhouse party were far from charming Kilnsey, and a shadow crosses me when my thoughts return to that happy visit, and I remember that in little more than a year that bright, happy, joyous girl, then so full of life and fun, was called to her eternal rest.

> "My Lord has need of these flowerets gay,"
> The Reaper said, and smiled;
> "Dear tokens of the earth are they,
> Where he was once a child."
> LONGFELLOW.

I always feel thankful to my old friend Mr. Knowles for introducing me to the quiet charms of Kilnsey, far from railways and telegrams. He was a good all-round sportsman. I regret that I have to write in the past, for he also has gone home. The following little story shows how he could be wrapped up in the art of dressing flies. People who are no longer young will never forget the intense frost of 24th December 1860, when the thermometer descended some degrees below zero, and the Clyde and most of the rivers in Great Britain were frozen over, and even the Thames was blocked up by ice. As one of the effects of the severe frost, about three o'clock in the afternoon of Christmas Eve I saw a horse with icicles at least a foot long hanging to his nostrils. To return to Mr. Knowles. On Christmas Eve Mrs. Knowles and some guests went to an evening party, and returned home after midnight; they were astonished to find Mr. Knowles so engrossed in dressing flies that he had let the fire go out.

In the next chapter Druidale will again be found in his beloved Isle of Man, quite imbued with the idea that he has developed into an accomplished fly-fisherman.

CHAPTER IV

THE DRUIDALE FISHING EXCURSION AND BIVOUAC

We are all so happy as to have a fine fresh cool morning, and I hope we shall each be the happier in the other's company.—VENATOR.

THE month of June 1859, weather lovely, scene a stable in the pretty village of Onchan; *dramatis personæ*, six youths whose ages varied from twenty-one to sixteen; they are discussing where they shall go for a real good time of it. Some of them had circumwalked the island during the previous Easter with a donkey and cart to carry their impedimenta and a tent to sleep in, and the weather had been atrocious, in fact so bad that kind farmers had housed them for the night several times. After much discussion it was decided to encamp in Druidale. Druidale may be said to be the highest portion of the river Sulby, which flows into the sea at Ramsey after a course of about eleven miles. The Sulby river partakes of two distinct characteristics, the lower portion from Ramsey to the village of Sulby, about four miles (much more by the river), being for the most part sluggish, with streams here and there, and flowing through a country much of which is agricultural; and the higher portion through a deep pastoral valley with very steep sides, along a stony or rocky bed with frequent cascades and deep pools. As we go a-fishing the charms of Sulby Glen shall be done justice to, to the best of our ability, in another chapter.

The preparations for our departure took up a considerable time. The donkey-cart was loaded with the tent, various pots and pans for the culinary department, a blanket

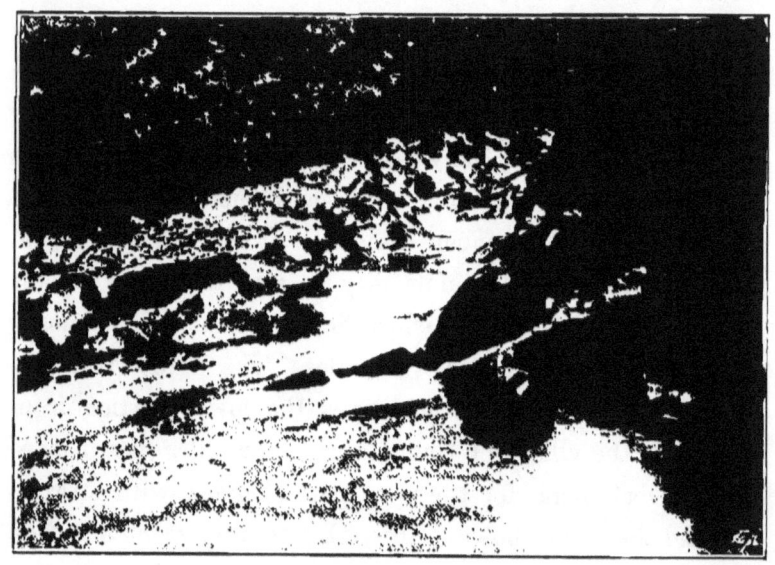

DRUIDALE.

for each person, and other things; the kettle and some more things were slung behind the cart, which added to our gipsy appearance. At six o'clock in the morning of Monday the 13th day of June, Oliver Graham sounded the bugle and we were off, and then there came an addition to our party in the person of a boy of about thirteen, Granby Calcraft by name, who was destined to be the terror of the party, as, boy though he was, he was armed with a revolver. Granby, who had been watching our preparations with great interest, asked to be allowed to accompany us; we signified our consent subject to his mother's approval, which was given, and he soon overtook us with the revolver in his pocket. The weather was fine, but there was a fine cool head-wind which blew the dust off the road in clouds, and made our journey for some time very uncomfortable. On we journeyed, along narrow country roads hemmed in with high banks covered with gorse, which being in full bloom presented a beautiful appearance. To the west we had a fine view of Greeba Mountain, a little to the right of it Garraghan, and to the north-east Beinn-y-Phott Mountain. In about two miles from Onchan we cross a white bridge over the river Glass, which after joining the Dhoo falls into Douglas Bay.

At this stage an important discovery was made; we had forgotten a precious leg of mutton, which had the night before been hung up in our larder, the stable. Charlie and Milburn at once returned for it, and the rest of the party resumed their journey. Rather less than a mile farther on, passing a plantation on the left, we come to a fork in the river. The stream to the right is called the East Baldwin Stream, and rises at the foot of Beinn-y-Phott; the stream to the left is called the West Baldwin Stream, and takes its rise between Colden Mountain and Garraghan. Our course is up the West Baldwin Stream, and we have to reach the West Baldwin valley by a very rough road, only a cart track up one very steep incline and down another, when we reach a fair road which carries us to the end of our journey. Presently we pass through the pretty little village of West Baldwin, with its white-washed bridge over the river, near which there is an old mill. The valley is beautiful, well wooded; gorse in flower in profusion, wild roses on the hedges, honeysuckle here and there, and the lofty hills forming a fine background; the sky of deep blue with an occasional passing cloud; the song of the cuckoo resounds up and down the valley.

As it was intended that our patient donkey should have a rest at Injabreck, Harrop and I went fishing up the river, in which I soon captured 17 trout with the upstream worm, and then rejoined the party with the donkey. We found them resting near the picturesque ivy and fern-clad bridge immediately below Injabreck, amid delightful scenery. Injabreck House was built many years ago by an English gentleman, who extensively planted the estate and thereby created a little paradise among the mountains. Seen from the mountains above, the place looks enchanting, and in those days it enjoyed a solitude which might have been enjoyed by a hermit, being an unknown place to the ordinary tourist, and haunted only by the contemplative man.

Charlie and Milburn had overtaken us, and the former had gone up a small stream which flowed from the left through a narrow rocky gorge, where grew beautiful ferns, and amongst them much of the hartstongue and maidenhair, to try for a few trout. Charlie delighted in those small streams where you have to push the grass and brambles aside in order to put in the worm. After partaking of a luxurious lunch, consisting of biscuit and water, I resumed fishing, and was soon joined by Charlie, who had caught a fine trout of at least three-quarters of a pound in the small stream. Presently we observed the others with the donkey and cart struggling up the steep hill which leads to a sort of pass between Snaefell and Beinn-y-Phott. As the poor donkey could not drag the load up the hill, they had fastened a rope to the shafts, and were pulling after the manner of trace-horses; we roared with laughter at the ludicrous spectacle they presented, but we were soon added to the number of donkeys. After much hauling, tugging, and shouting, we at length reached the top of the hill, whence we had a splendid view; on the right Snaefell, the monarch of Manx mountains, to the left Beinn-y-Phott, in front Sartfell, and in the distance Peel Hill and Peel Castle.

We had now attained an elevation of about 1200 feet, being above the range of cultivation,—a region of heather, bent grass, and rushes, a fine place for snipe and also for woodcock on their first arrival. We were at the source of the Sulby river. Here we got to the junction of two roads, the right leading to the base of Snaefell, and the one nearly straight forward to Druidale, in the upper part of which we intended to pitch our tent. As the heather was very fine we plucked a lot for our bedding, and in about two miles more we arrived at the fork of two little streams, which united formed the Sulby river.

On the banks of the stream proceeding from Sartfell there is a fir plantation, well sheltered and facing Snaefell, and from the plantation a view down Druidale. We decided to pitch our tent in the fir plantation. Our arrival caused great consternation to two carrion-crows (the hooded or Norway crow, a great rascal), which had built their nest in a larch tree, never thinking of such an incursion. We at once pitched our tent, and dug a trench round it in case of rain, and then prepared for dinner. With slabs of slate-stone, which we found on the road, we built two fireplaces—two sides and one end, and two narrow stones across to rest the pan or kettle on; then we gathered fallen wood and dry fern, with which we made our fires. The kettle was placed on one fire and the frying-pan on the other, and in the frying-pan were placed mutton chops and bacon, the spluttering of which was music to our ears, for we were so hungry, we were ravenous.

Our meal consisted of mutton, bacon, preserve, and bread and cocoa, and we all felt that we had never enjoyed a meal so much in our lives. It was 4.30 P.M., and we had had nothing substantial since breakfast. "Now then," said one of the party, "every man wash his own plate, knife, fork, spoon, and cup," which we accordingly did in the stream. We then spread our ling for bedding in the tent, and lay down to rest for about two hours, after which we felt ready for tea, which consisted of tea and bread and butter. We mashed our tea in the kettle.

During the evening several farm men and boys and a few girls visited our encampment, and were much surprised at our proceedings. About ten o'clock we prepared for bed; we took off our coats, waistcoats, collars, and boots, and rolled ourselves in our blankets and lay on the heather, our feet meeting at a common centre, the tent-pole. We were all very tired, and most of the party were soon asleep. I was just beginning to doze, when Milburn who was on my right gave me a nudge, "Harry, Harry, did you hear that noise? I believe there is some person outside the tent."

"What," I said, "are you sure that you heard some one outside the tent?"

"Well, I'm sure I think I did," said my nocturnal disturber.

"Well," I replied, "you had perhaps better awake Harrop," who was then snoring most monstrously, and had our best means of defence, the gun, under his head.

"Harrop, Harrop, listen, don't you hear some noise outside?"

"Wha, wha," drawls Harrop sleepily, as he rolls over and

mutters some unintelligible words, "wha, wha, what, go to sleep."

"But," says Milburn in a louder tone, "don't you hear some sounds outside the tent?"

Harrop, who was now thoroughly awake, said that he did; he capped the gun, Milburn cocked the pistol, and I took hold of the hatchet, and we all prepared for the worst. Milburn, who must have been the bravest of the party (he had been to America, and was therefore supposed to have had many a brush with the Indians), cautiously crept out of the tent to reconnoitre, with the pistol at the present: he shortly returned with the welcome intelligence that all was quiet, and that the donkey must have caused the noise; so, without more ado, we rolled ourselves up in our blankets and slept soundly until one o'clock, when we all awoke simultaneously and were much surprised that it was not later.

After much talk and commotion we again fell asleep, and slept till about 4.30, when we got up; our ablutions were performed in the stream, and the process of dressing, as may well be imagined, did not take long. The fires were lighted and preparations for breakfast commenced. Breakfast consisted of trout and bacon fried together, bread and coffee, the cream for which was donkey's milk. The donkey fortunately had a foal, so we substituted ourselves for the foal. It took about an hour to prepare breakfast, and we sat down to our first morning meal in Druidale about half-past five o'clock. The weather was bright and chilly, and no wonder, considering our altitude and the air from the north. Some of the party were enjoined to remain all day in care of the camp.

About half-past six o'clock Charlie and I started off to Mr. Brooke's house, about a mile off, to ask permission to fish in his part of the river. Mr. Brooke was the owner as well as the occupier of the Druidale estate, consisting of several thousand acres. He was a Yorkshire gentleman, who had taken up his abode in lonely Druidale many years before, and there devoted himself to farming a large tract of wild mountain land. His society consisted of woodcock, snipe, and other wild birds and trout. He was a widower and lived alone, excepting for a few farm servants. I never heard that he was fond of either fishing or shooting, so I cannot imagine why he buried, or perhaps more correctly, exalted himself in such a wild place, many miles from any one in his own rank. He had two sons, one a barrister in London and the other in Australia. Mr. Brooke was down, although we arrived at his mansion before seven o'clock, so said a typical dark-eyed Manx maid who admitted us.

In order to obtain an audience of the Lord of Druidale it was necessary to march through the kitchen, thence through a very small room, and we were in the presence of a fine-looking man, with white hair and whiskers, sitting in a room of fair size, with a handsome-looking sideboard at one end. He was engaged in writing. As we entered the room, the sanctum of the Lord of Druidale, in rushed two little pigs, which were soon expelled by the maid. Mr. Brooke received us, vagrants as we were, most courteously, and he appeared very much amused when we informed him that we had encamped on his estate. He laughed most heartily, and hoped we should enjoy ourselves. He most readily gave us permission to fish on his estate, also to shoot rabbits; in fact he gave us a *carte blanche* to do as we liked. He very much wished us to take breakfast with him, but we explained that we had already had breakfast at the camp, and we were impatient to try conclusions with the trout, so after thanking him very warmly for his kindness we bade him adieu. I elected to walk about a mile down the main river and fish up to the camp. Charlie, with his usual predilection for small streams, decided to operate in the Snaefell stream, which runs between Snaefell and Beinn-y-Phott.

For the most part Sulby Glen is very narrow, the sides being very steep, with rocks here and there, and the stream is to a great extent a succession of cascades and pools, some of considerable depth. In many places rocks overhang the stream, adorned with ferns and mosses, which grow most luxuriantly. The croak of the raven is occasionally heard, and the hawk is rather common. A kingfisher is occasionally met with, but there are not any water-ousels in Man, so common by the rivers in England.

I commence in a sharp run, out of which I take three or four trout; then I approach a pool under a high rock, and cast the worm into the stream above the pool. The worm glides under the rock, a sharp tug, and I am fast to a lively herring-sized trout, a fine fish for Mona, and he is soon in my pannier; then on I go up the rocky glen, catching trout after trout in pool and stream, and occasionally missing a whopper in the deep holes. On one occasion I dropped my worm from a high bank into a deep pool below; it caught in a briar hanging over the pool, about six inches from the water. A lively quarter of a pounder rose to the worm, and paid the penalty. As I am passing rather a high rock by the side of the stream a sparrow-hawk darts out of a crevice high up, and I soon saw that there was a nest, which appeared perfectly easy to reach; so I climbed up the rock, but, alas, I could not get my hand nearer to the nest than about half a yard. Unless I could walk on air the nest could not be mine, and I had to leave the hawk in undisturbed possession to complete her domestic duties.

On arriving at the camp I found Charlie there. He had caught 25 trout, and among them two beauties, one of two pounds and the other close on a pound. I said to Charlie, "How did you land that monster" (we did not use landing-nets), "and where did you get him on ?"

"Well," said Charlie, "you know where the stone slab crosses the Snaefell stream near the junction of the stream; I got him on in the deep pool just below. He ran me round and round the pool for ever so long, and at last got under a big stone in deep water. I was determined to get him, so I went into the water up to my middle and in the end got him out with my hands."

"Then you had to duck your head in."

"Yes, I had," he said, "but he was worth the ducking."

"Bravo, Charlie!"

I had 29 trout, and Mackenzie, who had also been fishing, 7; so we had 61 trout for our larder. About five o'clock we took tea—which consisted of bacon, trout, bread and preserve—which had been prepared by some of the party.

During our absence fishing, Graham and Granby had been enjoying themselves in their own fashion: one of them had swarmed the tree with the carrion-crow's nest in it, and brought down four unfortunate young crows; the crows were tried and condemned to be shot with the pistol. The poor birds were shot in detail, shot for shot, till all was over. After all, the hooded crow is a rapacious bird, and has been known to attack sickly lambs.

My diary states that "in the evening we wrote our journals

and read novels, and some of us wrote home." The trout problem was discussed, what should we do with the trout we caught; we could not possibly eat them all ourselves. The non-fishermen suggested that we should not catch so many. We did our best to eat them, as we had trout at every meal. Charlie suggested that we should salt them.

Several visitors called to see us as on the previous evening. We formed quite an entertainment for them, and the lads and lasses danced on the green to the music of the river; and we watched the rays of the setting sun with ever varying colours on Snaefell until the sun set behind the hills to the west.

On the morrow it was decided that it was my turn to rise early to light the fires, so I rose at the untimely hour of half-past four o'clock and lighted the fires, and afterwards with the assistance of some of the rest prepared our morning meal, which as usual consisted of coffee, bacon, trout, and bread, also of some eggs, a present from Mr. Brooke. After breakfast Harrop, Milburn, and I went fishing, the former in company, and I alone; Charlie remained to guard the camp; some of the rest went to Ballaugh, a village four or five miles off, to buy some bread. I took about the same portion of the river as on the previous day, and caught 16 trout. Bearing in mind the complaint of a glut of fish, I made a short day of it, and got back to the camp at three o'clock and dined luxuriously on trout, bacon, bread, and coffee. One of my trout was a beauty close on a pound. Harrop and Milburn returned to the camp with 23 trout between them.

After they had had the usual meal, Mackenzie, who must have been a born cook, assisted by myself and some of the others, made a roly-poly pudding. It was fearfully and wonderfully made; the dough was a compound of flour and donkey's milk, and the interior gooseberry jam. The dough was kneaded in fractions, on flat stones, which were then joined together, the preserve inserted, and rolled up in the most approved manner. The mass was tied up in a towel and boiled in the coffee-pot.

Charlie and Granby, who had gone to the important town of Kirk Michael for a little quiet dissipation to relieve the monotony of Druidale, after the Ballaugh party returned, got back at the untimely hour of seven o'clock. They brought some salt with them, with the view of salting trout. On their arrival the pudding was taken out of the pot amid loud cheers, and was pronounced by all to be excellent, and a vote of thanks to the maker of it (Mackenzie) was proposed, seconded, and unanimously carried.

The diary states that "we retired into the tent at nine o'clock, and occupied the interim between our retirement to the tent and getting to bed in writing our journals and reading novels" (the journals appear to have been considered important, and no doubt each writer intended at some future time to publish his experiences for the edification of a grateful public).

We lay down to sleep at eleven o'clock. I may state here once for all that tobacco was burned in the tent every evening for the purpose of exterminating the little gray gnats, which bit our faces with brutal ferocity; and when one of the party was deputed to clean trout by the stream, another accompanied him for the express purpose of burning tobacco about the face of the performer, whom I may call the gutter, in order to keep the gnats from worrying him.

The diary states that "nothing occurred to disturb our nocturnal slumbers," so it may be presumed that the gun, pistol, and hatchet had had a salutary effect on the donkey. A hatchet always reminds me of the two fellows who quarrelled about nothing, and accordingly resolved to fight a duel about it (nothing). They tossed for choice of weapons, and the fellow who won the toss selected hatchets. The other fellow objected; the winner insisted; then the other fellow said, "If we fight with hatchets, one of us is certain to be killed." The winner brutally replied, "Of course." Result, the other fellow declined to fight.

On the following morning, Thursday, we all rose at a quarter to six (we were gradually getting to more civilised hours): the diary does not say anything about our ablutions, so it does not appear whether at this stage ablutions were considered necessary or not. After the usual breakfast, Charlie, Milburn, Graham, and I started off to fish. I went alone as is my wont, and resolved to do the gentleman and fish fly. The trout rose nicely although the sun was bright, and nearly all the trout took the black spider (small feather from a starling's shoulder or neck hackled on brown silk). It was nice practice casting under the trees into the narrow pools. I fished up; there would have been little use in fishing down in such low clear water and bright sun. We reached the camp early in the afternoon, the result of the day's catch being Charlie and Milburn with worm 41, Graham with the same lure 1, and I 17 with fly. Harrop had remained in camp as caretaker, and he amused himself with shooting rabbits. The usual meal was partaken of. Harrop started for home, Rockmount, St. Johns, about seven o'clock, for which bereavement the survivors condoled with one another. However, he took with him a large basket of trout to the relief of our larder. In the evening, we occupied ourselves in the usual way, and as the gnats were more troublesome and voracious than ever, much tobacco was burnt.

On the next day, Friday, we rose about six o'clock, and as it was our last complete day in camp we all felt rather sad at the idea of going home on the morrow. We had not at all tired of camp life: we had lived together in perfect harmony, no quarrel or unkind words had caused friction. We were a happy family.

After the usual breakfast, Charlie, Mackenzie, and I went off fishing, Charlie and Mackenzie using worm and I fly. The weather was bright; rain had not fallen for a considerable time. Charlie killed 45 trout, Mackenzie 12, and I 18. These details are instructive as showing the superiority of worm over fly. Many trout in difficult places like Druidale can be caught with worm where there is not a chance with fly, but I felt more satisfied with my fly-caught trout than I should have been with three times the number killed with worm.

On reaching the tent early in the afternoon, we were much pleased to see Mr. and Mrs. Harrison of Rockmount, their daughter Georgiana, and our camp fellow Harrop, also Dr. Booth, who had the curiosity to visit our camp. They had just regaled themselves with tea, and appeared to be much amused with all they saw; and I have no doubt that our neglected personal appearance, faces disfigured by the gnats notwithstanding the consumption of tobacco, our spotless linen, and such like trifles very much entertained them.

The diary is silent as to ablutions; memory does not supply the blank. I can recollect gutting the wretched trout by the stream, alternately worried by gnats and smoked with burning tobacco until I was nearly choked, and washing my hands afterwards. Can we have drifted into the band of the great unwashed in less than a week? Mr. Harrison was a most worthy gentleman; he was then, and had been for many years, a member of the then self-elective House of Keys; he had travelled a good deal in Africa, and collected many trophies of his travels, such as Kaffir spears and ostrich eggs. He was a great collector of books, and in addition he read them. He was a prominent member of the Manx Society, and edited many of the books published by that society. He was a great collector of curiosities of many kinds; he had a very fine collection of birds' eggs, most of them collected by himself; also of old coins. Mrs. Harrison was a most amiable lady. I remember her smile, when her husband once laid it down that a lover should never despair when the lady says "no," for if he will only persevere the fair one is in the end certain to say "yes." "Was not it so, Mary?" he said: then the eloquent smile. Doctor Booth may be described as a right-down jolly fellow, with his heavy white beard and whiskers. He was one of the most hearty men I ever met. He was an angler, so was Mr. Harrison, and they often in company with a mutual friend, Mr. Brookhouse, from the same village as the doctor, Manchester, fished the Manx streams for the bonny trout. The doctor was chiefly remarkable for his immense library, which took up most of his house. He had a mania for books, and he was supposed to be a confirmed bachelor. Mr. Harrison and his friends used to fish with Indian grass lines, which Mr. Harrison had procured in some of his travels, but I do not think that they were suitable for fly-fishing, because they were so light and limp.

Our visitors had been so considerate as to bring us two loaves of bread, which were very acceptable, and we had much pleasure in giving them trout to their heart's content. They started on their return journey to Rockmount about half-past six. Milburn had remained about the camp all day, and had killed a fine curlew, which no doubt was resident on the hills for domestic purposes, but the "Wild Birds Protection Act" had not in those days been thought of, even in England.

Tea was discussed, prepared, and partaken of, and consisted of the usual viands. Our conversation was full of regrets that it was to be our last night in camp in full view of Snaefell, the intervening heathery moor with stacks of peat drying for winter consumption, and lovely Druidale, with its chafing and foaming brook rushing over its rocky bed. We all regretted leaving the sparrow-hawk in undisturbed possession. We had all tried in vain to reach the nest, it looked so easy, so near and yet so far. On this our last night we retired into the tent at nine o'clock; about ten we took off our coats, waistcoats, and boots, rolled ourselves up in our blankets, and, according to the diary, "of course we all slept soundly" on our heather bed, lumpy though it was. How cheaply man may live should he only please, and what a lot he can do without, or rather with what a little he can do!

The morn of Saturday dawned all too soon, and we rose from our couch at a quarter to seven. We prepared breakfast for the last time, which consisted, according to the diary, of the usual edibles. We had quite learned to do without beef or mutton; we found that bacon, trout, and bread were quite sufficient to support life on, and we had an unlimited supply of water at our feet, also of trout,—and what more can man want? Alcohol was unknown in the camp. Shortly after breakfast, all except Charlie and myself set out to ascend Snaefell, the summit of which was about four miles off, and they left us to clean the pots and pans, and cook the dinner.

During the morning our kind friend Mr. Brooke called, and he told us that he was going to Douglas, and that as he should most likely see our father there, he would be very glad to take any message for us which we might wish to send. He also pressed us to make his house our quarters on the night of that day and Sunday. We thanked Mr. Brooke for his great kindness, and explained that we were under orders not to prolong our stay among the mountains. Our worthy parents were confident that we should catch our death from colds, and we knew that they would be anxious about us, whereas we were all in perfect health, with our faces bronzed with the sun and blotched with the gnats. Mr. Brooke wished us a safe journey home, and proceeded on his way to Douglas. I pottered about the camp, fishing here and there, and caught 4 trout, one of which was a good half-pounder. Charlie and I prepared a sumptuous dinner in honour of our last day, to the entire satisfaction of the whole party, and on the return of our Snaefell excursionists about one o'clock, we dined in the open air as was our wont. For a wonder, there was no fish cooked; the menu was as follows:

    1st course, ham, potatoes, and bread.
    2nd ,,   rice pudding with currants.
    3rd ,,   bread and preserve and cocoa.

The dinner was done full justice to.

We talked for some time, and offered up incense which ascended in blue smoke until it was lost in the ethereal blue. The Snaefell party had much enjoyed their climb; they had had a splendid view all round the island also of the Cumbrian

Mountains, the Mull of Galloway, and the Mourne Mountains, Ireland.

At three o'clock we prepared for our departure. The packing of our baggage into the cart occupied us two hours, and about five o'clock all was ready; two salutes were fired, the bugle sounded, and three hearty cheers given, and off we started. It was uphill work for the poor donkey, until we crossed the ridge and reached the descent to Injabreck, which we had had so much difficulty in surmounting in the journey out. Now the situation was reversed; we had to hang on behind the cart to prevent the cart from running down the donkey. How beautiful Injabreck looked as we descended the hill, the fir woods, and the winding valley with the stream meandering at the bottom; anon the song of the cuckoo is heard as we pass through the vale, and the crake, crake of the landrail in the long grass; and the weather is perfect. Home was reached at a quarter past nine o'clock. The diary concludes by stating that about 90 trout were taken home, and that none of us ever enjoyed an excursion more than we enjoyed the Druidale Fishing Excursion and Bivouac.

Druidale, after a few more visits to the streams of Mona, thinks he is now qualified to distinguish himself in the rivers of the larger island, so he fixes upon the Derbyshire Wye that he may learn the "wherefore."

CHAPTER V

THE MAID OF HADDON

Come, scholar, let Maudlin alone; do not you offer to spoil her voice.—PISCATOR.

HAVING succeeded in capturing a few trout in the river Wharfe, I was conceited enough to suppose that I was qualified to wage war against the well-educated trout of the Derbyshire Wye, but I was then only a boy of twenty, therefore excusable. I prevailed upon my friends Joshua, Tom, and Dick to accompany me. Tom did not profess to be a fisherman; he went for a loaf.

We left home for Rowsley on the 6th of June 1861 and reached the Peacock Hotel about nine o'clock, after a journey from a station a short distance from Bradford of rather more than five hours. Travelling must have been slow in those days. The landlord at the Peacock at that time was Mr. John Cooper, and he furnished us with fishing tickets, from which we ascertained that artificial fly only was allowed, and that fish under ten inches in length could not be killed. Seeing that I considered a quarter of a pound trout a beauty, the restriction appeared most prohibitive. Rowsley is situated near to the junction of the rivers

Derwent and Wye, and is therefore a very convenient fishing station.

It was arranged that on our opening day Dick should fish in the Derwent, and Joshua and I in the Wye. About nine o'clock I commenced in the beautiful Rowsley meadows. I was quite charmed with the beauty of the scenery: park-like green meadows dotted with fine trees, the river meandering along with its numerous bends, some of which appeared to go backward. Fairy nature evidently designed the river to afford the greatest possible quantity of water in the least possible space. It really might in some parts be described as like a cork-screw. It was the feast of the May-fly, the water was covered with green and gray drakes.

In those days I pinned my faith on Stewart's black spider, and rarely fished without it. I had received the impression that there was no use in fishing with a large artificial fly, such as the green drake. I had not then even heard of the dry fly. However, I had dressed a few green drakes—no doubt in a wonderful manner—only to be tried if small flies failed. The weather was very bright, and the water low and clear. After fishing for some time I succeeded in capturing a nice trout of just the regulation length with my favourite black spider.

Shortly afterwards I observed a good fish feeding on the drakes under some low branches of a tree; it was a difficult cast, but I managed to get my black spider over him. He declined it again and again; I took off the black spider, and substituted one of my own green drakes, made a good deal smaller than the natural fly. At the second cast I was in him. Now came the tug of war: the situation was difficult and the fish was game.

However, in about a quarter of an hour he succumbed,

and I grassed a beautiful trout of one pound in weight. Not long afterwards I encountered the keeper, who looked at my fish, and asked how I caught the big one, and I replied with the green drake. "Do you know, sir," he said, "that the green drake is not allowed here?"

I explained that I had caught the fish with an artificial fly. I verily believe that he thought otherwise. I afterwards caught one more trout, making three, with the black spider. By about four o'clock we had fished up to Haddon Hall, which was formerly a fortified mansion occupied by the Earls of Rutland. At this time the fish were not taking, and we met Tom on the loaf near the Hall; he had been wandering about the old mansion. I will now quote from a wonderful journal of one of the party.

"On his (Tom's) assurance that the Hall was well worth going over, backed by the fact of a very pretty girl being the guide, we determined to go. After getting some ginger beer at the cottage we proceeded to the Hall, headed by the pretty girl. We found our guide full of fun and very amusing. She appeared to be thirteen or fourteen years of age, and wore her hair in long curls, of a pretty flaxen hue. She was dressed in a black dress and black straw hat. We must have spent at least two hours with her in the Hall. Not one of us had any wish to part company with her in a hurry.

"After some difficulty in getting to know her name, we learnt that they called her Dissey. Her name in full was . . . daughter of . . . who resides at Bakewell. This bonny lassie resides with her aunt close to Haddon Hall.

"After fully enjoying her ladyship's company, we fished our way to the inn, where we arrived at nine o'clock."

I well remember the pretty maid of Haddon. One can

imagine how her dress would set off her light complexion. What a long story she warbled out about the old Hall in her sweet musical voice, and how charming was her confusion when we interrupted her recital with questions! How our good Father Izaak would have enjoyed the fair maiden's company! Perhaps he would have asked her for a song, to which the aunt in the cottage might have replied instead of the mother. Izaak Walton's milkmaid was a maiden fair; might not the fair maid of Haddon have been one of her descendants?

Our friend Dick succeeded in capturing two trout of the regulation size.

On the following morning Joshua and Dick went up the Wye, and I up the Derwent. The weather was cloudy, with slight showers. I found it impossible to do justice to the Derwent without waders, and I did not possess such articles. The fish came short, and I missed a good many rises. However, I managed to catch three trout in the Derwent, and then proceeded to the Wye between Fillyford Bridge and Haddon Hall. The water was again covered with the drakes, which were contested for by the trout and the swifts. It was interesting to watch the birds swoop down and take the drakes off the water. It was most difficult to get even a rise from the fish. I spotted a large fish feeding fast on the drakes. I threw my drake over him, and he succumbed, and proved to be a grayling of a pound and a quarter. I then fished up to the island without any result. How beautiful the scenery is hereabouts, and how quiet the lovely island and the water rippling round it! Here I disturbed a couple of wild ducks. What a paradise for trout and grayling!

The weather was now brilliant, too much so for the fly-fisher.

I retraced my steps and found Joshua and Dick near Haddon Hall. The keeper was fishing with the former's rod, but he did not succeed in getting a rise. Dick told me that he had enjoyed a very pleasant hour with the maid of Haddon.

I will again quote from the journal, which states: "At the time that Dick saw this charming piece of human nature, he had only caught one fish, and on his showing her the contents of his basket, the maiden said with a sly look, 'I suppose you call this good sport?'" What pungent sarcasm, so delightful from the lips of a pretty maiden!

However, time is getting on; we must not linger much longer in the green meadows, so we wind up, I having caught three trout and one grayling, and Dick a trout and a chub. At this juncture Joshua discovered that he had lost a landing-net, which had been lent to him by the boots of the Peacock. It is conjectured that he found it a useless encumbrance. What with hunting for this valuable landing-net which could not be found, we arrived at the Peacock at 4.20, and the train was timed to leave at 4.40, during which time we had to dine, pack up, and get to the station. Thus ended a pleasant visit of two days to the pleasant meadows of Rowsley, which still lingers delightfully in the memory, as all good things should do.

After a lapse of eighteen years, I again visited the Wye in September 1879, in company with my brother Charlie, business matters having led me into the neighbourhood. On Monday the 29th of September, we commenced operations at Fillyford Bridge. I was again charmed by the beautiful river and the scenery. The trees were assuming their autumnal tint, the meadows were verdant. It was a treat to wander by the river. There had been some heavy rain on Sunday and the water was white. After a dense fog in the early morning, the weather became bright and hot, and it was quite calm. I did not get a rise until nearly opposite Haddon Hall, when I hooked a good trout, which got off. I afterwards hooked several trout and grayling, but all got off. It was not my day.

We visited Haddon Hall. It was as though time had stood still for eighteen years. There was the maid of Haddon, a pretty, fair girl of about fifteen, who wore a black dress and a black straw hat. It was like a dream of the past, but the then maid of Haddon was not quite so vivacious as the maid of yore, but she had the same old story told in much the same way. She said she was a niece of Dissey, and that Dissey was married and lived at Bakewell. It would be interesting to know for how many years the guide to Haddon Hall has been a fair girl with black dress and hat, and for how long the same family have held the post. I really must visit Haddon again and interview the present maid of Haddon. The Hall looked just the same, and one's thoughts wandered back to the time when hawking parties assembled in front of the Hall, pretty maidens and handsome swains with hawks on their arms, seated on their gay-looking horses, with dogs looking eager for the sport.

I am reminded of the strange conduct of a sparrow-hawk which I witnessed a few years ago. On a dull December afternoon I was walking from the village of Waddington to Waddington Station. The road was a broad lane with grassy sides, with high thorn fences on both sides. I observed a bird with strange fluttering flight alight close to the hedge on the left side of the road. In the distance I saw a horse and cart, attended by two boys, advancing. As they neared the place where the bird had alighted, the bird rose and flew over the hedge into the adjoining field and alighted close to the hedge. There was a gap near and the boys ran after the bird, and in a short time they emerged, one of them having in his hand a sparrow-hawk, which clutched the remains of a blackbird in its claws. The bird's eyes looked so bold and fearless. The boy had caught the hawk on the ground; the boy said the hawk would not leave go of the remains of the blackbird.

On the following day we again fished. I again hooked several fish, but with the same result as the previous day. The water was covered with flies. Thus I fished for two days in the Wye and scored a blank, but I much enjoyed wandering along the banks of the beautiful Wye, a very queen of a stream for the trout and grayling. The reader will now follow Druidale into Wales in search again of pastures new, and with certain encumbrances.

CHAPTER VI

WALES—CLWYD, ELWY, LLUGWY

No life, my honest scholar, no life so happy and so pleasant as the life of a well-governed angler.—PISCATOR.

IN the month of June 1874 I introduced myself to some of the rivers in the Principality. I located myself with my encumbrances at Rhyl. I can fully recommend Rhyl to paterfamilias. The sands are such as children delight in; in addition the air is decidedly bracing. I soon discovered that it was not at all a bad place for the angler. A glance at the map will show that the river Clwyd flows into the sea at Rhyl. Up to Rhuddlan Castle there is no trout fishing, because up to that point the river is practically an estuary, and the tide even flows some distance above the Castle. About a mile above the Castle the rivers Clwyd and Elwy unite. For a great distance above the junction the Clwyd is sluggish and deep, with high banks, and unsuitable for trout fishing. The Elwy is quite different, being a charming succession of pools and streams, and the banks generally low.

I soon ascertained that there was an angling association at Rhyl, and that day-tickets could be obtained for half-a-crown. On the 13th of June, having provided myself with a ticket, I proceeded by rail from Rhyl to Rhuddlan, and wended my way up the banks of the river. In passing, I much admired the old castle with its ivy-clad walls, and speculated as to its past history. I was much pleased with the formation of the river, which was alternate pool and stream, and looked very likely indeed. In proceeding through a thick, reedy place I flushed a mallard; no doubt his mate was near. The river was dead low and the sky cloudless, and I had decided to confine myself to fly.

When I arrived at the junction I elected to proceed up the Elwy, which looked much more likely than the Clwyd, and I fished to above the cathedral city of St. Asaph, which is prettily situated on rising ground about equidistant from the two rivers. The vale of the Elwy is delightful, being well wooded, and it was a treat to wander by the sparkling river; but I found the trout very wee, and I had to return many mites to the water. I kept five, and they were rather wee anes. I made a mental note that if I had devoted more time to the main river, I might have done better.

On the 16th I was off again to the river; the water and weather were the same, and all the conditions appeared against the fly, but there was just one element in my favour, rather a cool air from the north. I fished every yard of fishable water and met with my reward: by the time I got to the junction I had creeled 16 nice trout, the best of which weighed three-quarters of a pound. I then fished for some distance up the Clwyd, but did not increase my score.

On the 20th the weather and water were still the same, and I was once more at it. On arriving at the junction I had 15 fish. I proceeded some distance up the Clwyd and caught 2 more, making 17—not bad considering the low state of the water and the brightness of the weather. Then came the wish for really good sport. Distance always lends enchantment to the scene, and it is ever so with fishing. The knowing ones at Rhyl thought that there was good fishing at Bettws-y-Coed and Capel Curig, so on the 25th of June I journeyed by the lovely Vale of Conway to Bettws-y-Coed, and after lunch at the Waterloo Hotel, I proceeded up the Llugwy to the Swallow Falls, which I much admired. I then commenced to fish down the Llugwy.

At the head of the Vale loomed mighty Moel Siabod, upon the top of which hung an indigo-blue thunder-cloud. Mutterings of thunder were occasionally heard, but the storm passed off in another direction. It was bright and hot in the valley. The bed of the river was broad and stony, huge stones lying promiscuously scattered, and helping to form numerous little pools, wherein trout were rising nicely— generally out of reach, as wading was not permitted. As the banks were thickly wooded, casting was difficult, and I only managed to capture three trout. I felt that if I only could have waded out and cast among the big stones I could have caught a lot of trout.

On the following day I went by coach to Capel Curig, and was much charmed by the beautiful scenery *en route*. As we neared Capel Curig there was a splendid view of Snowdon; the weather was most brilliant. After lunch, about twelve o'clock, I went down to the lake with a view of fishing. There were plenty of boats but no boatmen about, not even a small loafing boy. However, I got into a boat, and alternately rowed and fished, but I soon got tired of that game. A little farther on there was another lake, connected with the lake I was on by a shallow channel. I moored my boat and fished the channel, and as I progressed I saw a black bull and the black bull saw me. Not liking his looks, I decided to wind up and regain the boat. The bull decided that he would like to go to the boat, so the end was that we both trotted in the direction of the boat. As I had the start I rolled into the boat with the horns of the bull much nearer than I liked, and soon had hold of an oar, which Mr. Bull declined to face. I only caught two wretched little trout.

In the evening I asked the waiter if the bull were dangerous, and he said that he had chased several persons, but had not succeeded in catching any one so far. The waiter expressed his conviction that an umbrella was a good implement to ward off a bull with, the way being to open it and present it to his face, when there would be a bull's run. The probabilities are, that when a bull runs after a person he does not intend to commit grievous bodily harm, but an average person has not the courage to give the bull a chance to signify what his intentions really are.

I have on several occasions been routed from portions of rivers which I have wished to fish by bulls, and I have never tried conclusions with them unless under favourable conditions. On one occasion, in Sulby Glen, I was followed by a bull for some distance, the bull being on the other side. I could not stand being shadowed by a bull all day, which did not look free from doubt. The position was favourable—a low wall on my side of the river, and some trees convenient, should the bull charge. So I fired a volley of stones at the bull, one of which hit him on the nose. Away the bull ran down the vale, and I saw him no more.

After dinner I tried the river in the cool of the evening, but without success. The river looked very likely.

On the following morning I again tried the lake for an

hour and a half, but fruitlessly, and I then betook myself to the river and fished for about two hours and caught four nice little trout, which were very beautifully marked. After luncheon I bade good-bye to beautiful Capel Curig, and took advantage of the coach to Llanberis, and as we drove through the magnificent Pass of Llanberis and descended the hill, we feasted our eyes on the green lakes lying below, and the village of Llanberis cosily by; then by rail to Caernarvon with its old castle.

Having to wait some time for the coast train to Rhyl, I strolled about the town. It happened to be market-day, and I heard Welsh spoken on all sides. Welsh and nothing else did I hear spoken. What charming peeps we had from the train of the Menai Straits, so blue and calm under the evening sky, a deep glow in the west, where the sun had set, reflected on the water.

To make up for the sport at Bettws-y-Coed and Capel Curig, I must have one more day in the Clwyd, which I had forsaken, angler-like, for pastures new, and the Clwyd was kind and forgave my desertion. On the 30th of June I was off betimes in the morning to Rhuddlan. The weather was windy with slight showers, but the river was very low. However, the wind was up, so I did not care how low the water was. The trout rose well, and as was my wont when I arrived at the junction I turned out my creel and counted 24 trout. I then fished for some distance up the Clwyd, and caught 3 more, making 27 trout for my last day in the Clwyd in 1874. This excursion has made Druidale a confirmed wanderer, and we next find him after the trout on the banks of the Cumberland Eden.

CHAPTER VII

THE VALE OF EDEN

I in these flowery meads would be,
These crystal streams should solace me.
"The Angler's Wish"—PISCATOR.

WHAT more beautiful, more quietly beautiful vale is there in England than the vale of Eden, sheltered for a great distance on the east by the Pennine range, the summit of which is Cross Fell, 2893 feet above sea-level, with its snowdrifts, which often linger until far into May, and sometimes until midsummer-day? In the distance there are the Lake Mountains to be seen, and among them the monarch Helvellyn. The river Eden rises amongst the mountains in the north-west of Yorkshire, whence it flows through Westmorland and Cumberland into the Solway Firth.

From Kirkby Stephen to the cathedral city of Carlisle the vale is singularly beautiful, being generally well wooded; and the soil, where exposed, being of a ruddy colour, blends harmoniously with the green of the meadows and the varied hues of the growing corn. The houses in the vale, being generally built of red sandstone, present a warm, cosy look, a striking contrast to the gray, cold-looking houses of the West Riding of Yorkshire.

the artificial production of trout in order to keep up the stock. When, however, we consider the natural advantages which the river possesses, its magnificent volume of water and freedom from pollution, we need not be surprised at this abundance of trout life. In addition, the river is singularly favoured with numerous small tributaries, which are admirably adapted for the trout in their spawning operations. As the vale of Eden is so well sheltered from the east wind, and the soil is generally light and porous, the climate is mild, and the river an early one considering its northern situation.

There is generally a bountiful hatch of March browns about the end of March and the whole of April, so the trout soon get into fair condition. The feast of March browns is followed by that of the creeper and the stone-fly, and when the trout are well on these dainties, they are difficult to capture with the artificial fly; but at this time even, many of them cannot resist the seductions of a large light March brown, which they doubtless mistake for the stone-fly. In addition to these royal feasts, freshwater shrimps are numerous, and may be the reason why many of the trout are of a delicate pink when cooked. An Eden trout, when in the pink of condition, is very beautiful, so beautifully marked with red spots, and the other colouring difficult to describe. Their flesh is most excellent.

It might be expected from the large size of the river that the trout would average a considerable size. The usual average, however, is about three to the pound, but when fishing with worm, minnow, creeper, or the natural stone-fly, a greater average is frequently obtained. As an instance, on one occasion an angler made a large capture with the natural stone-fly in the neighbourhood of Langwathby, and selected

28 of the largest to send to a friend, and the 28 trout weighed 14 lb. With the exception of the portion of the river under the control of the Carlisle Angling Association and the Yorkshire Anglers' Association, the fishing is in private hands. The proprietors and farmers, however, are very generous in giving leave to fish, and the public have free access to some portions of the river, notably in the neighbourhood of Langwathby. Visitors at the Tufton Arms Hotel, Appleby, have access to all the waters of Lord Hothfield.

In the seventies the Penrith Angling Association preserved a considerable portion of the river, extending from about Temple Sowerby to Lazonby, and annual tickets were issued at a guinea each. I first fished in the Eden about the year 1877, and I took up my quarters at the lovely village of Kirkoswald, accompanied by my friend, Mr. Frederick Ellis, an enthusiastic angler. Kirkoswald is somewhat remarkable for the singular position of its church and the belfry, the church being in a hollow, and the belfry at the top of an adjacent hill.

There is a picturesque mansion called The College, standing in well-timbered grounds on the banks of the river, immediately below Lazonby Bridge. Some distance above the bridge there are some very interesting caves in the red sandstone rock, which are well worthy of a visit.

In the year 1878 I took a season ticket from the Penrith Angling Association, and made Temple Sowerby my headquarters. I put up at a most comfortable old-fashioned inn, kept by Mr. and Mrs. Oliphant. Temple Sowerby is about two miles above the junction of the Eamont with the Eden, and is a very pretty village. There is a village green, shaded with some large trees, a fine view of the Pennine range, culminating in Cross Fell, and of the distant Lake Mountains; also of the mountains among which Eden takes its source: just the place to idle in and dream life away.

Although the Penrith Association has become defunct, fishing may still be obtained in the neighbourhood, as the landowners and farmers are most generous souls, and there is about a mile of fishing attached to the inn, the King's Arms. The river here is all that can be desired: charming pools, streams, and flats; lovely reaches shaded by trees, under which the fly may be thrown. In addition there are three small tributary streams, which often afford fair sport, especially the Levenette. During the year I made three visits to Temple Sowerby, but I did not effect much execution amongst the trout, as I only killed 51, and on my best day I only creeled 11 trout. Nevertheless I spent days of happy contentment.

I renewed my acquaintance with the Eden in the year 1881, in company with Mr. Ellis and his son. We took up our quarters at the Tufton Arms Hotel, Appleby. I believe that Appleby has the honour of being the smallest municipal borough in England. The old part of the town is situated in a hollow on the banks of the Eden, the new part on rising ground, tending towards the railway station.

The principal objects of interest are the old parish church and Appleby Castle, the Westmorland seat of Lord Hothfield, the latter being perched on an eminence on the right bank of the river, consequently a conspicuous object for miles. Two very steep conical green hills, offshoots of the great Pennine range, to the eastward of the tiny town, much enhance the beauty of the scenery. May though it was, there were deep snowdrifts low down the sides of the mountain range, Cross Fell in the distant background, with its corona of spotless snow, and in the far distance, on the west, the Lake Mountains in the neighbourhood of Ullswater, with streaks of snow on their sides.

Appleby is a snug, well-sheltered little town, and is situated amid beautiful scenery. There is a very pretty walk on a footpath to the north-west of the town, up a steep ascent near the river, whence there is a beautiful view of the river many feet below; on one side, a high wooded bank, the other side being low, with green meadows. This part of the river is called the St. Nicholas Home, and is famed for its good fishing. There is every reason why Appleby should in the course of time be a favourite health resort. It has many facilities, excellent railway accommodation, miles of excellent fishing, and a vast extent of beautiful scenery to explore; and, best of all, the air is bracing and salubrious.

On the evening of our arrival, Saturday the 7th of May, we fished near the Castle. I had the felicity of one rise, and the trout, a monster of unknown weight, took away two flies. On Sunday we attended service at the most interesting old parish church, and in the afternoon we took a long walk up the river and made our plans for the morrow.

Monday was a very bright day, with a cool wind from the north, water very low and clear. I decided to fish up in the direction of Ormside. For upwards of a mile there is a reach of deep calm water, very good for large chub; the consequence was, that I had to walk about two miles before I commenced to fish. In the neighbourhood of the railway bridge and upwards, there are some beautiful streams, but, alas, there was no rise on. I made a long day of it, and fished until past eight o'clock, and although I used worm as well as fly, I only captured four trout.

On the following day I took the train to Kirkby Thore, and fished from about ten to three o'clock. The weather was very hot and cloudless, and the water low. There are some lovely streams and pools about Kirkby Thore, and trout were numerous. I pricked and hooked an undue number of fish compared with those I caught. In the end I captured only seven trout, all on a small blue dun, which was not so bad after all, considering the bright weather and low water. I enjoyed watching the swallows, sandpipers, wagtails, dippers, and other birds flitting here and there, and at times the cuckoo's clear note rang through the pure air.

I was so pleased with the Eden at Kirkby Thore that I hoped to revisit it at some time, and I was not long in doing so. In April 1885 I was favoured by the courteous agent of Lord Hothfield at Appleby with a season ticket for his lordship's water in the Eden, so on the 22nd I journeyed to Kirkby Thore and took up my quarters at the Bridge Inn, which is charmingly situated on the banks of Trout Beck, a nice stream which rises among the Pennine range and about 200 yards from the Eden. On my arrival I discovered to my dismay that Lord Hothfield had only one farm in that neighbourhood, occupied by a gentleman called Mr. Tom, who had all the sporting rights over the farm. I called at the farm and saw Mrs. Tom, who at once gave me permission to fish, and I wrote letters to Mr. Westmorland and Mr. Graham, two landed proprietors, who gave me most courteous permission to fish on their estates, so I was all right. The weather was wet and disagreeable, such a contrast to the brilliant weather on the occasion of my former visit.

On Thursday the 23rd there was a considerable fresh in the river; it was a worm or heavy minnow water. I commenced operations in Trout Beck with worm, but only got two bites. I then put on a small Devon minnow, with which I caught one trout at the head of a mill-race. Finding the Beck unproductive, I went down to the river, and with worm caught one fish and hooked two others. I soon satisfied myself that the fish were not on the worm, so I walked up to a likely place for minnow, but there was a man there, trying the natural minnow. I watched him for some time, and he had not a run. He said, "They may come on at any time." After he had left the place I tried it over with a small sole-skin minnow, with which I soon caught two trout. Then I ran a good fish which took the minnow literally, and I was left lamenting, as it was the only sole-skin minnow I had. I then resumed the Devon, with which I caught one more trout, making five in all. There were five other men fishing, all of whom had very light creels, so it was clear that the fish were not on the feed that day.

On the next day, Friday, the weather was most unpleasant —rainy, with a strong wind partly down and partly across the river. As there were several men on the windward bank I decided to fish from the leeward bank, and as the wind was so strong I generally had to let my flies drift below me under the bank, which is not favourable for hooking and retaining fish. My tail fly was a quill March brown, my first dropper orange partridge and my second a red palmer. I caught a fish here and lost a fish there in the usual way. About eleven o'clock I observed a local hand on the opposite bank fishing a portion of the river which was fringed with low willows for about 150 yards. He called out,

"How are they doing?"

"Middling," I replied. "How are you doing?"

Local hand. "Pretty well."

While he was in my view he sat down and solemnly smoked a pipe. I fished a considerable distance below him, and then reversed my steps, fishing here and there on my way back to mine inn. About four o'clock I again passed him, still amid his favourite willows.

"Well," he shouted, "how've you gotten on?"

I replied, "I've caught about a score. How many have you got?"

Local hand. "Well, I've caught twenty-five, and I've got them all hereabouts, but I think they've about gi'en over rising."

No wonder, thought I, seeing he had been a fixture there all day. That fellow was taking it easy and no mistake. He knew what he was about. He evidently knew the advantages of being the man in possession. I made a mental note of this experience. When you secure a really good piece of water in the Eden, stick to it and fish it over and over again, giving occasional rests, and you will be rewarded. Some reaches in the Eden are especially productive, and especially those places fringed with willows. I ended my day with twenty trout.

My next and last day, Saturday, was a most unproductive day. There was a muddy fresh in the river. The weather was very windy, with occasional showers and bright sunshine, and in the afternoon there was thunder. I tried both the Beck and the river with Devon minnow, worm, and large flies, and the result was, one trout with worm and one with minnow; the result of my excursion therefore was twenty-seven trout. However, I much enjoyed the excursion, and felt satisfied

F

that under favourable conditions good sport might be obtained in the Eden at Kirkby Thore. We will in due time return to the beautiful Eden in another place when we record the doings of the Yorkshire Anglers' Association. Reverting to Druidale's former visit to the Eden in 1878, an epoch in his career had come, and will be told in the next chapter.

CHAPTER VIII

THE AIRE, SKIPTON

But, my loving master, if any wind will not serve, then I wish I were in Lapland, to buy a good wind of one of the honest witches that sell so many winds there and so cheap.—VENATOR.

IN the month of February 1879, I became a member of the Aire Angling Club, on the nomination of the late Mr. George Ellis of Castlefield, Bingley, a good all-round sportsman. How well I remember his tall stalwart figure by the riverside, and his good-natured jovial countenance at the annual dinners of the club, which were most pleasant re-unions. The late Mr. J. R. Tennant of Kildwick Hall, who might be called the father of the club, was usually present at the dinners, and it was quite a treat to sit next to him and receive the broadsides of his voluminous flow of conversation, especially if one wanted to devote one's whole attention to the comestibles, for Mr. Tennant was one of those good-natured individuals who do not insist on their hearers contributing their due quota to the conversation.

In Mr. T. H. Dewhirst of Skipton the club have a most courteous honorary secretary, who has for many years ruled with beneficent sway over the affairs of the club, cordially assisted by that veteran angler Mr. William Naylor of Keighley, who is well known as a salmon-fisher on the Lune, and as an occasional contributor to sporting papers. He was and is a doughty literary opponent, and he is a bold man who will tackle him. The late Mr. Pritt found this out when he and Mr. Naylor (N. of K.) fought the great battle of the blue dun, or rather over the derivation and meaning of the north country word "bloa" or "blae," which is used to describe certain flies such as water-hen bloa and snipe bloa.

The fly-fishing waters of the Aire Club extend from Carlton Bridge, a little below Skipton, to Gargrave, a distance of more than four miles. The fishing for the whole distance may be described as delightful, such a fine combination of pool and stream. The stream has a great advantage in that it can be fished from the banks, and one drawback is that the banks are generally high, with the exception of the part above Inny Bridge, the consequence being that waders are convenient, so that the angler may stand in the water when fishing where necessary, and not be perched on a high bank, in full view of the trout.

It takes some practice to learn to fish the Aire in a satisfactory manner, and a person new to the water should not expect much sport at first. The trout frequently rise well at the fly, and they take minnow freely. They are remarkable for their firmness and delicacy of flavour; they run a good size, and fish over a pound are frequently taken, especially with the minnow. There is no doubt that the dry fly could be practised with success, as there are many glides favourable for that mode of fishing, and I believe it is now practised to a considerable extent.

I commenced my acquaintance with the Aire on the 4th of

March 1878, in company with a member of the club, Mr. Frederick Ellis of Highfield, Dewsbury, whose guest I was. We proceeded to Inny Bridge, about two miles above Carlton Bridge; whilst we were putting up our rods we were pounced upon by the two respectable old gentlemen who were then the watchers for the club, old Bob and old Sam. The former, who considered himself a past grand-master of entomology, examined our flies; he pronounced my friend's flies as no good at all, but mine, which were much smaller, all right. The old gentleman then paddled away.

Mr. Ellis. "What shall I do about these flies of mine? Bob says they are of no use."

I replied, "Never mind old Bob; we will try our own flies, and if mine kill and yours do not I will set you up with some of my flies."

Mr. Ellis proceeded above the bridge to offer his abominations to the trout, and I walked some distance below to offer them the correct thing. I flogged away for over half an hour and never had a rise. I then rejoined my friend above the bridge and found him jubilant; he had caught three fish.

"Well," I said, "I cannot get a rise; what are they taking?"

"Oh, they are taking this fly," he said, and he showed me a fly dressed on a No. 3 hook, the celebrated water-hen bloa, only that the body was ribbed with silver tinsel. My friend with his usual generosity gave me a similar fly, which made me quite happy as I soon commenced to catch trout with it. Of course the reason was that it was early in the season and there was a good water, hence the trout were much more likely to take a large fly than a small one, as all would-be anglers should note. My first day's sport in the Aire was by no means brilliant, but I was quite satisfied; I killed 6 trout.

After I became a member of the club I distinguished myself on my two first days, March 4th and April 1st, with two blank days. On the 12th of May I managed to catch 3 trout, and my first respectable day, July 23rd, I killed 13 trout. It must be borne in mind that I resided nearly twenty-five miles from the river, and went for the day only, as and when I could find time without regard to weather or water; and when men fish under such conditions, their success must be very uncertain. My best baskets of trout were :—

1879.	July 23			13 trout.
	August 14			12 ,,
1880.	May 31			13 ,,
	July 31			15 ,,
1881.	August 4			13 ,,
	August 9			15 ,,
	September 20			18 ,,
1882.	May 22	.		17 ,,
	June 12	.	.	19 ,,
	June 26	.	.	18 ,,
1883.	April 21	.		22 ,,
	September 13	.	.	14 ,,

I only give the captures of one dozen or upwards, as I consider one dozen above the average. Of the 535 trout killed by me when a member of the club, 464 were caught with artificial fly, 61 with worm, and 10 with minnow, and the largest trout weighed 1 lb. I did not care how low the water was, provided that there was a nice wind up stream so that I could fish up.

At first old Bob the keeper was quite disgusted with me because I persisted in fishing fly up stream. On one occasion

I was fishing up in a nice fly-water; the weather and water were perfect, but the fish would not rise. Old Bob came to me and said—

"You will never do any good until you fish down like other folk. Now just go up there and fish that run down, and you'll get some fish."

To humour the old boy I did so; no result.

"Now, Bob," I said, "you go up the next run and fish it down, for of course you can catch them."

Bob did so and he did not get a rise, so I considered that I got a rise out of Bob. The great difficulty was to get a day with a nice wind up stream, as a south-east wind was necessary. The wind was generally west or north-west, and blew down between the high banks as though through a funnel, which made casting up, if not impossible, very difficult.

I will proceed to describe the sport I had on my best day. I commenced at Carlton Bridge at ten o'clock and fished carefully up. The water was dead low, the weather was cloudy with a cool east wind up stream. I fished to a deep pool a few yards below Carlton foot-bridge without a rise, and in that pool I killed my first trout at eleven o'clock; then the fun began, and I fished up to Inny Bridge, killing fish both in the pools ruffled by the breeze and in the streams, catching trout after trout. I reached Inny Bridge at three o'clock and counted my fish, and there were 22, the largest close on a pound, 17 of which fell to the female March brown and 5 to the yellow snipe. There were many olive duns on the water. Being quite satisfied I wound up and caught an early train home. What a contrast to my previous day's fishing on the 14th of April,—water very low, weather alternate cloud and sunshine, fresh north-west by west wind, result 3 fish.

As a rule it is difficult to catch trout with the fly during bright sunshine.

On the 22nd of May 1882, I killed 17 trout with the fly, got broken by trout four times, and returned 10 trout under the limit (eight inches) to the water; weather very bright, water very low, but the wind in the right quarter up stream. When the water is low an up-stream wind is absolutely necessary for success, because in that case the streams do not afford sufficient fishing ground.

It may be interesting to give a list of the flies with which I killed the trout in the club water, which I do so far as I am able in the order of merit :—light March brown, yellow light snipe, orange partridge, black spider, blue dun, yellow dun, orange starling or snipe, yellow partridge, maroon partridge, blue partridge, maroon starling, brown dun, yellow landrail, orange landrail, golden dun midge, green spider, peacock dun, red palmer, yellow curlew, coch-y-bundy.

Upon the whole the Aire is a much more easy river to fish than the Wharfe or Ure, and it is much easier to catch trout with the fly in low water, provided there be a breeze up stream, than in the Wharfe or Ure. There are not those long flats of shallow water to puzzle the fisherman, which abound in the other rivers. In addition, wading in the Aire is very easy, as the bottom of the river is not paved with large stones like the Wharfe and Ure. I have killed altogether 599 trout in the Aire, 521 of which were caught with fly, 68 with worm, and 10 with minnow, and the total weight was 176 lb. 8 oz.

CHAPTER IX

THE IRT, CUMBERLAND—AFTER SEA-TROUT

I am glad of that; but I have no fortune: sure, master, yours is a better rod and better tackling.—VENATOR.

IN the autumn of the year 1879, I was imbued with the desire to go sea-trout fishing, or, to say more generally, to endeavour to capture some specimens of the migratory salmonidæ. Where to go was the momentous question. In the end, after consulting the *Angler's Companion*, I decided to go to Calder Bridge, on the Cumbrian Calder, whither I started on the 1st of September, regardless that that day was the feast of St. Partridge.

On the journey I discovered that the hotel at Calder Bridge was some miles from the railway station, so I wired to the landlord to send to meet the train. Brother anglers, take warning where you wire to, and how you word your telegram. Picture my amazement when I alighted from the train and found a handsome carriage and pair awaiting my arrival, and my sense of mortification when I was deposited at the hotel door and received in state by the landlady and a posse of servants, who took charge of my luggage, a wretched shabby black leather bag and rather ancient creel. I felt very small.

The landlady said, "I thought you would be bringing your lady with you, so I sent the carriage for you." Ah! they expected two belated honeymooners no doubt, who were supposed to have more money than wit, and no wonder, when the porterage of the miserable telegram cost five shillings; and bear in mind that I arrived between eight and nine o'clock at night, just the honeymoon time.

After dinner (of course they had prepared a sumptuous dinner for the expected distinguished guests, and as I was the only one, I dined in solitary grandeur) I lighted a cigar and strolled into the garden. A turbulent stream ran by the garden, and at one part formed a pretty cascade. The roar of the falling water sounded melancholy, and I felt sad and lonely. If I had had my lady with me, I should no doubt have felt all right, and listened to the falling water as to sweet music. I should have welcomed even my friend Brown, who always when supposed to be two miles down the river suddenly appears in view about 100 yards ahead disappearing round the next bend.

By the morning my spirits had returned, and I strolled into the garden to examine the waterfall. In the pool below the fall I saw several sea-fish of about half a pound in weight, and my spirits rose with anticipation. The scenery was beautiful: a lovely well-wooded valley, with the mansion of Calder Abbey; the Abbey and a fine park studded with fine trees; the narrow valley of the Calder above; in the distance a fine view of Scawfell and the adjacent mountains in the neighbourhood of Wast Water. The surroundings were indeed charming.

After a conference with the village blacksmith, I decided to fish down to the sea. The village blacksmith is often an authority on matters piscatorial in Cumberland, so when deficient in local knowledge hie whither

> Under a spreading chestnut tree
> The village smithy stands,

and consult the smith

> With large and sinewy hands,

and he will tell you all he knows, and lend you his rod, if you ask him, which he wields with

> The muscles of his brawny arms
> As strong as iron bands.
> LONGFELLOW.

The smith informed me that he generally found trout flies on fine gut better for sea-trout than the usual monsters on sea-trout gut.

I soon found myself in a narrow valley with the rapid stream at the bottom. It looked likely enough, but the weather was horrid; a heavy gale blew up the valley from the sea, and made fishing a toil instead of a pleasure. The result was a fish, called in Cumberland a herling or sprod, of half a pound, and two small yellow trout. My flies were worried by parr, which were a great nuisance. The sea was magnificent, huge waves breaking on the shore.

I decided to seek fresh pastures, and after consideration I fixed on the Ehen which flows out of Ennerdale Lake, so on the following morning I drove to Egremont, went to the principal hotel, and after ordering dinner, strolled down to the bridge which spans the Ehen. I was surprised to find the water quite red, caused, I ascertained from one of the usual idlers on the bridge, by the ironstone mines in the neighbourhood, and he further informed me there were plenty of sea-trout in the river, but that they were caught by bait or spinning. I decided that this was not good enough. In addition, I did not like the place, it was not rural enough; but the question was, where to go to. I inspected the old castle, and then returned to the inn for dinner, not knowing what to do next.

Fortunately I met a very pleasant gentleman at dinner, in whom I confided. He said that he went regularly to a small village on the Irt, called Holmrook, on business, and that it was a very pretty spot; that not being an angler, he could not say anything about the fishing, but that he knew that the landlord had salmon nets. Just the place, thought I. I wired to the landlord of the Holmrook Inn to send *a trap* to meet me at Drigg Station, and in the evening I arrived at Holmrook. I was charmed with the place at first sight. The inn is close to the river, which can be seen from the windows. The scenery is all that can be desired. The inn is called the Lutwidge Arms, landlord, Mr. Abraham Brocklebank, who combined the occupations of innkeeper, farmer, miller, and salmon-fisher. On the following morning I rose with great expectations and breakfasted at half-past seven o'clock, and decided to walk to a little village called Santon Bridge, about two miles and a half up the river, and fish down to Holmrook. The weather was beautiful, the air was so fresh and crisp after the rain in the night. As I walked up the well-wooded valley, I had a splendid view of the mountains at the head of the dale, Wastdale. The atmosphere was unusually clear, so the mountains were seen to great advantage.

The tiny village at Santon Bridge has lovely surroundings, pine woods, the river a nutty brown colour flowing under the picturesque bridge into a large pool below. The condition of the water was perfect. That pool must yield something good thought I. I fished the pool most carefully—result, one wee trout, which I returned to the water. Below the pool the river is unfishable, because of a dense wood, for about a quarter of a mile. There are very pretty walks in the wood and fine views of the river, which for some distance is very rocky with frequent pretty cascades. A rustic summer house appears fairly to overhang the river at its most romantic part, and below is a foaming cascade, flowing into a deep rocky pool. Getting out of the wood, the dale becomes more open, and we are in Irton Hall park, and we see the Hall on the top of rising ground on our left, whence there is a lovely view of the valley of the Irt and the mountains in the distance.

The surroundings are indeed beautiful; the weather is perfect. We can enjoy ourselves whether the fish will take or not. There are some lovely reaches of water before me. In a well-looking pool immediately in front of the Hall, I had my first rise and pricked a good fish. One of my flies was a large black spider with silver tinsel. When attaching this fly to my cast, I had some doubt about it; it appeared groggy at the head, but as it bore what I supposed was a strong pull, I in an evil moment attached it. When you are among good fish, discard any fly when there is the least suspicion about it. I cast over the pool again and saw the whole thing happen. A fish of about two pounds rose from the depths of the pool and sucked in the fly; as I saw him turn downwards I struck gently, and, alas! the line came back. The fish had taken the wretched fly, alas! *mea culpa*.

I hooked two more good fish in that pool, both of which got off. A little lower down I hooked another good fish with the same result. I did not get any more rises from sea-fish, but I caught a nice half-pound yellow trout, which was the sole occupant of my creel. Thus ended my first day in the Irt, a day of mortification, which only made me keener than ever to try conclusions on the morrow.

On the morrow the water had considerably fined down, and having decided to wear waders, I drove to Santon Bridge and fished the same water as on the previous day. I hooked two fish in the rough water below the wood, and landed one, a half-pound herling or sprod. A little below there is an island, and just above the island I hooked three good fish, all of which got off. I afterwards caught two brown trout, so I had three fish to my credit.

In the evening my friends Dick and Joe arrived, so we formed quite a merry party, and discussed our plans for the next day. I decided to try a small stream, the Mite, about two miles off, for trout, which I was informed were numerous. I trudged the two miles, and tried some likely looking pools near the sea for sea-trout, but without success. I then wandered up the stream, alternately trying worm and fly, and wound up with eleven mity trout; they were wee anes. Dick fished from Santon Bridge and caught one small trout.

The morrow being the Sabbath, we walked across the fields to Irton Church, about two miles, and much enjoyed the walk through lovely scenery. On Monday we drove a long way up Wastdale, nearly as far as Wastdalehead, with the intention of fishing down the river. The streams and pools were all that could be desired, but we could not beguile the fish: it thundered several times, which may have accounted for our bad sport. I only caught four small trout. The natives said that most of the trout went to Wast Water at that time of the year. There certainly appeared to be very few trout in the river. My friends saw two fine salmon in a pool above Santon Bridge.

During the evening the village blacksmith came in for a glass and a chat, and we bemoaned with him our lack of sport. The smith was a mighty fisherman. We chaffed him about the fish and the fishing, and promised to take all the fish he might catch on the morrow at 1s. 6d. a pound, and a bargain was made. We were all in fun, never thinking that the result would be as it turned out.

On the morrow, Tuesday, I rose early and commenced fishing about Holmrook Bridge about seven o'clock, and fished until a quarter past eight without a rise. After breakfast I fished up as far as the next stone bridge, hooked one fish, and pricked another. When we assembled for dinner, we asked our fair waitress what sport the smith had had. The maid looked very knowing, and said we should see after dinner; more she would not say. After dinner, in walked the jovial smith with two salmon and a sea-trout on a tray: we could hardly believe our eyes: they were clean run fish as bright as silver; the salmon weighed seven and a half and seven pounds respectively. He had killed all with fly, at noon, close to the inn. We kept our bargain. In the evening I fished for some time and killed one herling.

I met a great fisherman near the bridge, Colonel Mawson, of Manchester, who was wielding an eighteen-foot salmon rod. The gallant Colonel had become so enamoured with the place that he had built a pretty Swiss châlet for a country residence, and passed much of his time there. In answer to his inquiry as to my sport, I told him that the fish when hooked would not stick on, and he replied, "Just the same with me; it has been so all the season." Dick killed a herling the same evening with the smith's rod, which was a caution for weight.

On the following day, Wednesday, I resolved to try the water below the bridge almost to the sea, most of which is deep and sluggish. After trying fly for some time unsuccessfully, I tried a yellow devil-killer, mounted with three sets of treble hooks, with which I hooked a good sea-trout, which got off: another fish rushed at it, but did not take it. After trying the devil-killer some time longer without any result—excepting sticking one of the hooks above the barb in one of my fingers, which caused much pain in getting out—I resumed the fly, and was soon fast to a sea-trout of about two pounds which fought furiously, but in the end the hold gave way and he was free. Shortly afterwards I hooked another good fish—alas, with the same result. I then sat down and smoked a pipe to relieve my feelings: I had no one to vent them on. I came to the conclusion that sea-trout fishing was not my forte. Ultimately I creeled two yellow fins and one small brown trout.

Thursday the 11th of September—my last day—broke with a heavy atmosphere, with every appearance of rain. I elected to try the low water again, and I fished in vain with fly, artificial minnow, and devil-killer, and never touched a fish excepting one wee trout. At half-past one the windows of heaven were opened and the floods descended, and there was a great rain, and I continued fishing for some hours in the downpour.

On the following morning the river was bank full with a yellow fresh. There was a great run of fish. As the landlord drove me to the station, we saw several local hands worming in the flood, with piles of fish on the ground by them.

The Irt, Cumberland—after Sea-Trout

The landlord said, "Look there, you ought to be coming instead of going away." "It was ever thus," I replied. "I am always wrong."

No doubt I missed a good thing. With a fair amount of luck or fortune, whichever it may be, fair sport may be obtained in the Irt in the autumn with sea-fish. I was informed that the up-stream worm in clear water was often very successful, and that the fly was very uncertain. There is no doubt that the Irt is a very poor river for brown trout, which I surmise are kept down by the voracious sea-fish. The late Mr. Burns-Linder was extremely liberal in granting leave to fish in his water about Irton Hall.

CHAPTER X

THE URE, ASKRIGG

I will keep you here for a month, but you shall have one good day of sport before you go.—PISCATOR.

THE Ure or Yore is one of the largest rivers in Yorkshire, and rises in the neighbourhood of Lunds Fell about 2100 feet above sea-level, not far from the source of the Eden. There are a great many small tributaries, very favourable for the trout in their spawning operations. The district is most interesting, and there are several waterfalls—notably Hardraw Force, having a fall of nearly 100 feet, near Hawes, and Millgill Force, about 70 feet, near Askrigg, both being on tributary streams. The bed of the river in most places is covered with large rounded-off stones, which render wading difficult and laborious.

Trout and grayling are numerous, and the local hands say that there are more trout than grayling. The higher portion of the river may be divided into two sections: number one from the source to Yore Bridge, which is under the control of the Hawes and High Abbotside Angling Association, and number two from Yore Bridge to Aysgarth, a considerable portion of which is under the control of the Wensleydale Angling

Association. As the subscriptions are only nominal, and the men of the district ardent fishermen, the river is very much fished. It is all very well for men in the neighbourhood, but if when the angler has come from a distance he shall find the local men out in force, which he assuredly will do should the water be in order, the game is hardly worth the candle.

I do not know a better formation of river than the Ure from Hawes to Aysgarth—any river more favourable for trout; and if that length could be preserved by a club of about eighty non-resident members, it would probably afford the best fishing in the Ure. But after all it would be a pity to deprive the hard-worked labouring man of his bit of sport. It is rather remarkable that the trout above Yore Bridge differ much in colouring from those below; the former being remarkable for their golden bellies, and the latter being much lighter. Askrigg and Bainbridge are very convenient places to put up at. During the holiday season a good many visitors put up for some weeks at Askrigg, whence they explore the surrounding country. Askrigg is situated on a slope at a considerable elevation above the river, hence the air is very bracing. It is only a few minutes' walk from the Moors, to which there is a fair carriage road, but the ascent is very steep.

Like many other places in the Dales, Askrigg was in years gone by of much greater importance than it is now. The church dedicated to St. Oswald is rather an elongated structure, and was evidently built for a larger population than at present.

My friend James and I went to Askrigg on the 22nd of October 1880, and we put up at the King's Arms—landlord then Mr. Richard Mason. Our object was grayling fishing. The weather was very cold and wet, with some snow; also sharp frosts on some nights. I fished on three days, but owing to the unfavourable weather had not much success. On the two first days I killed seven grayling with fly: on the last day a heavy flood came down, and at night, as I was returning home, snow fell heavily. I was so favourably impressed with the river that I was anxious to try it again under more favourable conditions, but in this I was disappointed. As I journeyed to Askrigg via Northallerton, on the 25th of August 1881, heavy rain fell, and the river was over the banks.

On the following day the valley formed a large lake, and it was quite impossible to approach the river; in fact, the exact whereabouts of the river could not be ascertained. Fishing was quite out of the question. In the morning I took the train to Aysgarth to view the falls, and I was well rewarded: such a mass of dashing, raging, foaming, seething, roaring, wild waters. How awful it looked; think of a man tossed like a cork on that wild waste of waters. For half an hour I sat watching the turbid flood, then I returned to Askrigg and explored the Millgill Force, amid the rocks and trees one sheer vast fall of peaty waters.

On the following day, Saturday, I took the train to Hawes, and commenced in one of the tributaries, as the river was still very heavy. I tried with worm and artificial minnow, but without the least success. I then went to the main stream and caught two trout with minnow; one of the trout was exactly a pound in weight, and literally gorged with worms. I then, as the water was clearing, changed to fly, with which I caught one grayling and hooked some nice fish, but they came so short that I could not manage it.

On Sunday afternoon I walked up the river. There was a large porter-coloured fly-water, and the trout were rising.

Prospects for the morrow seemed good; but, alas, at night heavy rain set in and destroyed my hopes.

On Monday there was a heavy muddy rising fresh, and the weather was very rainy with some distant thunder. I tried both worm and Devon minnow in the afternoon for about two hours, and had two runs with minnow.

On Tuesday the water was a heavy fresh, and I took the noon train to Hawes and fished down with minnow and fly, and I killed one trout with minnow and one with fly. To compensate for the bad sport there was a nice company of ladies and gentlemen at the inn: the custom of the house was to have a meat tea at seven o'clock. In the evening we amused ourselves with cards and other games. I was the only fisherman. There were several amateur artists.

On Wednesday there was a heavy porter-coloured fly-water, and I fished above Yore Bridge and killed four trout and one grayling with fly.

On Thursday the 1st of September, there was a full clear water, and the sport improved and I killed eleven trout with fly. I had a great misfortune. A considerable distance above Yore Bridge, in a lovely pool, I hooked something really good. As it was a difficult place to land a good fish in, I decided to pull him about fifty yards below. He went down beautifully —he knew where he was going and I did not. A sudden stoppage and I was fast. I waded a little out to prospect, and I saw that the trout had run under a water-logged piece of wood with some debris attached. I saw the trout distinctly, at least a pound and a half. The net was not of sufficient strength to get to him and scoop him out with, so I rolled over the wood in hopes that I might get my line clear; but a smash followed, and I lost the whole fly cast.

On Friday, my last day, I fished above Hawes and killed nine trout and one grayling with fly ; one of the trout weighed three-quarters of a pound.

The total result of my fishing was twenty-eight trout and three grayling. As will have been observed, the water never got settled. The fish came short to the fly. I had had too much rain, too much of a good thing. As I became a member of the Kilnsey Angling Club in the following year, and as the Ure and Wharfe are somewhat similar, I had no inducement again to visit Askrigg.

Druidale, having in this and the previous chapters endeavoured to instil into the young the love of fishing, will in the next four chapters try to teach them how to become successful fishermen.

CHAPTER XI

FLY-FISHING FOR TROUT

You are to know that there are so many sorts of flies as there be of fruits.—PISCATOR.

IT is generally conceded that fishing with the artificial fly is the most enjoyable method of fishing for trout, and it is also the most intellectual, for the angler has always to exercise his mind as to the kind and size of fly to use on any particular occasion, and he may exercise his ingenuity in the creation of some fancy insect, which may be attractive, for it is well known that some excellent fancy flies are not imitations of any known living insect.

A fisherman who does not make his own flies loses half the pleasure of fishing. After a little practice it is quite easy to make hackled flies, and a little more practice, plain-winged flies. The angler has only to carry out the plain instructions contained in Jackson's *Practical Angler*—which are the most simple instructions I know—and he can imitate the flies comprised in Pritt's *North Country Flies*.

The man of ample leisure may study Mr. Halford's elaborate book on *Floating-Flies and how to dress them*, and after much practice succeed in copying them to his own satisfaction. The north country angler need not encumber himself with a multiplicity of flies. I name a few flies which will kill in their respective seasons, and should the list be increased, I doubt whether there would be any gain in efficiency. They are :—

1. Blue dun (water-hen bloa).
2. Winter brown (light woodcock).
3. Little winter brown (dark woodcock).
4. March brown (male and female), winged.
5. Yellow snipe (taken for olive dun).
6. Purple dark snipe.
7. Orange partridge.
8. Yellow partridge.
9. Blue partridge (gravel bed).
10. Yellow dun (moor poult).
11. Iron-blue dun (dark watchet), winged and hackled.
12. Black spider.
13. Brown owl, both yellow and orange.
14. Red spider.
15. Brown dun (winged).
16. Greenwell's Glory.
17. Knotted midge.
18. Woodcock fly (hook, No. 2, 3, or 4; wings, mottled feather from a woodcock's wing; body, gray hare lug ribbed with gold thread; legs, ginger hackle).

With regard to the female March brown, the best feather for the wings, so far as my experience goes, is a small feather from the inside of a hen pheasant's wing, of a fawn shade—not the dun feather. A great many pheasants have not the particular shade. The body, fur from a hare's ear, ribbed with gold thread; legs, ruddy partridge hackle—or if the flies on the water have a ruddy appearance, a ruddy feather from the outside of a landrail's wing or the neck of a cock grouse; tail, strands from the tail feather of a partridge.

The body may be varied by ruddy fur from the neck of a wild rabbit. I dwell so much on this fly because the flies usually procurable are made with feathers of too much of a blue or dun shade, and are not nearly so attractive as flies made of the feather which I have endeavoured to describe. I will give one wrinkle as to fly-making : wax the part of the thread which is not required for making the body of the fly with cobbler's wax, and the other part—that is the part with which the body is to be formed, which is in some flies of a rather bright colour—with colourless wax. Thus made the hook will firmly adhere to the gut, as cobbler's wax appears to be the best for that purpose.

Gut or Hair.—Flies are attached to gut or horsehair. Gut may easily be attached to an eyed hook by means of a knot. Hair cannot be so attached satisfactorily ; therefore, should the angler fish with hair, he must tie the hook to the hair. Flies attached to hair have one great advantage over flies tied to gut (I mean by means of thread) : they are not liable to go at the head or to come off the hair, as flies on gut are liable to do if kept for a few years. Gut is liable to rot ; hair will last for many years.

The Fly Cast.—The length of the cast should not exceed the length of the rod. A hair cast should be made as follows : two top lengths, treble hair twisted ; third length, double hair twisted, then single hair tapered so much as practicable. Until about May the finest undrawn gut may be employed ; afterwards it is generally advisable to use drawn gut, unless in a good water. Hair has some distinct advantages over gut. It never fridges; it never appears to get worn out ; it falls much more lightly on the water ; it is easier to cast ; it rarely gets entangled—a shake will commonly make all right. It is well known into what an entangled mess drawn gut often gets. Good hair is to a considerable extent transparent. Stained gut forms an opaque dark line, plainly visible in clear water, and on a bright day it appears to the angler's eye to shine like silver; but as the trout is below, it may not appear so to the trout. In order to appreciate the difference between hair and gut, immerse some hair and gut in a glass of water, and hold the glass up to the light; the hair is much less visible than the gut. Reverse the position, and place two casts of flies, one on hair and the other on gut, into a pool of clear water on a bright day, so that the eye of the observer may look down on the casts. The hair is almost if not entirely invisible; the flies are plainly visible. The gut is shown by a thin dark line with the flies attached, and the line appears to reflect the sun's rays.

There is one incident which appears somewhat peculiar: as the hair cast alights on the water, it is plainly visible to the eye of the observer; the gut cast is almost invisible. It may be because the gut sinks immediately on striking the water, and the hair does not. Hair is very much inclined to float, and is therefore admirably adapted for the dry fly. When it is advisable that the flies should sink, as in early spring, gut should be used in preference to hair. Hair should not be used in narrow weedy streams, but only where there is plenty of room for play, as in most northern rivers. A trout of upwards of a pound may be easily killed with hair, but it would not be prudent to attempt hair where trout of upwards of a pound are common. Really good hair is difficult to procure, and the difficulty has been increased by the cruel and spoliating practice of docking horses' tails, whereby the horse is robbed of a portion of its most beautiful and useful appendages; the tail was designed by nature for the horse's comfort, to enable him to switch off the flies. For some incomprehensible reason, man has decided that a cocktailed horse is a thing of beauty : by the ordinary laws of progression man will decide in due time that a horse ought not to have a tail at all, and cut the whole of it off. The mane will go next, and the horse will look something like a tailless cow.

As to the Reel or Casting Line.—The best lines are made of oiled silk, tapered, and the weight of the line must be proportioned to the weight and length of the rod. The lighter the line an angler can throw, the more lightly the fly cast will alight on the water. A heavy line is liable to cause drag.

As to the Reel.—The weight of the reel should be proportioned to the length of the rod, and there should be a slight check, so that fish may be struck from the reel. There is now a plethora of choice in reels, so the angler may suit his own idea of what a reel ought to be capable.

Fly-Hooks.—I think the Kendal sneck bend has not yet been beaten. Bronze hooks have for some years been in fashion, but I do not think they have any advantage over the blue. They appear to shine or glisten in the sun, which blue hooks do not. I certainly think that for dark flies the blue hooks are the more suitable, as the blue assimilates to the colour of the fly—the iron-blue dun for an instance. The size of the hook should vary in accordance with the time of the year, the state of the water and weather, and the river fished, to some extent. The most useful sizes are from Nos. 1 to 3.

The Rod.—The fly-fisher should be provided with at least two rods, one twelve feet long and the other from ten to eleven feet. The longer rod should be used when the angler intends to fish down stream, or when he may be inclined to supplement the fly with minnow or worm, or some other bait; the shorter rod when he intends to fish fly up stream. Of course he may fish with the longer rod with fly up stream—it is simply a question of strength. With a rod of ten and a half feet a man may cast incessantly without that sense of weariness which the use of a twelve-foot rod entails. The rods now in fashion are the built cane rods, and I prefer those made in two pieces with lockfast joints. A cheap cane rod should not be purchased. If a man should not care to give about £2 : 10s. for a cane rod, he may provide himself with rods made of greenheart, and it is a question yet whether a greenheart rod is not quite equal to a split cane for all practical purposes. A greenheart rod is more liable to break, it is true. A split cane rod is of great strength : with my twelve-foot rod I lug trout of upwards of half a pound in weight on to the bank, when fishing with worm in a flood. I never tried it with a greenheart rod.

The mode of Fly-Fishing.—There are two distinct modes of fishing, up stream and down, and ever since the time that Stewart published his admirable little book, *The Practical Angler*—which I recommend all would-be anglers to read and digest—the two methods have been much debated. Notwithstanding Stewart's most earnest injunctions to fish up, there is evidence that he did not confine himself to that method. As a general rule, fishing up stream should be practised, and I propose to endeavour to demonstrate when a man should fish up, and when down.

And first as to the cogent reasons for fishing up. Trout lie with their heads up stream, and when they take a fly at or near the surface they rise rather obliquely, and when they have captured the fly they return to their original position, and do not turn with their heads down stream, as some one once suggested to me. The result is, that when the strike is made, there is a good chance of the hook taking hold, because the strike is against the fish; whereas in fishing down, or partly down, the hook is apt to be drawn out of the fish's mouth. If an angler will watch trout rising below a bridge he will see exactly the performance of the trout, and fully appreciate the advantages of striking down.

A second reason is, because in fishing up he fishes the lower portion of pools and streams first, and does not disturb the fish above; whereas should he commence in the stream above the pool, the trout for many yards may see him, and in playing the trout he is liable to disturb the lower water. As a third reason, he can approach nearer to the fish without being seen, and can consequently use a comparatively short line, which is a great advantage. And as a fourth reason, the flies come more naturally down with the current. As some disadvantage, there is much more labour in fishing up. Fishing up is specially applicable when the river is low and clear; fishing down when in that condition is almost entirely unproductive.

After considerable experience, I have come to the conclusion that casting straight up a stream is often unsatisfactory, and letting the line hang straight down much more so. When fishing straight up a fairly strong stream, the slightest drag imaginable must be made, so that the fish may be felt the moment he takes the fly, otherwise ten to one he is missed. The most fatal time is when the line is across the river but rather above the position of the angler, then a little turn of the wrist downward is generally successful. Should he see trout rising under a bank on the side of the river whereon he stands, although there may be a good water, drifting the flies down to them is generally futile. He should fish for such trout straight up, if he cannot approach them from the other side. When there is an apparent rise of trout, the angler should almost always fish up, unless rendered impracticable by the wind.

Before treating further on fishing up stream, it is convenient to explain the old method of fishing down. The angler progresses downwards, and fishes the water down in detail. In casting he throws the line across the river at about a right angle, and allows the flies to drift with the current until the line shall have described a semicircle. When the cast has got to the full extent, it hangs below him down the current, and for a few moments he raises and sinks his flies; in fact he causes the droppers to bob from time to time on the surface, and thus doing, when the water is somewhat discoloured, he often rises and hooks fish. I have watched Mr. Coates of Kettlewell—who has accounted for a great many trout during his long life—fishing in this manner, and his baskets of trout testify to the success of the method when the trout are on. And the system has this advantage that the rise is felt, and the trout strike themselves.

A man whose eyesight is bad may have fair sport in this mode of fishing, whereas, if he were to fish up, he would have little success, as he could not see the rises. Early on in the season, say until the end of April, when there is generally a fair volume of water in the rivers, also at other times when the water is in good volume and there is little if any apparent rise of trout—I use the word apparent because the trout may be taking the flies as they hatch before they reach the surface —fishing down often does more execution than fishing up, as

I have frequently proved. By fishing down in the manner I have described a great deal of water is covered with very little labour, and the sweep being great and prolonged, the flies sink considerably and are readily seen by the trout. One instance may suffice. It was at Kilnsey. There was a good brown fly-water, and I elected to fish down. When I got down to Cox's plantation, which is a very good lie for trout, a nice breeze up ruffled the water, so I decided to walk to the bottom of the length and fish it up. I fished it most carefully up, and did not get a rise, and I did not see a rise. I then fished it down and soon caught five trout, and missed several. The only rises were at my flies.

We will now go to a river such as the Wharfe, the Ure, or the Eamont, on a day at the end of March or the beginning of April, and we will assume that the March brown has not yet put in an appearance. The water is in nice condition. We may use three or four flies if we like, but I prefer three. As we wish our flies to sink easily, our casts are composed of the finest undrawn gut, which has cost at least six shillings a hank, and we pin our faith on two casts made up as follows:— No. 1. Tail fly, blue dun (water-hen bloa); first dropper, winter brown; and second dropper, orange or red partridge. No. 2. Tail fly, yellow snipe (olive dun); first dropper, winter brown; and second dropper, purple dark snipe.

There is no use in beginning before ten o'clock, as the hatch of fly will not come down before eleven o'clock, but we commence about ten and fish down stream. A rise cannot be seen, but we cast where we think the fish ought to be, and feel for a rise. The trout are most likely to be in the slow streams, the eddies by rough streams, and towards the tails of pools; also at the heads of pools where the streams begin to slacken. We pick up a fish now and then, when the flies are well sunk. In about an hour a few olive duns come down, and shortly perhaps the blue dun and the winter brown, the last-named fluttering in the air and then flopping on to the water. The rise has begun, and will last perhaps for half an hour or more. It may now be advisable to fish up stream.

Having illustrated fishing down stream we will now return to fishing up. Imagine a nice day in May when trout may rise fairly for some hours; they begin to rise about nine o'clock, should the weather be favourable. The water is moderate and quite clear. Three flies may be used, about two feet and a half apart. The following cast will probably be effective: tail fly, yellow dun or yellow partridge; first dropper, blue partridge; second dropper, purple snipe or black spider. We first soak our cast and get line out gradually, until the line is about half as long again as the rod or rather longer; allow the line to go behind to its full extent to avoid a crack, and impel it forward by a sharp motion of the wrist, taking care at the conclusion of the cast to keep the point of the rod well up, in order that the flies may alight lightly, and that only the fly cast may be immersed so far as practicable. The cast having been made in the required direction, as the flies float down the stream gradually raise the point of the rod, and when they have come down opposite they should not be allowed to get below the angler, but the cast should be repeated. The angler must fish from the low shore or bank, whenever he can, because fishing from a high bank above the trout is not conducive to much sport.

The angler approaches a pool into which a strong stream enters, and the tail of the pool is rather a shallow glide. The trout are rising, one or two in the tail, some under the far bank where the water rather shallows, and some at the head of the pool. Should he fish the head of the pool first in the approved old fashion, he will probably hook a good trout, which will run right down the pool and put down all the trout. He must begin at the tail, and try for all the rising trout in detail. He may thus secure four trout in that pool. The tail fly should be made to alight about a foot above the trout. The flies should be kept as near the surface as possible, and for that purpose it is useful to whirl the line in the air a few times to take off the wet, and here hair has a great advantage over gut.

We now come to a long streamy flat rather shallow; the opposite side is a grassy bank, and under the bank trout are rising. We so place ourselves as to cast across, but rather up over the rising trout. We drop the tail fly close to the grass, a little above the rise; and before the line can get below, the angler must cast again. We then come to a rapid stream in the middle of the river, with back waters on both sides of the stream. We fish the back waters on our own side up, next we wade in and fish the rough stream up; but we do not touch a fish in the rough stream, so we try it down in the old style and perchance get one or two fish out of it. We then, and not until, wade farther out, and fish the slack water on the far side of the stream upwards.

The best time for the fly in the daytime is from April to the end of May. When the trout are well on the fly they generally take well from about ten o'clock to two, and they often come on again about five o'clock and take till sunset. Excellent sport is often obtained in June on a cool or showery day. In July sport is generally very bad, even in a good fly-water. Towards the end of August, and from that time to

H

the end of the season, good sport may be obtained. The brown owl is then a useful fly, also the iron-blue dun, the best hackled imitation of which is a small bluish feather from the back of a merlin on a body of blue mole's fur ribbed with orange silk, head orange.

Most of the flies I have named will kill in the autumn, especially the red spider and brown dun; the latter is made as follows: wings from a starling's quill, body brown silk, legs ginger hackle. The most useful size of hook after April is No. 1, and I doubt whether any real advantage is derived from smaller hooks, because the misses are so numerous, as I have always experienced when fishing with the iron-blue or knotted midge, which I dress on No. 0 hooks. In striking a fish, when fishing up, the strike should be as sharp as possible, and down stream, but care must be taken in fishing with hair not to strike so hard as to cause a fracture, and the fish must be gently humoured in his first wild rush. The fish should at once be drawn down the stream, and netted as quickly as possible. In fishing small streams of which the charming little streams in Mona's Isle are types, the streams are so narrow that the cast must be almost straight up or down, therefore the angler should fish up at all times if possible, and he will soon appreciate the value of the slight drag before indicated, in order that he may feel the little trout immediately on their contact with the hook.

In the summer months, when the days are hot, good sport may often be obtained after sunset. The angler should commence with small flies. The brown owl, black spider, and yellow dun, also the coachman, are often effective. After about half-past nine o'clock, larger flies may be used, and should the angler wish to make a night of it he may have recourse to the bustard, which is supposed to represent a moth. I have always found evening fishing very uncertain, and have never killed more than ten trout in an evening's fishing.

I recommend every man or boy who wishes to become a good angler to read Stewart's *Practical Angler*, but I must state that I think that if Mr. Stewart had lived to attain the age of sixty years, and republished his book shortly before his death, he would have considerably modified some of the opinions expressed in his *Practical Angler*.

CHAPTER XII

CREEPER AND STONE-FLY FISHING

With the green drake and the stone-fly, I do verily believe I could some day in my life, had I not been weary of slaughter, have loaden a lusty boy.—PISCATOR.

THE creeper is the larva of the stone-fly; an imitation of either is practically useless, one might just as well fish with an artificial worm: trout will now and then go for the imitation, but they will not take it into their mouths. In the early summer the female fly runs over the water and deposits her eggs, which in due time hatch and become the creeper. The creeper can be used most successfully about a fortnight or so before, and until the stone-fly is "up." It is not at all uncommon to see a few stone-flies in April, but in the Yorkshire rivers the average time for the fly in force is about the last week in May. For the angler's guidance, I give the time for a few years in the Wharfe at Kilnsey.

1887	. . May 27	1893	. May 18
1888	. . June 7	1894	. May 27
1889	. May 24	1895	May 23
1890	. May 20	1896	. May 17
1891	June 3	1897	. May 27
1892	June 2		

In order to find creepers, turn over the stones near the side, where a sharp stream flows, not in the actual current, but by the side of the current. As the creeper comes to maturity, he crawls on to the dry stones, and then his outer shell comes off and adheres to the stones. When these shells are numerous, it is apparent that the stone-fly is up, and the mature fly is found under the stones out of the water. The male fly is called the jack, is dark and about half the size of the female. The wings lie flat; the body of the female is rather yellow underneath, and she presents a plump appearance. The male is very nimble, and therefore difficult to catch. The female being more portly, is caught with comparative ease. The best article to keep either creepers or stone-flies in is a circular slightly oval tin article, about seven inches in diameter and a little more than an inch in extreme depth, perforated with small holes and having a circular hole about three-quarters of an inch in diameter, which can be closed up by a sliding lid with spring action, by means of which the flies can be taken out of the article when required for use. It is advisable to get either the creepers or flies the evening before they are required, and a little damp moss should be put into the article.

The question arises as to the kind of rod to use. It cannot be too long; it is a question of the angler's strength. So far as my experience goes, a single-handed rod is preferable to a double-handed, because the cast must be made with much gentleness in order that the bait may not be flicked off the hook. For a man of average strength, a twelve-foot stiff fly-rod appears to be the best made of built cane, greenheart, or some other approved wood; the best reel line is one of oiled silk, proportioned to the weight and pliability of the rod.

The cast must be of fine-drawn gut, and about eight feet in length. Two hooks should be used, tied almost close together one above another, with the shank in the same direction, not inverted. About the best size of hook is No. 3 sneck bend, or even No. 4 if the trout are not shy. In order to bait either the creeper or the fly, insert the upper hook in the shoulder and the lower near the tail. The mode of fishing with either bait is much the same: cast up stream with as long a line as can be controlled, or cast partly up and partly across and well under the opposite bank. The creeper is often most successful in the necks of streams.

The stone-fly should be cast in the streams in which trout are likely to be lying, and this can only be ascertained by experience. Trout will often take the stone-fly in the glides at the tails of pools, especially if there be breeze on; also in the flats close to the gravelly shore. When creeper-fishing, it is desirable that the bait should sink; and if necessary for that purpose a small shot may be used as a sinker, or better still a swivel. When the line stops, and there is probably a fish at the bait, pause about two seconds, and then strike down gently but rather sharply.

The angler having cast his fly up the stream, the fly comes floating down and he must ever be on the alert; there is a little dimple and the fly disappears: pause a little, and then strike, and in all probability the fish is duly netted. Sometimes the fish flop at the fly, and do not take it. They are more inclined to flop at the large female than the small male or jack; and if flops are numerous, the jack may be more successful. Trout often take the fly when sunk, and sometimes better than on the surface. As the line comes down, gradually raise the point of the rod, and when it gets in a line with the angler he must cast again; it is not advisable to let the bait get below.

The most suitable day is when there is a nice breeze up stream, and in default a calm day. The angler should commence in good time in the morning, say at nine o'clock, and if the fish are inclined for the stone-fly they will generally take until about two or three o'clock. Some men begin about sunrise, but such early rising is the exception among men who merely fish for pleasure.

During the stone-fly season the wind has often a most aggravating way of blowing down stream, which is not conducive to good sport; but even if there be a gale of wind down the river some sport may be obtained. The best plan in such a case is, not even to attempt to fish up, but to throw the bait so far as possible across the river, and let it drift down under the bank; under such circumstances the bait is certain to sink under the surface, but that does not matter, and some sport may often be obtained in the pools. In this mode of fishing an undue number of misses must be expected.

Fishing with the stone-fly, however, is very uncertain, and the reason may often be accounted for by the presence of the black gnat in immense swarms, as that cuss to fishermen is the harbinger of the stone-fly. The fish frequently refuse the stone-fly altogether when the cuss is in force, and in that case the up-stream worm is often attractive. On one occasion I fished the stone-fly from the Falls, Kilnsey, to some distance up Kettlewell Beck, and only captured one trout. As I was going home that day I was anxious to get a few trout to show that I really had been fishing, so I put on the worm and very soon captured eleven good fish at the fag end of my day. I had practically wasted almost the whole day over the stone-fly.

The best condition of water appears to be a little after a small fresh, when the water has got quite clear. I once tried in a good porter-coloured fly-water, but the trout would not look at the stone-fly. I had to have recourse to small artificial flies, with which I did some execution. Even in very low water, with a bright sun, good sport may be had. I have had fair sport in all sorts of conditions of weather and water, save in a real fresh. Of course in this mode of fishing much time is lost in baiting, more than with the worm.

At best, sport with the stone-fly is very uncertain; if they will they will, if they won't they won't. They often prefer the small flies on the water. On one occasion I observed a three-quarters of a pounder feeding voraciously on the small flies. I floated my fly over him repeatedly, but he refused it; I put on a small fly cast and cast a yellow curlew lightly above him, and at the first cast I had him. It may here be remarked, however, that when the trout are fairly on the stone-fly, little execution can be done with the artificial fly. There is one great advantage in the stone-fly—that the best trout are commonly caught with it. The season is short, only about a fortnight. In the north of England the stone-fly is called the May-fly. It seems singular that trout will not take the floating imitation, whereas the green drake artificial is fished with so much success by our brethren in the south of England. The tyro will please to note that in order to become an adept in casting the stone-fly, considerable practice is requisite. He should first become a proficient in the management of the up-stream worm.

CHAPTER XIII

WORM-FISHING FOR TROUT

You are to note that, till the sun gets to such a height as to warm the earth and the water, the trout is sick and lean, and lousy, and unwholesome.—PISCATOR.

AT the outset it may be stated that trout will take the worm at all seasons of the year. Worm-fishing may be divided into two branches: the clear-water worm, and the flood worm. There is considerable skill required in fishing with the worm in clear water. Trout do not take worm in clear water freely as a rule until they have become satiated with fly, which generally is about the end of May, and this is particularly so in the large streams or rivers; but in some places—the Isle of Man to wit—they take worm freely during the whole fishing season. In June and July, they often take worm with great impetuosity. After the middle of August, their eagerness for the worm decreases, and at length it becomes difficult to kill six trout in a day with it in clear water, and then they will often go for the minnow.

So far as my experience goes, the trout taking fly almost always refuse either worm or minnow. They will take the worm, when they get off the fly. Worm-fishing in clear water should not be practised until the fly becomes impracticable, which is generally about the middle of June when the rivers are low and the sun bright, for under such conditions the fly after the middle of June is of little use in the daytime. The angler is then justified in having recourse to the worm. Some persons allege that the water cannot be too low for the clear-water worm, but this is a fallacy. After a long-continued drought trout take worm very badly, and they will not take it freely until there has been a fresh, and the reason appears to be because in hot weather the water becomes full of minute forms of life; the river-moss swarms with little things which have the appearance of tiny eels. The trout no doubt find these atoms more to their taste than worms. A good fresh washes away and probably destroys most of these tit-bits; worms come down with the flood, and the trout are reminded that such a thing as the worm exists. Trout, however, appear to pick up a good many worms when the water is low.

I do not venture to give an opinion as to the condition of weather best for the clear-water worm, because I have had excellent sport on fine days, wet days, showery days, cloudy days, calm days, and windy days in the proper worm season. The most certain time of the day appears to be from about eight o'clock in the morning to two o'clock in the afternoon. If the weather is very hot, a commencement may be made shortly after sunrise, should the angler like to make the sport of fishing into a labour. Most sport will be obtained in the streams, where the trout lie at this season: they appear to like to bask in the sun. The swift narrow guts or necks are very good, particularly when they swirl under the opposite bank.

The low shallow flats, especially at the gravelly side, are

often very good in a wind. As soon as the worm alights, there is often seen the wave of a good fish making for the worm ; when the wave ceases, he has seized the worm. The eddies by large stones are also good, also the thin tails of pools ruffled by the breeze. The best bed is a gravelly or stony one free from moss. Trout seldom take worm when they are among the moss—they are looking after something else. The roughest streams should be fished, even when they form a sort of waterfall, and the fish caught in such are some of the best in the river. There are occasions when for some reason or other trout cannot be caught in the places I have indicated. Then the pools should be tried. The worm may be dropped lightly over some willows into the calm water under the willows, or the worm may be cast as far as possible into a deep pool and allowed to sink. In this manner a few nice trout may be captured after the angler has slaved for hours in the streams without success and nearly wasted his day.

Having attempted to make the would-be worm-fisher understand when and where to capture trout with the worm in clear water, I make suggestions as to the weapons of attack. The rod cannot be too long for such rivers as the Wharfe, Eamont, or Ure, but the longer the rod, the greater the fatigue. A double-handed rod is much more fatiguing than a single ; and it is often convenient to try fly should conditions turn out to be favourable, and if a man is encumbered with a double-handed rod he cannot fish fly with success up stream. I am therefore in favour of a single-handed rod, twelve feet in length, built rather stiff, of split cane or greenheart. If a man is strong enough to use a longer rod with one hand, all the better. The reel line should be of oiled silk, the same as used for fly. The cast should be made of either the finest undrawn gut or drawn gut, and should be about eight feet in length. The most effective tackle for this mode of fishing is the so-called Stewart tackle of either two or three hooks. The best sizes are Nos. 3 or 4 Kendal scale. Should this tackle not prove successful, one hook should be tried, size about No. 10 or 11.

In baiting the Stewart tackle, the top hook should be stuck into the head of the worm, then a twist given and the second hook impaled about the middle of the worm, then another twist and the third hook impaled near the tail. When baiting the two-hook tackle, after impaling the top hook there should be two or three twists before impaling the lower hook. In baiting one hook, the worm should be impaled at the very top of the head, and the worm pierced to about three-quarters of an inch from the tail, care being taken that the whole of the hook is covered, and that the barb should not be exposed.

The best worms are the bluish worms which are often found in digging potatoes, but all worms of a suitable size should be taken, as the trout will take any worm when he is on. The only objection to freshly gathered worms is that being full of earth they soon break. They should be put into damp moss for two or three days before being used, or if moss cannot be procured, into chopped grass moistened. If the worms have been rather long in moss a little cream improves them. The angler should fish from the low side : a typical place is a long stream, shallow on the low side and gradually deepening toward the opposite bank, which is rather high. At the head of the stream there is a swift narrow neck. After well soaking the line, he should get out line of about the length of the rod, and then cast overhead, allowing the line to go to the full extent behind without a jerk, and then with a slight exertion of the wrist impel the worm gently upward as far as he can. As the line comes down with the current, the point of the rod should be gradually raised, and the line should not be allowed to get below the angler.

Fish may be lying all over the place indicated. They may be in the very thin water close to the edge, so the first cast should be made there, and thus the angler should cast until all the water has been fished to immediately under the opposite bank. When the line stops, there may be a fish, or the hooks may have stuck on the bed of the river: if using more than one hook, pause about three seconds and then strike gently down; if fishing with one hook, pause a trifle longer. When a trout is hooked pull him down stream, and net him as soon as possible. If fortunate in not missing fish, five or six trout may be got in this run. Should a fish be hooked and get off, he may alarm most of the fish thereabouts.

The narrow neck will probably yield the best fish—two or three perhaps, with luck. When fishing the shallow flats ruffled by the breeze most attention should be directed to the sides, and the angler will soon find out from a little observation the likely places in the flats. To be a successful up-stream worm-fisher, a man must be a close observer. When the stream ends in a long flat and the water is calm, the angler should make a detour to the stream in order to avoid disturbing the trout in the flat: they are probably in the thins close to the side, and if they see the man with the pole, they go scuttering up stream and convey the alarm to all the other trout about. It is rather singular that trout above a quarter of a pound in weight take the worm much more quietly than trout below that weight, so when a sharp tug, tug, tug is felt, the angler may expect only a small trout. Some trout have a way of taking the worm in their mouths and running off with it without attempting to swallow it, and in such cases the angler should strike at once.

When fishing with the worm in small streams like the little streams in the Isle of Man, I commonly use only one hook; and in this there is considerable advantage, because with one worm two or three fish may be captured, whereas with Stewart tackle only one as a rule. And what is really more enjoyable than to wander up a charming little stream rod in hand and only a bag of worms to think of, and catch a trout here and there and yank them out, no landing-net to bother one? But this yanking out sometimes ends in disaster. After yanking out a dozen or so of about two ounces each, the angler is liable to get careless : a bite, a yank which the angler cannot stop, alas ! the fish of the day, a real three-quarters of a pounder, has snapped the fine tackle in that big yank, and the angler feels as though he had lost his best friend. In such little excursions what a monster the solitary half-pounder looks among the little ones, and what a gallant fight he made ! Thus upwards he goes, fishing a stream here and a tiny cascade there as long as he may please, and when satisfied turn out his creel and count from three to five dozen trout which average about six or seven to the pound, but he has perhaps enjoyed the day more than the man who has fished the big river and caught fifteen trout or so of much larger size.

In fishing with the worm in a flood, the best time generally is when the water has begun to fall, when the trout to avoid the roaring flood are in the slack water at the sides. The angler should find out where trout do most congregate under such conditions, and when he has found such a place stick to it. Trout often lie just on the edge of the strong current.

The best plan is first to fish close to the bank or shore, then gradually farther out until the edge of the current is reached; and when the trout slacken wait five minutes, and then go on again. Always strike down. In this mode of fishing I prefer only one hook, and the cast must be weighted according to the strength of the water. The gut should be strong, and the cast need not be more than two feet long. The worm is commonly allowed to trundle on the bottom with the current, but a float would probably be more successful.

Enough, however, of this sort of fishing; the only excuse for it is when a man has journeyed far, and his time is limited.

CHAPTER XIV

MINNOW-FISHING FOR TROUT

I caught my last trout with a worm; now I will put on a minnow, and try a quarter of an hour about yonder trees for another.—PISCATOR.

MINNOW-FISHING is practised both with natural and artificial minnows. The manipulation of the artificial minnow is more easy than that of the natural, but the *modus operandi* is somewhat different, and it need hardly be said that the natural minnow is much more attractive than the artificial. The first consideration is the rod. In my view the best kind of rod is a rather stiff one about fourteen feet in length, and made up as follows: butt and middle piece whole cane, and top greenheart, furnished with snake rings; line fine oiled silk. The best tackle is known as the Ariel tackle, which is made up on three treble hooks tied at a distance proportioned to the size of the minnow, the sinker being a small serrated piece of lead to be inserted inside the minnow. The trace for the clearwater minnow should be of the finest undrawn gut—which is about double the price of drawn gut—from six to eight feet in length, and the hooks should be No. 1 Kendal scale. For fishing in discoloured water the trace may be a size thicker and the hooks No. 2, and the length of the trace may be reduced to about four feet.

I recommend a fourteen-foot rod under the assumption that the angler intends to confine his day's fishing to the minnow, for such a rod will not throw fly satisfactorily. Should he wish to be in a position to fish whatever may be the most attractive to the trout, I recommend a twelve-foot split cane or greenheart rod built rather stiff; but I must premise that it is much more tiring to fish with the fourteen-foot rod, and very good results may be obtained in all conditions of water with the smaller rod.

I will first treat of minnow-fishing in clear low water. The minnow, so far as practicable, should not exceed an inch and a half in length, and should be white underneath; if the minnows are dark or yellow they should be immersed for a night in a white earthenware vessel, which will have the desired effect. The line thrown is generally about the length of the rod. The most productive places to fish are the streamy parts of the river where there is a gravelly or stony bed and where there is a bank opposite, often fringed with trees and bushes close to the bank; also by the sides of large stones. When there is a breeze to ruffle the water the gliding tails of pools are often very productive, also the shallow flats close to the side, where the fish are prowling about grubbing for miller's-thumbs.

The minnow should be baited thus: first insert the lead so that the mouth of the minnow closes over the head of the lead, next insert the top hooks on the upper sides of the minnow, and the bottom hooks in or near the tail so that the tail may slightly curve; the curve causes the minnow to spin or wobble. Wading is almost indispensable; advance to the low side cautiously. The cast should be made underhand with a sort of swing upwards, as far as practicable on the near side and so that the minnow may alight with the least

I

possible splash, and in order to effect this object, at the time the minnow alights there should be a slight draw in the direction of the angler, which is effected by a jerk of the wrist. Draw the minnow gently down, gradually raising the point of the rod, and do not allow the minnow to get below; then repeat the process until all likely places shall have been fished.

When pretty far out, should the width of the stream permit, draw the minnow across the current, but always above. Drawing the minnow against the stream or allowing it to be stationary hanging down the river is generally unproductive. When the angler feels a tug he should lower the point of the rod for a few seconds, and then strike firmly but gently downwards and draw the fish to the side. The net should not be used if it can be dispensed with, because the hooks get fast in the meshes, and the fish in his struggles is apt to damage the tackle.

With regard to the best part of the day: from the beginning of the season to about the first week in June the best part of the day is generally after two or three o'clock, when the trout become tired of catching flies; afterwards first thing in the morning. I assume the angler is not keen enough to begin before eight o'clock or so, then they will commonly take until about two o'clock, but much will depend on the state of the weather. No fixed rule can be laid down as to when trout will take or not take any lure. I emphatically condemn this sort of fishing when fair sport can be had with the fly. The legitimate time for the clear-water minnow is from the middle of June to the middle of August.

With regard to minnow-fishing in a large or discoloured water, it is not very material whether the angler works up or down, but it is better to work upwards for the simple reason that trout lie with their heads up the river.

Trout often take minnow well, when the river is rising, about the time the ordinary bed is covered with water. Should the water get very high the worm will become effective, when the water has just begun to subside; when the water has begun to clear the minnow may become effective, and should the trout have gone off the worm the minnow should be used. Should the water be very big there are few places fishable, and those places commonly are the eddies or backwaters, and there will be most fish where the water is nearly still. The best plan in such cases is to cast up right under the bank and draw gently down, or if the current sets the other way reverse the position. Of course all the still water should be fished. When the water has got sufficiently low for the fish to lie in the broad flats or the thin tails of pools, the best plan is to cast as far as practicable across the river and to some extent upwards, and draw across the river until the minnow reaches the side below the angler; it is generally impracticable to draw so that the minnow can reach the side above the angler. The result of the cast which I have indicated is that for a short space the minnow will travel partly down and partly across, then straight across, and in the end a shade upwards; the object is to draw the minnow as little upwards as possible.

So far as my experience goes the best chance of hooking a fish is when the minnow is travelling exactly across the current, and this can be effected to the greatest possible extent by making the cast rather upwards. The old plan was to cast the minnow at right angles to the current—that is straight across—and allow it to describe a semicircle, and on the conclusion of the semicircle to give a sharp twist, and then draw the minnow upwards. The most fatal time then was at the moment of the sharp turn. When the trout are madly on the minnow it sometimes does not matter how the angler spins.

I have known trout jump out of the water for the minnow. As with the clear-water minnow, the angler should pause before striking. The trout will often go for the minnow when it is in the act of being drawn out of the water, and in such cases a miss is the usual result; never mind, wait a minute and repeat the cast, and he will probably come again with a determined rush to his fate. I do not for a moment advise the angler to confine himself to any particular mode of spinning for trout; he should try every method he can. Sometimes a zigzag motion will tempt a trout. Sometimes under the apparently most favourable conditions a single run cannot be obtained. In that case a large-sized fly may be efficacious if the water is not too much discoloured.

When fishing with the artificial minnow it is essential that the strike should be made immediately on the fish being felt, otherwise the fish would at once discover the fraud. Hence it happens that many more fish are missed than with the natural minnow.

A new method of preserving minnows has conferred a great boon on anglers, and the trout take them with avidity; minnows thus preserved have the advantage of being more tough than fresh minnows.

CHAPTER XV

THE KILNSEY ANGLING CLUB

From this time forward I will be your master, and teach you as much of this art as I am able.—PISCATOR.

IN the year 1882 I had the honour of being elected a member of the Kilnsey Angling Club, which now consists of thirty-five members, the honorary secretary then being Lieutenant-Colonel Nowell of Netherside Hall. The present honorary secretary is Captain Henderson, the owner of the Scale House estate near Skipton. The club was founded on liberal conditions, each member being allowed to be accompanied by a friend while actually fishing, but only members are allowed to fish with the natural stone-fly.

The natural stone-fly is held in great estimation by the members of the club, and it is considered a most fatal lure for the trout; and no doubt under favourable conditions very large baskets may be caught with it. But in truth the up-stream worm in low water at the proper time of the year is a much more reliable lure, and it seems rather singular that non-members should have been allowed the worm when they were not allowed to use the natural stone-fly; but the reason may have been that up-stream worm-fishing was not well understood or appreciated by the members of the club, and I believe that at the time I became a member the up-stream worm was not used to any appreciable extent, the members arranging so far as they could to arrive during a fresh, and fishing with worm or minnow according to the condition of the water, and graduating to fly when the water cleared, or

NETHERSIDE.

rather when it became of a rich porter colour, so popular with the members of the club.

It is generally admitted that trout are difficult to catch with artificial fly in the Kilnsey Club waters when they are low. The waters of the club extend from Netherside to some distance above Starbotton, a distance of about seven miles in the Wharfe, and from the meeting of the waters (the junction of the river Skirfare with the Wharfe) to about three-quarters of a mile above Hawkswick on the Skirfare, a distance of about two and three-quarter miles.

Netherside is distant from the meeting of the waters about two and three-quarter miles, and this portion is styled in Kilnsey Club parlance the river; the portion of the Wharfe above the meeting of the waters is styled Kettlewell Beck. A large deep pool called Armadale is formed by the confluence of the waters. To the left or east of the pool—by the custom of Craven called a dub—on slightly rising ground is a whitewashed farmhouse called Throstle Nest, from the grounds of which there is a beautiful view down the river. The house is shaded by large beech trees and looks singularly cosy, being sheltered on the east by the steep slopes of the lower part of Conistone Moor.

Across the valley is the famous Kilnsey Crag, with the hamlet of Kilnsey near the base. Farther down can be seen Chapel House and Netherside, and in the far distance the fells in the neighbourhood of Rylstone, which present a blue appearance. So far as scenery is concerned, the Kilnsey Angling Club are highly favoured; they could hardly have pitched their quarters under more favourable conditions. The air is remarkable for its purity and bracing qualities, which may be expected, as almost all the waters of the club are over 600 feet above sea-level. As a natural consequence the fishing is somewhat late. The Tennants' Arms Inn, the headquarters of the club, is most conveniently situated, being about two miles up the river from Netherside, therefore in the middle of what may be called the best fishing—that is the river.

It may be convenient here to describe the nature of the waters of the club, and their scenic surroundings. Starting at the bottom, Netherside, we commence our fishing in a sharp broad run which terminates in a long deep pool below, belonging to the Netherside estate; the next run is very similar. The surroundings are beautiful: the woods of Netherside on a steep craggy slope appear to overhang the vale; the gray mansion peeps out from amid the foliage, the green meadows by the river-side are here and there studded with the hawthorn and the hazel. Some distance on the left is Kilnsey Crag, and in the distance, above the vale of the Skirfare, the rocks on the slopes of Hawkswick Moor which bear the form of fortifications, and in the far distance Buckden Pike up Kettlewell Beck. Wending our way up the river, we come to a long flat, being the lower portion of Calcraft Dub.

It may be here explained that the upper portion of the Wharfe is remarkable for long broad reaches of calm shallow water called flats, the sides of which the trout love to haunt in search of miller's-thumbs or the creeper when in season, to the confusion of the angler, as the trout scuttle away at his approach and alarm the sensible trout which are in the stream or sharp run at the head of the flat. In a good water these flats—generally so unproductive in a low water—afford excellent sport with the minnow or fly according to the state of the water, so that the angler gets his compensation.

A few yards above Calcraft Dub are stepping-stones by which the river may be crossed at low water; then we come to a splendid reach of a combination of flat, dub, and stream, the pool being called the Gipsy Camp or Grayling Hole; then some more streamy flats until we arrive at the falls—there being two distinct low falls at about thirty yards apart, the intervening space being a bed of rock intersected with numerous water-worn channels which appear to have been scooped out by some strong force such as the action of ice. These falls and broken water at all times present a picturesque appearance, and in a flood the water rushes over the rocks with a mighty force.

Immediately above the falls is a rather shallow dub, headed by a sharp rather broad stream very good for trout, and a little stream joins the river on the left bank, and a little higher up another little stream on the right bank.

After a few more streams, we arrive at a long deep dub, near the head of which the White Beck from Kilnsey Crag enters the river. Above this is a combination of dub, stream,

CONISTONE BRIDGE.

and flat called Cox's Plantation, then a succession of streams until we reach the deep dub below Conistone Bridge. There is evidence that there has been a bridge here and over the Skirfare since at any rate the year 1150, as appears from the following extract from Burton's *Monasticon* under the head "Hawkeswych":—"William de Helte and his heirs gave the firmatio of his two bridges, one over the Shirphare and the other over Werf, with a road of thirty feet wide between them." The characteristics of the river are much the same up to Armadale, the meeting of the waters. The second pool below Armadale is called Broken Brow, down which tumbles a waterfall formed by a small tributary.

Proceeding up Kettlewell Beck we observe delightful streams, dubs, and flats, and a few cascades. At Black Keld Dub an interesting stream called Black Keld enters. About 300 yards up, the stream disappears under the rock and is

BROKEN BROW.

subterranean from the mountain Great Whernside. During a fresh this stream comes down very dark coloured with peaty water, hence the name Black Keld. Above Black Keld the river in several places passes over a bed of solid rock grooved with numerous small channels, and in some places there are holes having the appearance of huge footmarks, as if giants had passed along and left the impression of their feet.

Immediately above Kettlewell the river entirely changes

its character; the rocks cease and there is a succession of long still pools headed by short streams until after Buckden is reached, some distance above which the river resumes its rocky character. At Kettlewell a stream from Great Whernside joins the river, and the summit of the mountain is visible as if guarding the dale. The slopes on both sides of the dale are very abrupt and present a somewhat wild appearance, the green being mixed up with rocks, huge loose stones, and occasional hazel bushes and rowan trees, the usual characteristics of the Craven country.

The village of Kettlewell presents a very snug appearance, sheltered on all sides by the surrounding hills. Corn appears to have been grown in the neighbourhood in ancient times. "William de Arches gave a free passage for their (the Monks of Fountains) men, horses, cattle, and things over his land de Staverboten—or Stanerboten or Starboten—except over corn and meadow, from the east part of the Werf to the boundaries of Ketelwel" (Burton's *Monasticon*). The neighbourhood of Buckden and Hubberholme some four miles or so up the valley is beautiful, extensive plantations on the sides of the dale having been made by Sir J. W. Ramsden, Bart., the late owner of the Buckden House estate, which was acquired by purchase by the late Major-General Stansfield. Hubberholme is famous for its ancient church, which is well worthy of a visit.

We will now retrace our steps and wander up the Skirfare. Rather more than half a mile from the meeting of the waters is Skirfare Bridge, on the main road between Skipton and Buckden. This length may be described as principally a shallow flat, varied by a few sharp streams and shallow dubs, a favourite lie for trout of good size. The trout caught in the Skirfare are generally lighter in colour and more plump than those caught in Kettlewell Beck. A few hundred yards above the bridge is the Wash Dub, where sheep are washed in the early summer. This dub is an excellent place for good trout, and should the angler not be able to get a rise there, there is little hope elsewhere. A small tributary joins the river at this dub, which has its source on or rather out of Kilnsey Moor, as the stream flows in a volume from the limestone rock, as does also the White Beck at the other side of Kilnsey Crag. These facts tend to point out that there is a vast body of water within Kilnsey Moor. There are several streams of a similar character which are quite clear after a heavy rainfall. From the Wash Dub to the next bridge, Hawkswick Bridge, the river is a succession of flats with many sharp streams and shallow dubs. For some distance the river flows over solid rock, similar to the rocky bottom of part of Kettlewell Beck and intersected by similar grooved channels.

Above the Kilnsey Club water we come to Mr. Hammond's water, which extends for some distance above the next village, Arncliffe. The village of Arncliffe is singularly beautiful: a well-wooded dale with crags on both sides; an ancient bridge spans the river, immediately below which is the church with its ancient square tower, and not far from the church the vicarage standing in well-wooded grounds.

The Ripon diocesan calendar was planned in this secluded spot by the late Vicar, the venerable Archdeacon Boyd—venerable in the strict sense of the term—and Canon Kemp, the late Vicar of Birstall. The Archdeacon may be fittingly described as a Squire Parson, and he passed almost the whole of his long life among the Dale folk. He was a geologist, also an observer of the weather. For many years he measured the rainfall at Arncliffe, with the result that the rainfall there was ascertained to be about 60 inches per annum. Good trout fishing may be obtained by leave from Mr. Hammond, which is always given to visitors at the Falcon.

A short distance above Arncliffe, Cowside Beck enters the river; it is a rocky stream running through a narrow dell with very steep sides. Passing up the main river we reach the tiny village of Lytton. Hereabouts the course of the river is very interesting, one more instance of Craven potholes. For about a mile the river disappears, but the course is marked by a rocky or stony bed.

Fissures may be seen into which the water disappears. In times of flood the subterranean channel is not sufficient to take all the water, consequently the visible bed of the river is full of water, and as the flood water subsides the dry bed reappears. If these fissures were bridged over, there would be a mile more of good fishing, and to all appearances this might easily be accomplished.

Some distance above Lytton the river passes through a romantic rocky ravine, where there are numerous cascades and deep rocky pools haunted, it is said, by large trout. This part of the river is only a few miles from Upper Ribblesdale, but the ascent and descent thereto are steep and make up for the short distance. Among the hills the curlew and several other shore birds rear their young in spring, and it appears strange when taking a walk to hear sounds which are more commonly heard in our estuaries; and the birds are so tame. It is interesting to observe that wary bird the redshank hovering like a hawk overhead within shot, as you approach the neighbourhood of its nest, and piping wildly.

Snipe nest in considerable numbers on these Craven hills and moors. A walk in the nesting time on these wild uplands is most interesting, much more so than in the autumn when the grouse shooters are on slaughter bent.

I have endeavoured to describe the nature of the waters of the Kilnsey Angling Club as specially adapted for the bonny trout, but in doing so it appears appropriate to direct the

MEETING OF THE WATERS.

angler's attention to the beauties of nature in secluded places such as the surroundings of the Kilnsey Angling Club quarters, for every true angler must be a lover of nature, and especially so in her wildest haunts. There may be still opportunities for further interesting geological discoveries in Craven; it is only a few years since Dowker Bottom Cave, about a mile north-west of Kilnsey Crag, was discovered.

With regard to fish and fishing, there is no doubt that

rivers passing through a limestone country are favourable for the production and growth of the trout, more so than rivers passing through a slate-stone country like most parts of the English Lake District and parts of Wales. The limestone and limestone grit are exceedingly hard, and are little affected by the action of water in comparison with blue or green slate, consequently minute forms of aquatic life cling to the hard stones much more readily than to the smooth slate, and afford abundant food for the trout. In addition, moss has a way of growing on the hard stone, and harbours an immense quantity of aquatic forms of life, as may easily be observed on examination of the moss; and there is no doubt that trout feed amongst the moss, and the observant angler will have noted that there is little use in fishing with the clear-water worm over a moss-covered bottom.

The stone-fly is numerous in all the waters of the club, and affords most nourishing food for the trout both in the creeper stage and the perfect fly; and when the stone-fly season is fairly over, the trout are satisfied with insect food and become eager for the worm or minnow, and then the trout divide their attentions between the worm and the minnow according to the time of day apparently. Minnows are scarce in the club waters, but the numerous miller's-thumbs form a substitute for them, and when the trout are at the sides of the flats they are probably devoting their attention to the miller's-thumbs.

By the rules of the Kilnsey Angling Club, clear-water worm and minnow fishing are not allowed except in Kettlewell Beck until June 20th, that date being considered as the extreme limit of the stone-fly season. It may be said that the members of the club as a general rule fish the artificial fly until the stone-fly season, which commences about the 20th of

May or somewhat earlier or later according to the season, and lasts until about the middle of June. April and May are the best months for the artificial fly, and should a fresh occur during the stone-fly season trout take the artificial fly with avidity.

On a cool cloudy day in June a fair basket may be made with fly even in low water, provided that the trout are not too much absorbed with the stone-fly should it be out in considerable numbers. As a rule July is a bad month for the fly even in a much esteemed porter-coloured fresh, although the late lamented Mr. Pritt once killed upwards of thirty trout during such a fresh in July: this is the time for the deadly minnow, a good fly-water in July. About the middle of August the fly again comes into favour, especially in a good water, and continues until the end of the season. The clear-water worm is a most deadly lure from about the middle of June to the end of July, and should the trout not be on the worm the up-stream minnow will probably be successful.

In order that the captures of trout in the club waters may be appreciated, it is necessary to mention that a typical fishing day roughly extends from about nine o'clock in the morning to about five o'clock in the afternoon. If members adopted the course followed by the late Mr. Stewart, the author of Stewart's *Practical Angler*, and slaved from early morn to dewy eve with fly, worm, and minnow, according to the humour of the trout, they might often capture their 12 lb. of fish and thus qualify themselves to be considered worthy of the name of anglers; but how about the supply of trout? that is the question.

The reader will be anxious to learn the quantum of trout which may be considered to afford a fair day's sport from a

Kilnsey Club point of view. To this I answer, that 15 with the fly is considered a good day, about the same number with the clear-water minnow, and from that number to 20 with the clear-water worm; of course these numbers are often exceeded, but more frequently not attained to. So far as I am aware the greatest number caught with the artificial fly has been 52, and with the clear-water minnow and worm about 30; but I am confident that if a man were to do his utmost with the up-stream worm, he might easily exceed 50 during a long day on a favourable occasion, but this would not be true sport from a sportsmanlike view.

With regard to the size to which the Kilnsey trout attain, the general average may be stated at three to the pound. Pounders are rare, half-pounders are common, considerable numbers are caught from 10 to 15 oz. Out of 2756 trout captured by myself, only two exceeded a pound, and each weighed 1 lb. 2 oz., one having been caught with artificial fly and the other with the creeper. The heaviest trout that I am aware of weighed about one pound and a half.

Baskets of trout are not by any means uncommon when the average is about two to the pound. I give the following particulars as to the trout captured by me in the waters of the Kilnsey Angling Club from 1882 to 1897, both inclusive :—

No. with fly.	Worm.	Stone-fly.	Minnow.	Total.	Weight.
1241	871	401	243	2756	1018 lb. 3 oz.

showing an average weight of rather more than 5 oz. 14 dr., or nearly 6 oz.

It was at Kilnsey that I first met that most genial of anglers the late Mr. Thomas Evan Pritt, the celebrated editor of the *Yorkshire Post* Angling Column and the founder of the Yorkshire Anglers' Association. I regret that I have not any record of our first meeting, but it was probably at Whitsuntide 1883. He first appeared in my notes in April 1885 at Easter-tide. There was a very pleasant party at the Tennants' Arms, of which he was the life and soul. Alas, poor Pritt, we shall not have again thy merry laugh and joke. Among the party there were the veteran and always kind and courteous angler Mr. Thomas Halliwell, Mr. J. W. Reffitt, and Mr. Benjamin Hirst. I arrived on Thursday the 2nd of April; it was a cold day with snow showers, and I distinguished myself by falling down in the water, and I got soaked from head to foot and my hat went floating down the river. On entering the inn in my wretched condition, I encountered Pritt, who had just arrived, and he asked me in his inimitable manner why I had chosen to take a cold bath on such a day.

The event was in due time recorded in the Angling Column with most romantic variations, and I am indebted to the courtesy of the proprietors of the *Yorkshire Post* for permission to make the following extract.

The other day I was watching a friend who was fishing a very rough stream, at the foot of which, ten yards below where he was standing in the middle of the current, was a hole about eight feet deep. Suddenly his feet flew from under him, his rod and net disappeared, and he shot down the current like an arrow [bravo, Pritt!]. Fortunately he succeeded in laying hold of a projecting rock to which he clung with much affection, until at length he succeeded in raising himself and getting out: he was altogether out of my reach [quite true, veracious Pritt]. When his legs at length were hoisted out of the water, one foot was fast in the landing-net, which was itself in this way landed: and as luck would have it, one of the flies on his cast was firmly hooked in his coat, so that by merely dragging away at his line it was all off the reel; he also recovered his rod. When I ventured to inquire what was the object of this performance generally, his characteristic reply was, that I might be quite sure he was not doing it because he liked it.

This is really delightful; oh that the facile pen of Pritt had descended on me! At that time Pritt appeared to enjoy splendid health; and what jolly evenings we had at the Tennants' Arms! With Pritt to lead, the fun was fast and furious. My notes record that he at that visit lead in the fishing. On Good Friday he killed 20 trout, and on Easter Tuesday 19.

Some reference is made as to Mr. Pritt's success in fishing with large flies in the chapter on the Yorkshire Anglers' Association, when other members of the club were fishing with small flies, and the results of the fishing were as follows :—

Mr. Halliwell	5
Mr. Reffitt	8
Mr. Hirst	4
Myself	7

24 as against Mr. Pritt's 19.

I did not record Mr. Pritt's captures on any other days than on Good Friday and the Tuesday. In the following four chapters we shall proceed to illustrate fly, stone-fly, worm and minnow fishing, in the waters of the Kilnsey Angling Club.

CHAPTER XVI

FLY-FISHING AT KILNSEY

And before you begin to angle, cast to have the wind on your back, and the sun, if it shines, to be before you.—PISCATOR.

WE will now wander down the river in retrospect on a day in the leafy month of June. I only arrived at Kilnsey that morning, accordingly I could not make an early start; therefore I did not expect much, but how often the unexpected happens! It was the 17th of June. I walked down the river to Netherside with its overhanging woods. The hawthorns were in their full glory of bloom, and the air was sweet with the perfume. There was a nice light curtain over the sky to screen off the sun, and there was a pleasant breeze from south-west up stream which made a nice curl on the dubs and smooth flats: there was a nice clear fly-water, but not too much to render wading up stream difficult.

At eleven o'clock I commenced with a hair cast to which were attached three flies dressed on No. 1 hooks. I did not record the particular flies on the cast, but most execution was done with the yellow starling and the orange starling, the feather being taken from the inside of a starling's wing, one of the little yellowish dun or fawn coloured feathers.

THE FALLS, KILNSEY.

The water was dimpled here and there with rising fish, and I soon found that they meant it. I waded quietly up, and again and again cast over rising fish which invariably responded.

By the time I reached the Falls I had about eight trout; it was then that the sport began in earnest. Every nook and corner held a fish, and they rose with an avidity which is only too seldom experienced by me when at Kilnsey; and they were game—a nine-ounce trout which I hooked in the uppermost fall carried me down to the lowest fall, at least sixty yards.

Hereabouts I creeled about fifteen trout. In the rather shallow pool above the Falls I creeled several more, the last of which behaved with remarkable consideration. I spotted him rising. At the first cast I just pricked him; after a pause I cast again and pricked him hard: no use now, thought I, but I waited a few minutes and he came a third time, and, hurrah, he was fast! How he did fight! What a monster he appeared to be! But I soon found he was hooked foul: but the hair held, and he was in the end duly netted. He was a nice three-quarters of a pounder and the fish of the day.

It was now about five o'clock, and a slight rain began to fall. The rise continued, and I fished up to Conistone Bridge. By this time I had had enough of it. At my last cast I hooked and landed a half-pounder. I then wound up with 30 trout, weight 10 lb. 1 oz. I had not lost a fly. What a creel I might have had, had I fished a little longer; but I was more than satisfied. At night there was a great fall of rain, and the next day was Sunday—a *dies non* at Kilnsey, when the trout may flop at nature's flies and fear no evil. At Kilnsey they say a man who fishes on Sunday comes to a fearful end, but I never heard a precedent quoted. It is quite orthodox, however, to stroll by the river-side, watch the trout rising gaily, and wish it was Monday, so we walked up the Skirfare in the morning. There was what is called in the Dales a bold "flee-water" of a dark peaty colour : the trout were rising well in the pools and eddies, and wherever they could find a hold.

It was a lovely June morning with an occasional shower, which studded the trees and hedges with diamond-like drops which glisten in the occasional gleams of bright sunshine. As we near Dawn Dub a heron flops up, then a snipe rises from a sedgy spot, and almost at the same moment a couple of sandpipers from the shore, and fly piping down the river. Lapwings are about in the meadows, and screech as they whirl about in the air; one of them alights close to, and with one wing trailing as if broken, runs before, occasionally stopping and then running again. Anon the cuckoo sounds his soft note as he flies about. We are quite alone with the birds for our companions, and we feel the eternity of the surroundings, the foaming river ever flowing, and the eternal rocks above ever still. We retrace our steps, and as we pass under Kilnsey Crag we hear the not very euphonious bell of Conistone Church sounding across the dale, summoning a small band of worshippers to church. We respond to the appeal, and cross Conistone Bridge, looking as we go at the deep pool below and thinking very much about to-morrow.

As we pass through the stile to the churchyard, a group of Dalesmen stand with their eyes directed to the Skipton road, which can be seen trending down the dale for a mile or more. They are watching for the parson's gig—he comes from Rylstone. As the gig nears, they shamble into the church. As the parson emerges from the vestry, the harmonium gives him a welcome. A little mixed choir are already seated. A few Dalesmen are late, and as they pass up the aisle look conscious as though their entry created a great sensation—a stalwart young farmer among them who is sporting a span new Scotch plaid coat and evidently feeling that the eyes of all the girls are upon him, as he takes his seat with a bump and colours to his very neck. Thus about a score or so of worshippers are assembled. The singing is lead by a Mr. Chaffinch, and what so sweet as "spink! spink!"? There is a Miss Chaffinch too among the choir. The choir sing with the usual vigour of Yorkshire lads and lasses; the rank and file of the congregation, however, appear to be afraid of their own voices.

It would appear that when the church was built either the population was greater or the people were more devout, considering the size of the church. A wedding is a great event in these lonely dales; such excitement! And a christening is quite an event too: how shy the godfathers look—will they ever "name this child"? but fortunately the godmothers are generally equal to the occasion. A funeral is an event of the greatest importance and solemnity, and the Dalesmen; from a sense of respect combined with duty, journey from afar in their sombre black garments, some of which, swallow-tailed in shape, appear to be heirlooms. Service being concluded we all escape, *ego ipse* to dinner in the club-room—sacred to otters and other anglers—which I partake of in solitude, if solitude it can be called with the otters eating their dinner in the glass case.

The morrow has come. Where shall I go? I have all to myself. Choice breeds care; but the Skirfare looked so nice yesterday, and up the bonny river I walked about three-quarters of a mile above Skirfare Bridge, and began fishing a little after nine o'clock. There was a good water of a light porter colour. I must make the best of my time, for I must wind up at three o'clock. The trout came short for some time, but they gradually improved, and fish after fish found their way to my creel. At the Wash Dub I had a good fight with a nice three-quarters of a pound trout: it is nice work for a hair cast in a strong water. The killing flies were the blue

SKIRFARE BRIDGE.

partridge (taken probably for the gravel-bed) and the yellow and orange starling.

By the time I got to the meeting of the waters I had 22 trout. At the bottom of Kettlewell Beck I got 1, and thence to the Field Dub I got 8—making 31 in all, weight 9 lb. 7 oz. Alas! it was then three o'clock, and I left the trout still on the rise. Thus ended a very pleasant two days' fishing.

I fished two days in the Aire in the same month of June,

and my catch in the four days amounted to 98 trout. That month was apparently a very favourable one for the angler.

It has never been my good fortune to kill a goodly number of trout at Kilnsey in April with the fly; my maximum has only been 13, but they were good fish. It was the 15th of April 1884: the water was rather low, and there was a strong north wind down stream. I commenced at the meeting of the waters at half-past ten, and left off at Conistone Bridge a little after three with 13 trout which weighed 6 lb.—best trout 13 oz., and the killing flies were moor poult and winged yellow dun. During that visit I fished on four days and caught 43 trout, 17 lb. 6 oz. On my next visit, from the 3rd to the 5th of May, three days, I killed 58 trout, 17 lb. 9 oz.—best day 27 trout. These are fair sample baskets, and it is the exception to do better. I have had the best sport with the fly in the months of May, June, August, and September.

One more illustration of fly-fishing at Kilnsey late on in the season. It is the month of August, when the curlews leave the top of the hills with their young for a few days in the dales, preparatory to their flight to Morcambe Bay; Monday the 17th. We can never forecast the result of a day with the fly at Kilnsey; everything may appear favourable, and still the creel may get lighter as the day progresses. There was a nice clear fly-water about right for fishing up stream. I commenced at Netherside at half-past nine o'clock, but it was an hour before I caught my first trout. By two o'clock I had only 9, and at that time I had got to the White Beck Dub. The east side of the dub is fringed with willows and is shallow, the west side is deep: the dub terminates in a broad shallow where fish love to feed. Running up about the middle of the dub there is a gravelly ridge, which varies from time to time by the action of floods. Heavy showers began to fall, and the fish began to rise well.

I crossed to the shallow side and fished up, and in a short time killed 13 fish, and I was unfortunate in losing 4 trout owing to breakages. I fished with hair. Fishing up Cox's Plantation I killed 2 more. At five o'clock the weather became so wet that I gave up with 24 trout, weight 8 lb. 14 oz.— best trout three-quarters of a pound. The killing flies in order of merit were the blue dun (water-hen bloa), iron-blue dun (dark watchet), yellow dun, and landrail wing. These illustrations must suffice for fly-fishing at Kilnsey. Of course there are days recorded when the pannier is very light; a few times zero is recorded, but only a few.

I give a list of the flies with which I have captured trout at Kilnsey in the order in which they occur in my diary.

Black spider.
Orange partridge.
Yellow dun.
Orange dun.
Blue partridge.
Blue dun.
Yellow landrail.
March brown (male).
Light March brown (female).
Yellow snipe.
Yellow curlew.
Maroon dun (starling).
Orange curlew.
Olive dun (winged).
Brown dun (winged).

Coachman.
Cinnamon fly.
Quill gnat.
Purple dark snipe.
Hare-lug.
Little winter brown (dark woodcock).
Brown owl.
Iron-blue dun
Knotted midge.
Winter brown (light woodcock).
Red partridge.
Peacock dun.
Red spinner.
Woodcock fly.

The hackled yellow duns are made from the following feathers: under the starling's and young grouse's wings, and from the back of the hooded crow. Probably the best all-round flies at Kilnsey are in order of merit the yellow snipe, yellow dun, blue dun, orange partridge, yellow partridge, blue partridge, hackled iron-blue, light woodcock, and orange and dark woodcock. The hatch of March browns at Kilnsey has for many years been very spare, nevertheless in a good water considerable execution is done with the March brown. The yellow snipe is a great favourite, especially in spring.

Certain samples of fly casts have been indicated in the chapter on "Fly-Fishing." The dressings of most of the flies I have named are contained in Pritt's *North Country Flies*, and an angler who wishes to dress his own flies will find the book of great advantage to him.

CHAPTER XVII

MAYFLY-FISHING AT KILNSEY

And now I shall tell you that the fishing with a natural fly is excellent and affords much pleasure.—PISCATOR.

THE stone-fly is the May-fly of Kilnsey. About the middle of May several members of the Kilnsey Angling Club are in a state of expectancy, and about the 24th they are in a mild state of excitement, when a missive from the keeper arrives of which the following is about the formula :—

KILNSEY, 23rd *May* 18 .

Sir,

The May-fly is up.

Yours resp.

J. E. EMMOTT.

Now the time has come when the most important business pales before the importance of the May-fly. Lawyers desert their clients, doctors their patients, and business men their markets. They are mad to be at it: will the trout be mad on it, as they fondly hope? They arrive at Kilnsey some time in the evening, some by the Buckden bus—which is about a duplicate of the royal mail, and contains a mixed assemblage of the genus *Homo*, luggage, hampers, bitter-beer cases, soda-water cases, and an occasional dog thrown in by way of variety—others of more aristocratic tendencies by dog-carts, which are generally without the dog. After a hasty tea of the inevitable ham-and-eggs type, they rush to the river, to search for the flies for the morrow.

WASH DUB.

It is amusing, almost sad, to watch a respectable middle-aged gentleman, who has learnt not to sigh over his lost waist, stooping and laboriously turning over the stones in search of the nimble insects; how he blows and groans and blows at the agile jacks, which he cannot catch. At last, however, assisted by an active urchin, who fortunately comes on the scene, he fills his tin with the insects and returns rejoicing to the inn, where after his arduous exertions he partakes of much-needed refreshment.

During the May-fly season, the fly is much in evidence in the inn. It is found even in the bedrooms. It is an anxious time : how will the wind blow to-morrow ? will the cuss be on in force ? He no longer thinks of the bills he has to meet ; they may wait, the May-fly will not wait. It is the May-fly or nothing. He does not even think of his other favourite lures. He is on the May-fly whether the trout are or not, and whatever the trout may do he will be faithful to St. May-fly. Minnows and worms even cannot lure him from the faith once given to the saint.

Oh what a childlike touching faith is this ! when a man can leave all, his wife and family and all that he has, for the sake of his patron saint. Verily he stoops to conquer, and he has his reward. He glances at the smoke rising from the houses at Conistone across the river, as he dresses in the morning, and oh, joy ! the wind is up stream. He is devoutly happy : the saint is kind. He feels at peace with himself and all mankind. He sallies forth like our Father Izaak of old ; he baits the hooks tenderly with the living fly as though he loved him, in order that he may live a little longer. Perchance Nero impaled flies on a pin before he went fishing.

My first introduction to the May-fly was a sell. It was in May 1882, and up to that time I had not so much as seen one. It was at Kilnsey, and Mr. Reffitt was there. On the day of my arrival he came in with a pannier of 17 trout, which he said he had caught with fly. On the next day I slaved with artificial fly for 9 trout, and on arriving at the club-room, behold there was a dish of 23 fine trout, of some 11 lb. weight, caught by friend Reffitt again—"all caught with fly," he said. I felt desperate. What a fool of a fisherman I must be ! After a great deal of chaff at my expense my friend purged his conscience by making confession: all had been caught with the natural stone-fly.

It was not until 1884 that I initiated myself into the mysteries of the natural stone-fly. It was the 26th of May; the weather was bright and warm, water very low. I fished up Kettlewell Beck and killed 11 trout, weight 4 lb. 9 oz.—best trout three-quarters of a pound. It was a good beginning, for one of our best men with the May-fly only killed 5. The next day proved the uncertainty of the May-fly : I only caught 1 trout with it, and 1 with the black spider—the cuss was in force. The next day was another instance : with May-fly I got 2 trout, with artificial fly 2, and minnow 1. On the same day two other men got 2 each with the May-fly. What a failure it was!

In the following year the fly was late, and I had my first day on the 10th of June. The weather was fine and hot, and the water very low. I commenced opposite the inn, and fished up to Milehouse Dub in Kettlewell Beck, and left off at three o'clock with 10 trout. I went out again in the evening and caught 4 more, making 14 in all, weight 7 lb. 1 oz.—best 15 oz. I fished on three more days, and the sport gradually fell off.

	Trout.	Weight.
First day	14	7 lb. 1 oz.
Second ,,	12	6 ,, 0 ,,
Third ,,	8	3 ,, 8 ,,
Fourth ,,	3	1 ,, 2 ,,
	37	17 lb. 11 oz.

I did not fish the May-fly at Kilnsey again until 1888,

which was a very late season. My principal sport was as follows :—

	Trout.	Weight.
June 14	16	5 lb. 8 oz.
,, 15	15	5 ,, 6 ,,

On my two last days the trout were quite off the stone-fly.

The season of 1889 again illustrated the uncertainty of the May-fly: on the 27th, 3 trout; 28th, 9, and 3 with artificial fly; on the 29th, 16 with May-fly; and on the 30th, 4 with May-fly and 2 with artificial fly.

In 1890 the fly was up in good time and there was some fair sport with it. Seven members of the club were at it, and the consequence was that the trout became shy. On the 23rd of May I fished up Kettlewell Beck from about half-past eight o'clock to three. The weather was bright and hot, and the wind up stream. The water was moderate, and I killed 19 trout, weight 6 lb. 5 oz. On the next day I commenced about the same time and fished up the Skirfare as far as Hawkswick. The weather was bright, with a strong wind up stream. I ceased fishing at three o'clock, having creeled 16 trout, weight 6 lb. 9 oz.—best fish 11 oz.

On Monday the 26th I again fished up the Skirfare to Hawkswick. The weather was cool and windy, and I only killed 10 trout, weight 3 lb. 7 oz. The water had got low. On the next day I fished up Kettlewell Beck and only killed 4 with the May-fly and 1 with the artificial. On my last day I fished till about two o'clock for 4 fish. They appeared to have gone off the May-fly.

The season of 1891 was somewhat late, and so far as my experience went the fish were not well on the May-fly. On the 9th of June I killed 15 trout with it by about three o'clock.

In May 1892 I for the first time tried the creeper at Kilnsey, but I did not find it very attractive. On the 12th, after fishing with fly for some hours in the best part of the day for 1 fish, I soon caught 5 with the creeper, and had I commenced with creeper I should probably have done some execution with it. The Mayfly-fishing was injured by floods, and I had an opportunity of trying it in a good brown fly-water. It was the 4th of June. The weather was alternate cloud and sunshine, wind up stream. I fished in Kettlewell Beck and only killed 8 with the stone-fly and 1 with the artificial. Two other anglers who were out only killed 5 and 3 trout respectively. On the 7th there was a nice fly-water, and I killed 13 with May-fly, weight 5 lb. 4 oz. Mr. Reffitt killed 15. On the 9th I had some nice sport with the May-fly below the Falls, and left off at three o'clock with 11 trout, weight 5 lb. 2 oz.—best trout 14 oz. The weather was fine and hot.

In May 1893 I decided to give the creeper a fair trial at Kilnsey, so on the 4th I commenced with it and fished for hours, but only caught 4 trout. The water was very low, too low for any mode of fishing. As I was walking on the bank opposite the inn, near the top of the Field Dub, I saw a large trout leave a thin rapid. I noted the exact spot. The next day I fished the creeper from the low side, but my friend did not appear to be at home. That day I only killed 6 trout with the creeper, but they were good ones and weighed 2 lb. 13 oz. On the following day I again waited on my friend with the creeper, and he at once responded. He made a mad rush to the deep pool below, and made a gallant fight. He was a beautiful trout of 18 oz. I did not do much, however, but I left off at half-past two o'clock with 6 trout, weight 3 lb. 3 oz.

L

That was the very worst May-fly season I ever experienced: my best pannier contained but 7 trout. They would not have it.

In 1894 I fished the May-fly the first week in June, and although I could find plenty of flies, I did little execution. Perhaps the trout were past it.

The May-fly season of 1895 was a wretched one. The fly was up about the 24th of May. The water was very low, much too low for a fair chance of sport; the weather was bright and hot. I devoted eight days to it, commencing on the 25th, and only killed 48 with the May-fly, 2 with the artificial fly, 7 with the up-stream minnow, and 2 with worm, making in all 59 trout, weight 23 lb. 6 oz.—best day 12 trout, and best trout 11 oz.

On the 18th of May 1896 I went to Kilnsey with the view of giving the creeper a good try, but I found the fly up in force. On my opening day, the 19th, there was a north-west wind down stream, which made casting difficult. There were a few rain-drops, and gleams of bright sunshine. I commenced a little above the Falls, in the first streamy water, and soon began to pick up fish, and by the time I got to Byron Dub I had 17 trout, weight 7 lb. 8 oz.—best trout 13 oz. I did not fish after four o'clock. The next day the weather was a caution. A heavy north-westerly gale, with occasional pelting showers of rain mingled with hail, blew right down the river; to get a cast up stream was an absolute impossibility. Often the gusts of wind would blow the line clean out of the river, and blow the fly off the hooks. The only plan was to drift the line down stream under the opposite bank. Thus doing I managed to kill 5 trout, but I came in early as I was tired of being out in such a wind.

On the following day there was still a strong wind down stream, and the only course was to fish down with a long line before the wind. I had most sport in the dubs, but I missed many rises. However, I succeeded in killing 14 trout, weight 5 lb. 1 oz. My last day, Friday, came. The wind had dropped, and the weather was sultry and cloudy, and when I began to fish above the Falls there was a vast array of black gnats in possession of the river, and the trout were mad on them. Fish after fish refused the succulent May-fly, and by three o'clock, when I had to wind up, I had only 6 trout. A little before that time they had commenced to take the May-fly, and I dare say that had I remained out longer I might have made a fair pannier. Result of four days' fishing, 42 trout, weight 17 lb. 6 oz.

The May-fly season of 1897, the Diamond Jubilee of Her Most Gracious Majesty, was not kind. The season was late, the wind persisted in blowing down stream, and the fly did not appear to be in favour with the trout. The fly was fairly on at the end of May, and Tuesday the 1st of June was my first day. Mr. Reffitt, Mr. Godwin, Mr. Moiser, Mr. Fawcett, and I formed the May-fly Company. The start was delayed by a heavy thunderstorm, which lasted from nine o'clock to half-past ten, accompanied by heavy rain and hail, and there was a strong down-stream wind which militated against sport, and I had to be contented with 9 trout.

On the following day, in consequence of rain, there was a good fly-water. As the stone-fly did not prove attractive and the wind blew down stream, I fished down the Skirfare from Hawkswick and killed 12 trout with the yellow partridge, yellow dun, and black spider, and returned 13 undersized trout to the water. Alas! I missed an undue number of rises. On the four following days I only killed 23 trout, 21 of which were killed with the stone-fly and 2 with the artificial. The total catch in seven days was only 52 trout, weight 19 lb. 1 oz. The superiority of the clear-water worm was exemplified in three short days' fishing on 15th, 16th, 17th July, when I killed 51 trout which weighed 19 lb. 11 oz.—best trout a nice plump pounder, killed under the fall at the head of the Wash Dub.

A rather curious circumstance happened with regard to a trout of about three-quarters of a pound. I dropped my worm from a high bank into calm shallow water under a tree, and it was immediately seized: on approaching close to the bank I saw my quarry in company with four trout of at least half a pound each looking on and evidently wondering what was amiss. After wasting a lot of time in playing the fish, as I could not reach him with the net I attempted to lift him out, but the hold gave way and the trout regained his friends.

CHAPTER XVIII

WORM-FISHING AT KILNSEY

Nay, the trout is not lost; for pray take notice, no man can lose what he never had.—PISCATOR.

ANGLERS who look on worm-fishing with feelings akin to contempt, appear to me wanting in appreciation. There are days and days in the north country when the fly is practically useless, yes even the dry fly. I should like to know the man who could extract 20 trout from the Wharfe under certain conditions of weather and water at Kilnsey with the dry fly— I mean the conditions when the worm is so deadly.

It is Saturday, the 30th of June 1888. I elected to fish in the Skirfare, so I proceeded to a little below Skirfare Bridge. My rod was a twelve-foot built cane, which I use for all kinds of fishing. The weather was alternate cloud and sunshine, with a strong wind down stream, which rendered casting difficult. I began at ten o'clock, and was at once among them. They meant it from the first. A little below the bridge there is a rapid narrow stream, which flows under a tree. I threw into it—a great tug, and the worm gone. I bait and again cast—another big tug in the same spot, and another worm gone. "He will not take again," thought I. I waited a few minutes, and cast a third time—a third tug, and I paused a little longer than usual, and I had a well-fed trout of 13 oz., the best that day. By a quarter past four I reached Hawkswick Bridge, and turned out my pannier and counted 31 trout, which I afterwards found weighed 9 lb. 14 oz. rather below the average with the worm. On the 18th of July 1892 I killed 22 trout in the same water, which weighed 9 lb. 10 oz.

KETTLEWELL BECK.

It is not advisable, when the water is low, to fish in the same water two days in succession, and although there was a Sunday between, I decided on Monday the 2nd of July to fish in Kettlewell Beck. I commenced my day at the meeting of the waters at ten o'clock. The water was low, and the weather for the most part rainy, wind south-west. In the rough water at the bottom of the beck the sport began, and I caught 3 fish there. As I advanced upwards my creel got heavier and heavier, and my back ached with the load of fish. By four o'clock I had advanced to a little below Kettlewell Bridge, about three miles from mine inn. The fish were still taking; it seemed a pity to leave them. The Skipton mail would pass about half-past four. I must either take the mail or struggle along with my load.

After all, I had caught enough—more than enough; so I reeled up and walked up to the road to await the arrival of the mail. Soon the mail drove up—a waggonette drawn by two horses, and fairly packed with human beings and a collection of bags, boxes, and hampers. There was just room to squeeze in. It is a curious thing that the driver rarely admits that he is full—the number which the mail will hold appears to be an unknown quantity. We are soon deposited at Kilnsey, the first station on our road, and a stoppage is made there to receive the Arncliffe and Conistone mails and to allow thirsty passengers a reasonable time for refreshment, it being a distance of no less than three miles from the last stop for similar purposes. The arrivals of the morning and evening mails at Kilnsey are the events of the day. The small boys look on the mail driver with profound admiration, so do the rosy-faced maidens of the dale. I felt glad that I had not to trudge it.

In the privacy of the club-room I counted and weighed my spoils: 31 trout, 12 lb. 5 oz.—largest trout 11 oz. On this visit I fished on four days, and with worm, minnow, and fly killed 86 trout, weight 30 lb. 8 oz.

In the following year, 1889, during five days' worm-fishing in June, I killed 90 trout, weight 33 lb. 8 oz.—best trout 1 lb. They were short days and I did not wish to kill more than I did.

With one more illustration of the clear-water worm we

must be content. This time we commence at Netherside and try the main river. It was the 27th of July 1891. I commenced about half-past nine o'clock, and as the water was in fair order for the fly, I tried fly for some time, but I could not get a rise. There was a strong wind down stream, and after a short shower at the time I commenced, the weather was alternate cloud and sunshine. With the worm I at once began to pick up fish, and the stream at the head of Calcraft Dub yielded about half-a-dozen good fish. When I reached the Falls I had 19 fish. Above the Falls, in some excellent worm-water, I only got two more; and as I was returning home, I ceased fishing at half-past two o'clock with 21 fish—9 lb. 5 oz., heaviest 11 oz. The weather was apparently unfavourable for worm-fishing. The fact must be that when fish are hungry they will feed, whatever the weather may be.

We will conclude this chapter with something dreadful,— the worm in a flood. When men have travelled some forty miles, twelve of them being by road, for only a few days' fishing, they want to do something; and if there be a regular flood the worm is the only means, and that must be our excuse.

I arrived at Kilnsey on the 6th of July—the same month as last mentioned—in the evening. The weather was showery and much rain had fallen on the hills; the river was rising fast. The next morning the river was bank full, and the worm was the only chance. When there is a big flood there is no use in wandering about. The right policy is to stick to a place where trout must congregate to shelter themselves from the seething waters. The Field Dub is a typical place for this mode of fishing from the Conistone side. The banks on the Kilnsey side are rather high and are a verdant meadow.

On the Conistone side there is a gravelly shore, which in a

flood is covered with water. There is a backwater near the top of the dub, and hereabouts the trout congregate from a long stretch of water. Being so near the inn I selected this spot; but though so near, I had to walk nearly a mile by Conistone Bridge to get to it. The water was just right, about up to the turf, and very gradually falling. I began at ten o'clock, and I found the fish well on. I stuck to the same place till about three o'clock, giving the trout a rest now and then, and there killed 37 trout. I proceeded to the inn and despatched the fish by parcel post.

Afterwards, in order to spend the time until dinner, I amused myself with a Devon minnow, with which I killed 4 more trout, making 41 in all, weight 15 lb. 4 oz.—best trout 10 oz. The water had fined down to a good minnow-water. If I had procured some minnows and not lost time in despatching my trout, and made a regular day of it, the slaughter would probably have been something dreadful.

Thus it is I often cease fishing when the trout are still on, for when fish are easy to catch the sport becomes monotonous. Even in a flood the trout will not always take the worm.

On the last-mentioned occasion I fished on five days, and with worm, minnow, and fly killed 93 trout, weight 34 lb., and the best trout was three-quarters of a pound.

CHAPTER XIX

MINNOW-FISHING AT KILNSEY

And of these minnows you are to know that the middle size and the whitest are the best.—PISCATOR.

THERE are sometimes conditions of water and weather when worm would appear to be the best lure, but for some reason only known to the trout it is not so, and they will go at the minnow voraciously, and at the same time not touch a worm. Can they under such circumstances be really hungry, or have they recently had a surfeit of worms?

The first time that I fished with the minnow at Kilnsey is an illustration. It was on the 28th of June 1883. There was a fresh—either a worm or minnow water—so in addition to a bag of worms I provided myself with twenty minnows.

I commenced at Conistone Bridge at nine o'clock, on the Kilnsey side, with worm, with which I killed 2 trout. I soon found out that they were not on the worm, so I changed to minnow. The real sport of the day began just below the Falls. The splendid shallow flats were in excellent condition for the minnow. I generally cast out as far as I could, and drew the bait across the current. However, they were so keen that they took it in almost any position. One trout jumped out of the water at it, but did not get fast; the next spin he made sure of it, and I made sure of him. There was another angler on the other side worming, but he could not get a bite, and he watched me catching fish after fish. When I got to Netherside I had used all my minnows. I turned out my creel and counted 22 trout, only 2 of which were

KETTLEWELL BECK

caught with worm. They weighed 9 lb. 9 oz.—best 11 oz., about 7 oz. on the average.

I had a similar experience in the Skirfare on the 27th of May 1892. There was a big worm-water, and I walked up to Hawkswick Bridge with a view of getting some big trout, whose acquaintance I had made unsuccessfully before. Just below the bridge I at once killed a good trout with worm, but could not get another bite. Alas, I had not provided myself with minnows; I had only a small silvery Devon. With the

Devon I had numerous runs, but only killed 9 trout with it. I believe I should have filled my creel had I been provided with the real minnow. The result of the day was only 12 trout, 2 having been caught with the fly.

The following instance shows how trout may take both minnow and fly well at the same time. It was the 15th of September 1896; weather heavy showers, and water rising. As the water appeared to me too big for fly, I commenced with minnow below Conistone Bridge about ten o'clock. Mr. Ledgard, who confines himself to fly, crossed the bridge and made his way down to Calcraft Dub, where the late Mr. Thompson made such famous baskets. Mr. Shaw commenced at the Falls and fished opposite to Mr. Ledgard, with fly. The fish came well at the minnow, and I reeled up a little after two o'clock with 16 trout, which weighed 6 lb. 7 oz. —best trout three-quarters of a pound. Mr. Ledgard did very well with fly—27 fish. He said he found the water just right at Calcraft. Mr. Shaw, who is an expert hand, only got 11. In such a water there is no doubt that Mr. Ledgard had the better chance. By five o'clock a great muddy flood came down.

With regard to minnow-fishing in clear water, the best pannier I know of was made by Mr. Benjamin Hirst, in April, some years ago, in Kettlewell Beck. He killed rather more than 30 fish. Mr. Lupton has also distinguished himself with the up-stream minnow. When the trout are on the minnow in low water, it is nice sport, but one may fish for hours without a run. I have known a man stick at it from ten to three without a run, and then make up for lost time.

In April 1894 I was at Kilnsey. Owing to an error in the printing of the club rules, I came to the conclusion that the restrictive rule as to minnow-fishing had been rescinded. The water was low; there was an absence of fly, and the fish could not be made to rise. On the 10th I walked down to Netherside and fished up with minnow, and I had some nice sport. When I reached the Falls I had 9 trout. I expected to have some good sport in the streams above the Falls and those below Conistone Bridge, but I only got 2 more; then I could not get a run.

I have often had a few hours' nice sport with the up-stream minnow in low water, but I have devoted very few whole days to the sport; and when I have devoted a day, it has happened that the fish have not been well on the minnow. This is the sort of thing that happens: in the first hour or so one may get half-a-dozen fish and then all is over; or the reverse—one may fish for three hours without a run, and then capture the half-dozen. Of course the devotee of the minnow, like any other specialist, gets his big days which are talked about. He has days when he has to be satisfied with 4 or 5 as the proceeds of six hours' hard labour, when perhaps his friend may have killed 30 with fly.

CHAPTER XX

AN EVENING AT THE TENNANTS' ARMS, KILNSEY

And now let's go to an honest ale-house, where we may have a cup of good barley-wine, and sing " Old Rose," and all of us rejoice together.
—HUNTSMAN.

MONTH, September; time, between five and six in the evening. Four or five fishermen dribble in from the fishing, encased in their waders. They put their rods through the open window of the club-room, and then place them on the rod-racks. Some slake their thirst with bottled beer, and with a considerable amount of groaning stoop down to take off their waders. This arduous operation having been accomplished, they trot upstairs to dress for dinner, a very simple performance, which having been performed to the satisfaction of each, they shamble downstairs in their slippers to dinner—a simple meal consisting of a crop of beef, pudding, and tart, and oatcake and cheese, in most instances washed down by bitter beer, which each has placed by him in a jug appropriated to himself. After dinner they draw round the fire, for the evenings are chilly. Pipes are produced and incense is offered up.

Presently Mr. Halefield rings the bell, at the same time saying, "Now, gentlemen, give your orders." Enter Dora, the

CHAP. XX *An Evening at the Tennants' Arms*   159

maid of the inn and a general favourite. Various beverages are ordered, from whisky and soda to lemonade or coffee, and as the liquor decreases the conversation increases in a proportionate ratio.

Mr. Halefield (loq.). How dreadfully low the river is! If we do not have rain soon, we shall have a bad wind-up for the season.

Mr. Luder. Yes; we had some nice rain the other day at our

"THEY PUT THEIR RODS THROUGH THE OPEN WINDOW."

place, so I thought there would be a big fresh here. If I had known I would have stayed at home. By the way, Druidale, you did well to get ten trout to-day, but I suppose you fished the minnow.

Druidale. No; I honestly fished fly and nothing else: but you must bear in mind that I fished up stream—I could have done next to nothing fishing down as you fellows do in this sort of a water.

Mr. Halefield. This river is too rapid for fishing up, the flies come down too fast; you want a slow river for fishing up.

Druidale. But in the stone-fly season you all fish up with the natural fly; I cannot see the difference. By the way, did any of you ever try those new artificial stone-flies, the facsimile of the natural?

Mr. Halefield (to Druidale, with a laugh). Did you ever try the imitation worm?

Druidale (with warmth). I should think not; a fellow would be a fool to fish with imitation worms, when he can get any quantity of the real thing.

Mr. Halefield (with glee). Ah, I have caught you there. (Laughter.)

Druidale puffs at his pipe solemnly, and tries to look vacant.

After a pause, during which Druidale recovers—

Mr. Everleigh (loq.) What flies did they take to-day, Druidale?

Druidale. I caught most with a fly I call the brown dun, and some with the brown owl.

Mr. Garde (a good fly-dresser). Of what do you make the brown dun?

Druidale. Wings, starling quill; body, brown silk; and legs, cochin's ginger neck feather, or better still, a red feather from a grouse's neck. It is a capital killer in autumn.

Mr. Everleigh (who is a shooter). You did well, Druidale, to get a duck and a snipe right and left the other day; how did you manage it?

Druidale. In the morning, before breakfast, I took up my gun and walked in my slippers across to the Field Dub, to try for a heron. Of course I never see a heron when I want to do, and as I came back I walked by that little marshy pond near the river, about three hundred yards from where we are, and up jumped a snipe on my left and a duck on my right. I gave the snipe it first, and then the duck, and the duck was only winged and fell into the river.

Mr. Everleigh. How did you get the duck out?

Druidale. Oh, I walked in as I was and retrieved the bird.

Mr. Garde. Well done, good dog.

A knock at the door and the master keeper enters. Hallo, Jerry!

Jerry. Well, gentlemen, I've some good news for you: it's raining nicely.

Bravo on all sides, and a general rush is made to the outdoor, and the men receive the pattering drops on their upturned faces, and return with glee to the fireside.

Jerry. I think there will be a good fall.

Mr. Halefield. This is glorious; to think, when we were in despair, we may have a grand worm-water from nine to twelve, a nice minnow-water from twelve to three, and then a splendid fly-water. Have you any minnows, Jerry?

Jerry. I have a nice lot, and some good worms too.

Mr. Garde. It is all very well for you fellows with your worms and minnows, but as I abhor them I shall have to wait till three o'clock, I suppose, and in the meantime you fill your baskets. Hang it all.

Druidale. Do as the rest do, Garde, and cease growling.

Mr. Halefield. Now then, don't quarrel about worms and minnows. I mean to have another glass. (*Rings the bell.*)

Enter Agnes (Mrs. Inman, our worthy landlady).

Agnes. Well, you will all be pleased with this weather; it's raining and no mistake. You'll be in no hurry to go home now. I'm so glad. What can I get you?

Mr. Garde. What will you have, Jerry?

Jerry. I think I'll take a whisky and small soda.

Mr. Halefield. Will you have some tobacco, Jerry, or a cigar?

Jerry. Well, you know, sir, I don't smoke a pipe; I don't mind a cigar if you please.

Glasses are brought in and a cigar-box handed round, and all look happy and their faces beam rosily as they sit round the fire, and trout are caught or lost, and the why and the wherefore discussed as it ever has been and ever will be.

Druidale. Now, Jerry, I wish you would tell us about the members who fished here when you had not long been keeper. Mr. Thompson of Luddendenfoot was a good hand, was not he?

Jerry. Yes; Mr. Thompson was a very good fisher, about the best we ever had. He was a good all-round fisher: he fished fly, May-fly, worm, and minnow well.

Druidale. Had he always good sport,—could he always catch them?

Jerry. Well, you see, sir, he used to spend a good deal of time here. He would come for two or three weeks at a time, so he was pretty sure to get some good fishing days. He did not come for two or three days as you do.

Druidale. Can you remember some of his best baskets?

Jerry. Well, it's hard to say now from memory, but I have known him fill a 15 lb. pannier, and that would be about 40 fish; but he had his bad days as well as anybody else. He was fond of fishing on the opposite side below the Falls when the water was right. I have seen him make some rare panniers in Calcraft.

Druidale. When do you call the water right for Calcraft Dub?

Jerry. You want a good bold water, when it is about as high as the green sods, and you fish off the bank.

Druidale. Mr. Thompson died some years since, did not he?

Jerry. Yes; I can't just remember how long it is since. I could have cried when I heard of his death; I was that sorry. He was a right nice gentleman. I nearly always went out with him when he went fishing.

Druidale. Mr. Gleadhall caught an awful lot of fish, did not he? Was not he a good hand?

Jerry. He was a good hand with the fly, and considering that he was a short man, he threw a very good line. He only used fly. He used to make some good baskets; but you know that as he lived at Kettlewell, he was always on the spot and could pick his days, and that's a great advantage.

Druidale. Ay; there is no mistake about that. One day he told me that for one year he kept an account of the trout he caught, and that he was so shocked with the result that he did not keep an account again. The number was something over 1300.

Mr. Loder. Dreadful! dreadful! dreadful! Did he sell them?

Jerry. Oh no; he gave them all away to the farmers and the people about.

Druidale. The last time I saw him he told me that on one occasion he caught four trout at a time, on a hair cast, at the meeting of the waters, and that not one of them weighed less than half a pound.

Mr. Everleigh. Well done, Gleadhall. I suppose Mr. Field is a good fisherman, is he not, Jerry?

Jerry. Yes, sir, very good, about the best fly-fisher we ever had; but he fished nothing else. One day, I remember it very well, he killed 52 trout.

Mr. Loder. And Mr. Reffitt killed just the same number not long ago.

Mr. Everleigh. I hear that Raneley is bringing out a new creel made of alligator's hide, lined inside with the skin of a cormorant, and that it is to beat every creel out—even the tin thing he thought so much of and advised everybody to have.

Druidale. I see, Mr. Hawes, that you have your tin pot of a creel yet, *à la* Raneley. It looks quite dissipated, as if you were in the habit of rolling over it.

Mr. Hawes. Now, Druidale, stop your chaff; you know very well that when I was getting over a wall the wall fell and I fell with it, and the creel got bulged.

Mr. Loder (laughing, in which all joined). Did your weight make the wall fall, or did the weight of the wall make you fall, Mr. Hawes?

Mr. Hawes. What nonsense! you know that a puff of wind will often make these Craven walls fall.

Mr. Loder. It would take a strong puff to make you fall. (Peals of laughter, during which Mr. Hawes tries to look dignified.)

Mr. Hawes (designing to take a rise out of some one). Have you been to Arncliffe lately, Loder?

Mr. Loder. Yes; I took a walk there last Sunday morning with Druidale.

Mr. Hawes. Did you go to fish?

Mr. Loder. No; it is not considered proper to fish in these dales on Sunday, is it, Jerry?

Jerry. I never knew any of our members fish here on Sunday; the Dale folk would not like it.

Mr. Garde. I suppose the Dale folk have no objections to come here on Sunday, and have a glass or two and discuss the affairs of the neighbourhood, in fact, to enjoy themselves?

Jerry. Oh no; the folk here think a little gin in the water makes it more wholesome. This is a limestone country, you know, and they say water by itself does not agree with them.

HAWKSWICK BRIDGE.

Druidale. They would not like to be made teetotal by Act of Parliament.

Mr. Lader. No fear of that as long as we have a Conservative Government in power. If the Rads. could only keep in power for ten consecutive years there would be a grand sweeping liquor law made, and the Dale folk would have to drink their water without the little gin in it.

Mr. Halefield. Nonsense; do you think we have no drinkers among the great Liberal party?

Mr. Hawes. Why did you go to Arncliffe, Loder, if you did not go to fish?

Mr. Loder. I went for the beautiful walk up the dale, through the village of Hawkswick with its wild crags, and to feast my eyes on the rustic village of Arncliffe with the old church by the river, and the rocks wherein the noble eagle's eyrie used to be.

Mr. Hawes. Did you call on the venerable the Archdeacon in his cosy vicarage by the river-side—or perhaps you went to hear him preach?

Mr. Loder. No, I did not; we called at the Nest for some refreshment, which we needed after our four-mile walk.

Mr. Hawes. I suppose that is the kind of spiritual refreshment you and Druidale like, eh? and I suppose you worshipped at the shrine of the "Fair Maid of Arncliffe," and were as devout as if you had been in church, or perhaps more so?

Druidale. We saw the fair maid, and she regaled us with bread and cheese and beer, and with the sight of her pretty face; and knowing our weakness, she showed us a dish of lovely trout, caught by Toller the day before.

Mr. Halefield. Fie, Druidale! you have made your market; you ought not to look at pretty girls.

Druidale. My dear Halefield, I fear that you have been wanting in your devotions to our Father Izaak, who in his rambles met the pretty milkmaid, and listened to her love song, and then suffered the infliction of the mother's warning. I follow in the footsteps of our father, who loved the beauties of nature; and what is there more beautiful in nature than lovely woman, spotless as the driven snow?

Mr. Everleigh. I fancy that nothing would please Druidale more than the admission of the fair sex into our club. He and

Pritt made a vigorous attempt to admit ladies into the Yorkshire Anglers' Association.

Druidale. And of course, as you are a woman-hater, you opposed their admission. My friend Pritt is an upholder of woman's rights. I suppose you would confine them in a harem *à la mode* Turk.

Mr. Loder. I suppose if Everleigh saw a girl in knickerbockers he would keep his eyes shut.

Mr. Halefield. If you fellows are going to talk about women all night I may as well go to bed.

Mr. Hawes. We have had quite enough of the subject. I should like to know, Jerry, how long the natural stone-fly has been fished here.

Jerry. Before I became keeper. It was more than forty years since, in Bill Hesseltine's time.

Mr. Everleigh. Who began it?

Jerry. One of our old members, Mr. Thompson the Vicar of Addingham, who kept it to himself as long as he could. It happened in this way. There were several members fishing here about the end of May, and the weather was very bright, and the water low. They only fished fly. Mr. Thompson on several days brought in large baskets of trout, much bigger than usual, and he always said he had caught them with fly. The other members caught next to nothing, and they were quite wild about it, and began to think that Mr. Thompson caught the trout unfairly, so one day one of them watched Mr. Thompson, and spotted where he went to. He watched him from behind a wall and saw him constantly turning over the stones by the river-side; and then he saw that he was fishing up with a very short line, and he saw him catch several trout, and was some little time before he cast again. In the end he pounced upon him, and found him in the act of baiting the natural stone-fly, which we call the May-fly here; so the murder was out.

Druidale. So the rest followed suit?

Jerry. Yes; and for some years they had splendid sport. I am told that they got big panniers made on purpose. The May-fly has fallen off much the last few years. Mr. Reffitt appears to be our best hand at it now.

Druidale. You remember, Jerry, the great fly-minnow fisher who came here in September a few years since, when I was here?

Jerry. Oh, I reckon nout of him much. Mr. Lupton would kill two to his one with minnow. Mr. Lupton is the best minnow-fisher I ever knew, but then he uses a long rod made on purpose for the minnow.

Mr. Loder. And fishes little else, so he ought to know how to do it. What is the story about the great fly-minnow fisher, Druidale?

Druidale. I will tell it to the best of my recollection, and Jerry can help me out. In the month of September, a few years ago, I was in this place, and as I entered this room, Agnes (now our good hostess) was laying the cloth for dinner. "Well, Agnes, has anybody turned up to-day?" "Yes, sir, a strange gentleman came by the mail, and he is out fishing." "What sort of a fellow is he?" Agnes laughed and replied, "He is just like an old bachelor." "You are a clever girl, Agnes, but how do you tell old bachelors from old married men?" "Well," said Agnes, "he is so funny; he got some minnows from Jerry, and he made such a to-do about them. He measured them and would only have them a certain length."

Jerry (interposing). The gentleman came from London,

and I had got a letter from him asking me to have 200 minnows in readiness for him, exactly one inch and a quarter in length.

Druidale (resuming). As I was at dinner in solitude, Agnes entered. "If you please, sir, the gentleman has come in; have you any objection to his dining in this room?" (this sacred room, gentlemen!). "No," I said; "tell the gentleman he will be very welcome. Has he caught anything?" *Agnes.* "Yes, he has caught some very fine trout—I think larger than those you caught the other day." The fish, 15 in number, were brought in for my inspection, and a nice lot they were, about 6 lb. in weight. Presently the great London minnow-fisher entered the room. I welcomed him, and congratulated him on his success. He did not think much of it; he said he ought to have caught 10 lb. "Do you ever fish the fly-minnow? for the last five years I have only fished the fly-minnow; it pays best." I replied that I preferred the fly to anything else, and never fished minnow when the fly would take; that I had caught 15 a few days before with fly, and that at Kilnsey the fish generally took fly better than minnow. This he pooh-poohed, and said it was because I did not fish the fly-minnow. He then showed me his tackle, and his mode of baiting the minnow. The tackle consisted of drawn gut, to which were attached three sets of treble hooks with a small piece of serrated lead to be inserted inside the minnow. He impressed upon me the absolute importance of the minnows not being more than one and a quarter inch in length. "What sort of a fellow is your keeper?" he said. I replied that he was sharp enough, and knew what he was about. In the course of the evening Jerry came in, and he gave us minute instructions in the mysteries of the fly-minnow. He assumed a very superior air, as if Jerry and I were ignorant of the art of fishing. He would show us what the fly-minnow could do. He particularly examined Jerry as to the minnows in stock, and wound up by ordering him to get 400 minnows one and a quarter inch in size at once. I said to Jerry aside, "This is awful; he will ruin the river." Jerry laughed and said, "The trout will soon get used to it; wait and you'll see." On the following day I went home.

Jerry (continuing). The great minnow-fisher did very little afterwards. The next day he fished he got over deep in the water, and got a lot of water into his wading-stockings, and he got such a cold that he was in bed three or four days; also he had a bad finger. The day Mr. Druidale left he only caught 5 fish. I was out the same day and caught 16 with fly, so you see he did not do much with his 400 minnows.

Mr. Loder. A very good story, and shows the folly of conceit. The tackle is the Ariel tackle, and the best I know, but I think it is a mistake to dress minnow tackle on drawn gut; there must be a great many breakages. And think of the agony of a poor trout with three treble hooks in his mouth!—in all probability certain death.

Mr. Halefield. And therein lies a most potent reason to fish with fly, when fair sport may be had with it, on the ground of humanity; for I apprehend that few if any trout are killed with a small fly hook, whereas with minnow and worm hooks (particularly Stewart tackle) many fish must be killed. A humane sportsman should only fish worm or minnow as a last resort.

Druidale. I can give you a case in point as to Stewart tackle. On one occasion I fished in the Aire in a fresh with Stewart tackle, as I was out of the one-hook tackle, and lost several hooks. On my next visit old Sam the keeper brought me a

Stewart-tackle cast, which I identified as my own as it was made up by myself, and Sam said that he had found a half-pound trout dead in the river, with the hooks in his mouth. On another occasion in the same river, I caught a trout with fly, in the mouth of which there was a large rusty worm-hook; the poor trout was in bad condition. I think that minnow-fishing with drawn gut should be prohibited, as being cruel and leading to considerable numbers of trout being left to rot in the river. I know an angler who fishes little else but minnow, with drawn or the very finest undrawn gut, and he admits that he loses many trout owing to breakages.

Mr. Garde. The Kilnsey Angling Club has ever since its formation been regarded as a fly-fishing club principally, and I trust that all members will do all in their power to maintain the best traditions of the club. (Great applause.)

Mr. Loder. I wish we had old Pritt here to give us a real good story.

Mr. Hawes. Well spiced?

Mr. Loder. Perhaps you can give us one, Hawes? We are not soon shocked in this room, are we, Jerry?

Jerry. I have heard some good tales told in this room. I have known some of our members a bit light gi'en at times too, like other men.

Druidale. You must not tell tales, Jerry, about our members. They can do no wrong, they are immaculate; if a man can return a trout $6\frac{5}{6}$ inches long to the water, he must be above suspicion in all things.

A knock at the door; enter Mr. James Werfdale, a popular Dale farmer, with a "Good evening, gentlemen."

Druidale. What will you have, Mr. Werfdale?

Mr. Werfdale. Thank you, I will not take anything. I've

been to Skipton market to-day. I heard you were here, so I thought I would come in for a chat. I'll smoke a pipe, though.

Mr. Everleigh. Have you had any sport lately, Mr. Werfdale?

Mr. Werfdale. I have killed a few partridges and rabbits, and one hare.

Mr. Loder. Hares seem scarce.

Mr. Werfdale. Before the Ground Game Act was passed there were lots of hares; they are getting fewer and fewer.

Mr. Hawes. What sort of sport are they having with the grouse on Conistone Moor?

Mr. Werfdale. They have done pretty well.

Mr. Loder. I heard there was a woodcock killed a short time since; it is very early for woodcocks.

Druidale. It is too early for foreign birds; the woodcock in question was probably bred here. Many woodcocks breed in this country, more than most people are aware of. My own impression is that woodcocks bred here do not remain here in the winter. I believe that the woodcock is bound to migrate.

Mr. Hawes. What do you mean by being bound to migrate?

Druidale. I mean that the instinct of the bird compels it to leave the place where it was bred for some more southern country, and that consequently birds bred here go south— perhaps to the shores of the Mediterranean. The migration begins early in October, and birds found here after the middle of October are probably foreign migrants. The habits of the snipe are similar. We often flush snipe when fishing, and I believe they go away in October, and that the few seen here in the winter are foreign migrants. If you go to Bordley Moor in August you may bag ten brace of snipe if you can hit them. In September they become less plentiful, and the first bad weather drives them all away,—whither they go we know not. Mr. Geikè's work on the birds of Heligoland is most interesting. It appears that great numbers of dotterel are killed there during the migration.

Jerry. I could do with some dotterel feathers very well: they are very hard to get.

Mr. Loder. I vote we send to Heligoland for a cargo.

The "Migration of Birds" is here interrupted. A trap is heard to stop outside, then a great commotion in the passage, and Mr. Raneley rolls into the room, clad in dripping coat and hat, struggling with a mass of rods in one hand and a creel in the other, followed by Dora with a huge hamper and a portmanteau, which she deposits on the floor, thereby adding to the general litter of the room—hats, baskets, waterproofs, waders, brogues, and such like in promiscuous confusion.

Mr. Raneley (taking off his hat and shaking it, and bowing to the company profusely). Good evening, gentlemen. Good evening, gentlemen; pleased to meet you all.

Mr. Halefield. Allow me to introduce you to our new member. Mr. Raneley, Mr. Hooker. Mr. Raneley shakes hands cordially with Mr. Hooker, saying, "Glad to make your acquaintance, sir; I am very pleased to meet you."

Mr. Raneley requests Dora to get him some tea and ham and eggs, " and plenty of dry toast, Dora, and mind you poach the eggs; now mind, Dora, don't fry them with the ham."

Mr. Raneley (taking off his boots by the fire). I thought I should find you here, Druidale. Hi! hi! hi! hi!

Druidale. Why are not you after the partridges?

Mr. Raneley. You wish I was, do you? Hi! hi! hi! hi! you are not going to have it all to yourself this time! Hi! hi!

Mr. Raneley having struggled out of his boots, and put on an ancient pair of slippers down at the heels, paddled off upstairs to tidy himself; which important function having been accomplished, he soon re-entered the room and sat down to tea, and when he had satisfied the first pangs of hunger said, "Gentlemen, had we not better draw for our lengths to-morrow?"

Mr. Halefield. What's the good of drawing for our lengths now, when there may be a flood in the morning, and then we can go where we like?

Mr. Raneley. I always like to know my length the night before.

Druidale (with characteristic roughness). Raneley, go and recline your length upon your bed, then you'll be sure of it in the morning.

Mr. Raneley having finished tea is attacked by

Mr. Hawes. Now, Raneley, let us have one of your well-primed stories. We have not had a decent story to-night.

Mr. Raneley. Hi! hi! hi! I am sorry for that. You must have been naughty.

Mr. Raneley declines to be drawn.

Druidale. Are there any bulls about, Mr. Werfdale?

Mr. Werfdale. I've got a bull in the big meadow below the Falls, but he is quite quiet; but if you are frightened, I'll have him taken out.

Druidale. Have you sold any bulls lately, Mr. Werfdale.

Mr. Werfdale. No; I suppose you are thinking about the bull and the mushrooms?

Several exclaim, "Do let us have the story, Mr. Werfdale."

Mr. Hawes. If we are going to have a bull story at this time of night, we had better have another glass so as to enable us to survive it.

Agreed on all sides, and Mr. Werfdale is induced to have a wee tot, although it has been market-day at Skipton.

Mr. *Werfdale* (taking a sip and clearing his throat, went into action). Well, gentlemen, a year or two ago I had a young bull about a year old, so he ought to have been quiet enough. One day I was in the field he was in, and he came at me and knocked me down; I got up and he knocked me down again. As this did not suit me, I soon put the wall between me and the bull. I resolved to sell that bull. Not long afterwards I met Mr. Scarfield in Skipton. Mr. Scarfield said, "Have you a good savage bull to sell, Jim? I want a bull to drive mushroom gatherers from my meadow. I can never get a blessed mushroom; they get them all." "Well," I said, "I have got a bull savage enough for you; but you must take warning, Mr. Scarfield, he has knocked me down twice, and he is only about a year old." "That's just the bull for me," said Mr. Scarfield. "I'll teach those mushroomers to keep out of my meadow, that I will." A bargain was made, and I soon got quit of that bull. Not long afterwards, I again met Mr. Scarfield at Skipton, and he began talking about the bull. He said, "You must be frightened of bulls, Jim. He is as quiet as an old sheep; he is no good at all with the mushroomers, he won't go at them a bit; they have just all their own way." "Well, I know," I said, "that bull knocked me down twice, and that is quite enough for me. Mind how you go near him." Mr. Scarfield repeated, "I'm sure you are frightened of bulls, Jim." "Have a care, Mr. Scarfield." In a few weeks I had occasion to see Mr. Scarfield on business, so I called at his house. "Mr. Scarfield in?" I said to the maid who opened the door. "Yes, sir, he is in, but he is in bed." "What's to do, is he ill?" "He has had an accident, sir, but you can see him in his room." I was ushered upstairs. "Hullo, Mr. Scarfield, what's up?" "Oh, Jim, that bull has nearly been the death of me! if my man had not gone at him with a pitchfork, I should not have been here now. As it is, I've had enough of it; will you take that bull back, Jim?" "No, thank you; I've had enough of him." "I shall get quit of that bull, Jim," and he soon got quit of him.

Mr. Halefield. What became of that bull in the end, Mr. Werfdale?

Mr. Werfdale (solemnly). He was executed for wilful murder.

Uncomfortable sensation. Some of the company begin to think it might be prudent to ask Mr. Werfdale to take that other bull out of the big meadow.

Mr. Loder. Has any one here ever known an instance when a bull has seriously injured a fisherman?

No one appears to have known of an instance.

Druidale. I have heard of a case where a bull did appear on murder bent. It happened at Hawnby on the Yorkshire Rye. Three fellows were there fishing, and they had been informed that there was a dangerous bull about. They several times caught sight of him, but until the day the event happened they managed to keep well out of his way. However, on this particular day they came upon the bull all of a sudden. There was a general stampede; it was *sauve qui peut*. They all ran towards one tree, the bull in hot pursuit. As the unfortunate last man was swarming up the tree, the bull prodded him behind with his horns, and materially hastened his ascent.

Mr. Halefield. What happened next?

Druidale. When the bull saw his intended victims safely treed, he trotted off in search of further adventures, and then the trio sneaked down the tree, and came to the unanimous conclusion that that particular part of the river was not worth fishing in.

Mr. Raneley. Now, Druidale, you cannot expect us to go to our beds with a wind-up of two horrid bull stories, for the narration of which you are responsible, so please give us a really good story by way of an antidote, otherwise we shall all have nightmare—I mean night-bull.

Druidale. I know a good story about a parson and a barmaid, which has some seasoning at the end of it.

"Let us have it, by all means; there is certain to be something good where a parson and a barmaid are concerned," said one.

Druidale. Well, my dear fellows, you shall have it. Once upon a time I dragged my weary bones after a day's fishing in the Aire to the Skipton Station refreshment room, being overcome by a big thirst. The young lady at the bar, who was facetious, relieved me with a big drink, for which I was truly thankful, and she remarked, "You fishermen seem always thirsty; I have served several with big drinks this afternoon. A parson came in a short time before you, and oh, how he did make me laugh! I have not got over it yet. He said, 'I have got very wet; I got in above my waders, and I want to avoid catching cold; please give me a glass of whisky.' I gave him a glass of whisky, and he poured it down the right leg. He then asked for another; I gave him another, and he poured it down the left leg. Then he trotted out and said he would be all right. I thought he had better have put the whisky inside," and the young lady shook with laughter.

Mr. Raneley. Is that all?

Druidale. What on earth more do you want?

Mr. Raneley. The seasoning at the end.

Druidale. The seasoning, as I have told you, went down his legs, and that ended the story, so I have kept my word.

Mr. Raneley. A regular sell.

Druidale. If my seasoning is not pungent enough for you, enlist *Under Two Flags* and I am sure that even you will be quite satisfied.

Mr. Loder. Gentlemen, that story about the parson and the barmaid reminds me of a very good story about a parson and a keeper, and it is similar in this respect that the point or seasoning is at the end.

Mr. Raneley. Bravo, Loder! we can rely on you for a good story. Druidale is a humbug.

Mr. Loder. Once upon a time a parson went for a day's fishing to Malham Tarn, and Mr. Morrison's keeper attended him. The parson toiled for some hours without a rise. At length, when all hope was about extinguished in his breast, there was a sharp tug; the reel screeched, and oh, joy! he was fast in a good two-pounder. After some most exciting play the keeper skilfully netted the trout. He extracted the hook, and laid the trout on his two hands. "What a beauty he is," he said; "I never saw a better fed fish in my life." The fish, not liking the prospect of being food for Mr. Parson, gave one little jump and regained his native element. The parson said *something*, and I leave you ingenious gentlemen to guess what little word the parson said. That parson is an authority as to what an ordinary mortal may be permitted to say under similar aggravating circumstances.

Druidale. Bravo, Loder! very good. It is now Raneley's turn for a yarn to contribute something for the edification of the company. Come, Raneley!

Mr. Raneley. I submit that we have had plenty of yarns for one evening; let us start some interesting discussion.

Druidale. On the best mode of obtaining a supply of alligators for the manufacture of creels.

Mr. Raneley. Get out with you. I have often wondered what the origin is of the natural terraces on the sides of this valley which rise one above another: will any one start a theory?

Mr. Halefield. My impression is, that the sides of these Craven valleys were at one time cultivated, and that terraces were formed on the sides—which were then abrupt—in order for their more easy cultivation.

Druidale. My theory is, that the terraces were caused by the action of water, these valleys forming a great lake which gradually subsided, and that the terraces were formed in detail as the waters gradually subsided. You know how narrow the valley is at Netherside about two miles down the river. I apprehend that at no very distant date, speaking geologically, there was a huge barrier there which formed the lake, and that this barrier was gradually carried away by floods or by some convulsion of nature, or the action of water may have gradually worn the embankment, and thus left the present channel. A lake might now be formed at—comparatively speaking—small expense.

Mr. Loder. If a lake were formed extending upwards from Netherside to Conistone Bridge, Kilnsey would become very attractive, and a large revenue might be made out of the lake from boating and fishing alone. You all know that there is a valuable spring of mineral water near the meeting of the waters, and who knows what wealth of mineral waters might be discovered? Kilnsey might become a second Harrogate.

Druidale. Harrogate is increasing tremendously. It appears to me that the aristocratic element of Leeds and Bradford will ere long find Harrogate too populous for their refined tastes, for as the number of houses increases the atmosphere will become more and more polluted. What splendid air Kilnsey enjoys! how it is surrounded by mountains—Great Whernside more than 2300 feet above sea-level! An electric tramway might be made to the summit, from which the inhabitants might view the sunrise before breakfast or the sunset after dinner without fatigue. A railway might soon be made from Bolton Abbey up the dale, and the journey to Leeds or Bradford accomplished in little over an hour through beautiful scenery. Houses and hotels would spring up, and Kilnsey with its unrivalled advantages, and being so near the great centres of population, would be a popular pleasure resort.

Mr. Halefield. Where would the K.A.C. be then? the great charm of Kilnsey now is its solitude. Would you have Kilnsey, with its projected lake, a second Windermere? We should have to go to the wilds of Scotland or Ireland. . . . However, Kilnsey as it is will last my time out.

Druidale. You must thank Rancley for leading Mr. Loder and myself to such dreams of the future; if he had volunteered one of his refined stories as requested, you would not have had your minds disturbed by even the thought of the solitude of your dear sacred Kilnsey being disturbed by even the *crême de la crême* of Leeds and Bradford. But allow me to say a little more of the projected lake; being so far from the sea, and having an altitude of about 600 feet, it would soon freeze over, much sooner than Windermere, so there would be excellent skating, also splendid tobogganing on the steep sides of the valley. During a hard winter Kilnsey would have a winter season. I suppose you have some good snowstorms here sometimes, Jerry?

Jerry. Indeed we have. I have known all the roads blocked to the top of the walls. I well remember a tremendous snowstorm we had in December 1882. Mr. Dymond and party of six guns had arranged to drive grouse on Conistone Moor the last two days of the season. Snow was falling when they reached Skipton, but they determined to go on. They got an omnibus drawn by four horses and proceeded on their journey to Kettlewell, about fifteen miles. The storm got worse and worse, with a north-easterly gale. After great difficulty they got as far as Threshfield, and there they stuck in a tremendous drift, and could neither get forwards nor backwards. The driver was so benumbed with the cold that he had to be helped off the box. The party put up at the Old Hall Inn. The landlord had prepared a lot of geese for Skipton market; Mr. Dymond and party ate them all up. They had to remain there for three whole days, until the roads were cut to Skipton. Of course the grouse season was over by that time.

Mr. Loder. Think of the delight of going over the mountains on snow-shoes in a hard winter! No occasion to go to Norway—snow-shoeing only an hour from Leeds!

Mr. Garde. There will not be a railway up the dale in a hurry. You all remember what a fiasco the Skipton and Kettlewell railway was. The promoters having persuaded the High Court of Parliament to give its sanction, became more enterprising and promoted an extension of the line to Aysgarth, and thinking to enhance the beauty of Aysgarth Falls they projected a handsome railway bridge over the Falls. Mr. Ruskin arose and made a mighty growl, and the promoters failed to satisfy Parliament that a pretty railway bridge over the Falls would increase their beauty; so Parliament in its wisdom, and by way of a little mild sarcasm, was graciously pleased to sanction an extension to the village

of Buckden, which for some years, owing to the Sir Wilfrid Lawson tendencies of a local magnate, Major-General Stansfield, was without that boon to fishermen, a public-house. . .
In the end the promoters came to the conclusion that a bird in the hand was worth two in the bush, so in order to obtain repayment of the Parliamentary deposit, they promoted a Bill for leave to abandon the railway, which Parliament was pleased to pass. A happy ending for the K.A.C.

Enter *Dora*. It is ten o'clock, gentlemen. Do you want anything more from the bar?

Mr. Halefield. Is it raining yet, Dora?

Dora. Yes; it is a very wet night.

Mr. Loder. Glorious! we will have one more wet in honour of the night.

Mr. Werfdale. Well, gentlemen, I must wish you good night. Good night, and I hope you will all have good sport to-morrow.

Chorus. Good night, good night, Mr. Werfdale.

Jerry. Well, gentlemen, I must be going too. Good night.

Several voices. Come in in good time in the morning, Jerry, with the worms and minnows. Good night.

Shortly the fishermen light their candles, and with hearty good-nights shamble upstairs to their rooms, having first satisfied themselves that it is still raining.

CHAPTER XXI

THE TWEED

> Twined with my boyhood, wreathed on the dream
> Of early endearments, beautiful stream,
> The lisp of thy waters is music to me,
> Hours buried are buried in thee.
> "To the Tweed"—T. T. STODDART.

FOR years I had longed to throw a line in the bonny Tweed, the river which was the true love of Thomas Todd Stoddart; the river about which he sang and dreamed; the river on the banks of which the immortal Sir Walter Scott lived. What recollections the name invokes of Christopher North, Burns, and the Ettrick Shepherd!

Having visited the Tweed, I owe the trout in that noble river an apology. I was under the delusion that a man who can catch trout in the Wharfe would find the trout of Tweed easy victims. No such thing. The education of Tweed trout is almost perfect: the time may come when they will be so perfectly educated as to defy the wiles of the angler. The Wharfedale trout have not by any means attained to so high a standard as their brethren of the Tweed. Wharfedale anglers are just a bit conceited, and it is very good for them to wander to pastures new now and again, to get the conceit taken out of them. They generally return home in a meek and contrite spirit, and they are reticent about their doings. Some put their experiences into print, but they quite forget to state their captures. There is a great deal about scenery and that sort of thing : they might have gone off for the sake of the scenery, and thrown fishing in by way of a fill-up—as a sort of secondary object.

It was on the 21st of May 1886 that I travelled from Bradford to St. Boswells by the Settle and Carlisle Railway. What charming streams are passed on the route — Aire, Ribble, Eden, Eamont, Esk, Liddel. The Liddel looked so tempting that I longed to get out of the train at Newcastleton. I felt, Why go farther, when scenes so fair at hand? We put up at the Buccleuch Arms Hotel, myself and a friend who spent his time in sketching. After lunch I walked to the river across the fields, and a charming walk it is. The village of St. Boswells is about a quarter of a mile from the river. The footpath leads to a wooded bank or cliff, below which the noble river flows, some fifty feet below. My first view of the river was a sight to be remembered. About a mile of river flowing between green meadows, with noble trees here and there; across the river, Dryburgh Abbey peeping through the trees ; in the far distance, the beautifully wooded Eildon Hills, with Eildon Hall at the foot. I feast my eyes on the lovely view, and descend by a steep rugged path to the river-side. I then appreciate the magnificent flow of water—there was a good brown minnow-water. I was on the free trouting water, which is about three miles in extent, St. Boswells being in about the middle of it. About a mile and a half below St. Boswells is the Merton Water, the property of Lord Polwarth and leased to the Hon. Henry Brougham, the present Baron

Brougham and Vaux. Merton House, the mansion of Lord Polwarth, is about two miles from St. Boswells, down the river.

At half-past five o'clock I threw my first line in Tweed, and my lure was a preserved minnow. I tried it in vain; I did not get a single pull. I therefore changed to fly, with which I caught three small trout and two yellow fins, all of which I returned to the river.

Friday, 22nd.—The weather was very bright, and there was a good big fly-water, but this condition of things does not, in my experience, conduce to good sport: if the weather be bright, let the water be bright too. I began below the Cliff about half-past nine o'clock, and fished to below Merton Bridge with fly and minnow alternately. There was little, if any, fly on the water, and the trout were not moving. I reeled up at five o'clock fishless; I had only caught a few small trout, which were duly returned to the water.

However, I was so fortunate as to make the acquaintance of the celebrated Mr. Purdy, Mr. Brougham's keeper. He was a real canny Scotchman, and to some extent he reminded me of a distinguished statesman who is credited with having said that the object of language was to conceal your meaning. He would not commit himself to anything. The landlady of the Buccleuch Arms had told me of Mr. Brougham's mighty deeds with the salmon; how sometimes the dining-room floor was covered with big fish. I asked Purdy if Mr. Brougham was a good fisherman. Purdy would not commit himself one way or another; he said he was a lucky fisherman, and with that I had to be content. Purdy's house was almost on Merton Bridge. On approaching it, it had the appearance of a poaching establishment, salmon or some sort of nets being hung up about. I asked Mr. Purdy if I might try for trout in Mr. Brougham's water. Purdy did not exactly commit himself, but somehow or other I found myself under Mr. Purdy's guidance next day.

Saturday, 23rd.—Attended by Mr. Purdy I began the day below Merton Bridge. As the water was big, Mr. Purdy advised minnow, and I fished with minnow for some time, but could not get a run: asked Purdy if he thought I knew how to fish with minnow; would not commit himself. After fishing about half a mile, Purdy paddled me across the river at a grand pool under a red cliff, and there he left me to my own devices. Minnow being useless, I rigged up a fly cast. The weather was bright, and I flogged for an hour without success. Purdy had said that it had been a very bad trouting season. About midday I began to pick up a trout or two. There is a lovely sort of pool and flat under a wooded bank on the far side, just above Lord Polwarth's reserved water, in which I had some nice sport. A long cast, and there is the tug of a good fish. How that fish fought! but in the end I drew him to the gravelly shore—a lovely Tweed trout, 1 lb. in weight and in the pink of condition. He had taken a Kilnsey favourite, the orange dark woodcock. I reeled up at six o'clock with 11 trout, weight 3 lb. 5 oz.—my first success in Tweed. In the evening I was joined by Mr. James Withington, who was anxious to distinguish himself across the Border.

Monday, 25th.—Lord Polwarth had been so kind as to grant me a day's fishing in the reserved water near Merton House. I drove to the Hall, and walked through the gardens to the river-side. The Hall stands only a few yards from the river. The surroundings are very beautiful. The reserved water extends for about three-quarters of a mile. The water looked perfect; the weather was delightful—cloud and sunshine with an occasional shower. I began with fly at half-past nine o'clock, and as I could not get a rise, and could not see a rise, I sat down and waited for something to happen; and something happened in about half an hour. A fish rose in the tail of the pool I sat by; I cast neatly over him, and I had him, a plump little trout of 5 oz. There was then a good rise on, but somehow or other I missed many fish. They were much inclined to jump out of the water when hooked, like sea-trout, to which I believe Tweed trout are very near relatives. They are gray and quite without red spots, so different to the trout I was accustomed to; and they were so strong that I had to be careful, as I fished with fine-drawn gut. While wading near the side I was somewhat alarmed by something bumping against my legs; it turned out to be a salmon of about 14 lb. I got it on to the bank, and I found it was quite blind owing to the fungoid disease. The fungus was principally about the head; where there was no fungus, the poor fish was clean like silver, and in plump condition. I came to the conclusion that the fungoid disease is very rapid in its progress, otherwise the fish would not have been so plump. At five o'clock I reeled up with 15 trout, weight 5 lb. 2 oz.—best trout 12 oz. I felt that I ought to have done much better. The killing flies were orange dark woodcock, purple snipe, and light March brown. James got 7 trout in the free water, which was not at all bad.

Tuesday, 26th.—We had arranged with the Dryburgh keeper to ferry us across the river, opposite the Abbey, in order that we might fish the Abbey water, which is not open to the public. I commenced operations near to the venerable Abbey. The keeper advised me to try the creeper, as the weather was very bright; I did so, and he also tried it, but we could not induce any trout to take it. The gravel-bed was thick on the water, also March browns and yellow duns. The March browns had rather a red appearance. I put up a fly cast, and succeeded in killing 14 trout, weight 2lb. 15 oz. only—best trout 9 oz. Sometimes during the day there was a good rise on, but the trout were so wary! They would give a little pluck to know what was about, and go on rising often only a few yards off. I saw about half-a-dozen fellows fishing from the other bank, and although I watched them a good deal, I did not see a capture.

The keeper told me a sad story. The event had only happened a few weeks before, and had thrown a gloom over the place; it made our landlady quite nervous when she saw us drawing on our waders in the morning. "The poor young gentleman," she said, "slept in the room you are in. He went out in the morning, looking so bright and cheerful, and they brought his body back in the afternoon. Oh, I shall never forget it!" The gentleman was one of the two lessees of the Dryburgh fishery. He and the keeper were out trout fishing; the keeper was about 100 yards from the gentleman, who was wading in strong water, a little above a deep salmon pool. The keeper saw the gentleman stumble, and try to recover himself; he stumbled again, and to the keeper's horror rolled down into the deep pool. The keeper, who was wading, hastened down to the pool, but the wading, as I know, is there most difficult. When he got to the pool, the unfortunate gentleman could not be seen. The keeper went out in the boat, and the body was not recovered before an hour had passed. I asked the keeper how he accounted for the accident. "Well," he said, "the gentleman told me a few days before that he often felt dizzy when he was wading." That day James caught 3 small trout.

Wednesday, 27th.—Fished the same water with creeper and fly; creeper useless. Lots of March browns, yellow duns, and gravel-beds on the water. Fish rising well at the natural flies. Tried floating March brown, but I might as well have tried a bare hook. I changed my flies till I was tired of the game, and concluded with 5 small trout.

Thursday, 28th.—I decided to try new water to me, so I drove about three-quarters of a mile above Dryburgh Bridge. The scenery is lovely; a long reach of the river upwards is visible, festooned with overhanging woods. Wild ducks keep flying about, and water-hens scuttle across the river. Small sea-gulls are after the smolts, or whatever they can pounce upon. A heron lumbers up. Sandpipers flit from stone to stone. The swifts are hawking about, sharing the flies with the trout. There was a strong wind, so it was not easy to get the fly well over the fish. I caught many trout too small to kill; I could not induce the good trout to take my flies. I only creeled 4 trout. I met a local hand who showed me the contents of his creel; he had 15 trout, which I estimated at about 20 oz. He was killing the sized trout which I returned to the water. He said he kept all he caught. After dinner I fished until it was quite dark for 4 trout. When I reached the hotel I found the good landlady in a state of alarm; she was thinking of getting up a search party to find the remains of No. 2. I fancy she thought I was in most danger because I occupied the same bedroom as No. 1. Result 8 trout, weight 1 lb. 9 oz. James scored a "duck-egg."

Friday, 29th.—Having taken a fancy to the water I tried yesterday, I tried it again. The weather was very windy. There were some good fish rising, but they evidently knew a good deal too much. As the sun was bright I tried the creeper, with which I soon caught 2 trout, one of which was a nice fish of 10 oz. I only got one more run with the creeper, so gave it up and stuck to fly, with which I caught 5 small trout. As on the previous day, I returned many small trout to the water. My 7 trout only weighed 1 lb. 9 oz. I did not care to try night fishing again after the experience of the night before.

Saturday, 30th.—A regular field-day on Tweedside; the local masters of the art were out in force. The education of the trout was by no means neglected, and they were apt scholars in the art of self-defence. I began below Merton Bridge with creeper before nine o'clock. The weather was very windy and bright. I had three runs with the creeper, but did not score. There is a splendid pool a short distance below the bridge, and in this pool good trout were rising freely at March browns and yellow duns chiefly. At my first cast I slightly pricked a fish and then another, and then having satisfied themselves that my flies were the usual impositions, they continued rising madly. I tried a lovely floating March brown, which looked so natural, but the trout would not even bob their noses against it. I changed and changed my flies to no purpose. On my way fishing up the river I met in detail six local hands, all of whom asked what sport I had, and of course I returned the compliment. We were all alike, not a fish among seven men who professed to be anglers. Oh, shades of Stewart! where are the 12 lb. panniers which entitle a man to the name of an angler—alas, where?

But before reeling up at half-past one o'clock I actually

caught a magnificent trout of 2 oz. *O homines! O mores!* how am I fallen! I had gone to Tweedside with great expectations, and in eight days' fishing only killed 61 trout, weight 15 lb. But after all it is not to be wondered at. There is no close time; legions of local hands fish the whole year round with all sorts of lures, salmon roe included; they kill half-ounce trout and do not feel ashamed. The trout have no rest. The open tributaries are in the same condition. A gentleman informed me that he had had one day in the Leader, and had caught 25 trout which weighed about the same number of ounces, and that he was so satisfied that he did not intend to try it again.

The free length of the Tweed at St. Boswells would make a splendid club water for about fifty members who did not reside too near the river. St. Boswells is easily accessible from the great Yorkshire towns, and what a splendid trout fishery it would be with a little preservation and a limited number of rods!

CHAPTER XXII

THE BORDER ESK

> He stayed not for brake, he stopped not for stone,
> He swam the Esk river where ford there was none,
> But ere he alighted at Netherby gate
> The bride had consented, the gallant came late.
> Sir Walter Scott.

WHAT recollections of the old romantic times the Border land recalls, the land of poetry and romance, where English and Scotch often met on the war-path! How different now, when they unite against the salmon and trout in friendly rivalry, and old scores are forgotten! There must have been a good fishing water when young Lochinvar crossed the Esk in order to make his raid on Netherby Hall, in fact the poet must have imagined the river in flood. The angler is indeed delighted

> When ford there is none,

in order that he may have a chance for a "fush," for are not the Esk salmon a wee bit shy of the attractions offered by the angler, more so than was the fair maid of Netherby of the attractions of young Lochinvar, and was it not Mr. Francis Francis who said that the Esk salmon have a way of taking the fly with their tails or fins. But it is to be hoped that things are now changed, as most of the Esk and its tributaries are preserved by the Esk and Liddel Association,—and did not they make a raid on the poachers in the year 1892, and were not the poachers honoured by having their names endorsed on the fishing licences issued by the association?

In the neighbourhood of Scotch Dyke the Esk forms the boundary between England and Scotland, and about a mile above Scotch Dyke the Liddel joins the Esk, and also for some distance forms the boundary between the two countries. The fishery regulations of the association are somewhat complicated, as there are several classes of permits to fish, but it may be stated broadly that the Esk below Longtown forms one division. From Longtown to Scotch Dyke, a distance of about four miles, the fishing is reserved by Sir Richard Graham, Bart., of Netherby Hall. Above this the second division comes in, and the charges for fishing are less than in the lower water. A charge of £4 : 4s. per annum covers the whole of the waters of the association. For the water below Longtown a whole season licence costs £3, and a licence granted after July £2. Weekly licences are £1 and daily 5s., but the weekly or daily licence empowers the holder to fish in all the waters of the association.

The Esk is famous for its sea-trout and herling fishing. It has been conjectured that the herling is the sea-trout in its grilse stage, but this does not seem to be by any means quite clear. Intelligent local anglers are of the opinion that the herling and sea-trout which abound in the Esk are of a distinct and different species. The herling has a forked tail, and the sea-trout a square one. The herling varies in size from two to seventeen ounces, and the average weight is half a pound.

o

The sea-trout varies in weight from half a pound to five pounds. We have therefore this important fact, that at a certain stage of growth the herling and sea-trout are the same size, and this undoubtedly tends to show that they are of a distinct and different species. Herling ascend the river in order to deposit their spawn, and the spawn is deposited in September and October; they return to the sea in March and April. It is estimated that a herling of the weight of six ounces is eighteen months old. The question naturally arises as to whether a herling ever exceeds seventeen ounces in weight, and if so, of what nature it is afterwards. The forked tail is not an absolute indicator of species, for the parr has a forked tail, and the salmon a square one; it is therefore apparent that as the young salmo salar develops, the conformation of the tail alters. If it is reasonable to suppose that a herling may develop into a sea-trout, why should it not be reasonable to suppose or conjecture that a herling may develop into a salmon, notwithstanding that the growth of salmon in the sea has been proved to be so prodigious?

The sea-trout as a rule is a short and thick fish, while the herling is rather elongated like the salmon, and taken altogether the herling is more like a salmon than a sea-trout. That veteran angler Mr. Stoddart in November 1846, as stated in his *Angler's Companion*, amused himself with catching herling in the Esk above Langholm with salmon roe, and he states that of all the bills (herling) taken by him, not one weighed half a pound, and that without exception they were kelted females, that a few of them were black and of loathsome appearance, but that the generality, although lank, large-headed, and loose in the scale, retained their silvery coating. So Mr. Stoddart proves that the herling spawns before

November. The run of sea-trout generally commences in July, and the great run of herling in August.

Should the angler decide on a raid on the herling he has to consider where he had best locate himself, whether at Metal Bridge, Longtown, or Langholm. Metal Bridge is near Floriston Station on the Caledonian Railway, and is three miles below Longtown, the latter being ten miles from Carlisle on the North British Railway. There is no doubt that more herling are killed in the neighbourhood of Metal Bridge than in any other portions of the river. They are constantly coming and going with the tide of the Solway, which flows some distance above Metal Bridge, and when the tide is on the ebb is one of the very best times for the attack on the herling.

Should the angler locate himself, however, at Metal Bridge, and wish to spend a day in the upper waters, he would have to take the train at Longtown three miles off, which would be very inconvenient, whereas, should he put up at Longtown, he can easily take the train to Riddings Junction for the Canonbie waters or the Liddel, or to Langholm for the higher waters of the Esk. Riddings Station is only a few yards from the Liddel. The accommodation at Metal Bridge is very limited, as there is only one inn there. Longtown is rich in hotel accommodation, as is also Langholm.

Salmon and grilse are generally numerous about the end of August, but for some unknown reason are difficult to catch before October, and even then sport is most uncertain. The reason may be that the river is so much fished by local men, who are out in numbers whenever there is the least chance of a fish. Herling fishing is also very uncertain, and the worst of it is, that unless after a spate the night is often the only time when fair sport may be obtained, and if an average mortal fishes all day he is too tired to go out at night. When the water is low and clear, sport in the daytime is next to nothing with the fly, and even with the up-stream worm by no means certain. Local men say that about six o'clock in the morning is the time for up-stream worm in low water; but if the common trout take the up-stream worm well—as they often do—between eight and one, why should not the herling do so also?

Be this as it may, however, the herling is a funny little fellow. He generally either affords excellent sport or next to none. Like his relative the common trout, he sometimes rises what is called short, at other times with avidity, as if he intended to be caught. The correct thing appears to be to endeavour to catch him with what are called herling flies, but as a matter of fact such flies being large—at least twice as large as ordinary trout flies—are useless, except in the dark or in a discoloured water. In ordinary water in the daytime small flies of about the size of a medium March brown are the most successful, and the gut must be of the finest.

The Esk is an easy river to fish, especially so below Longtown. The bed of the river affords easy wading, but the angler must be on his guard not to get into a deep hole all of a sudden, as in some places one step would launch a man out of his depth, as happened to a veteran major who passed through the Crimean war almost without a scratch and narrowly escaped being drowned in such a hole.

The gallant major was fishing between Longtown and Metal Bridge. There was a fresh in the river; the sport was good and the Major's pannier was half full of herling. In a moment the gravel went shuttering under his feet, and he was over head. He left go of his rod and landing-net, and with the uttermost difficulty scaled the sides of the gravel bed, which was equal to an attack on the Redan, and he was devoutly thankful when he found himself on *terra firma* His pannier had turned upside down, and the precious herling were swallowed up by the river. The rod and landing-net wobbled down towards the Solway. An angler below felt a mighty tug : " Man alive, I have a monster," he thought, "and he is fast on ! " After some exciting play the thing was landed, and turned out to be the Major's rod. Some days afterwards an angler observed something sticking out of the sand of the Solway, which proved to be the Major's landing-net. The Major was thankful that his body had not wobbled down to the Solway, and then up with its tide.

Like many others who indulge in a taste for sporting literature, excited or incited by records of wonderful slaughter of sea-trout and herling therein periodically recorded, I had for long desired to distinguish myself amongst the salmonidæ of the Border rivers, and on the 2nd of September 1893 I took up my quarters at the Graham Arms Hotel, landlord Mr. William Bell, ably assisted by his handsome wife—or perhaps it would be more correct to say that the lady is assisted by her husband, for is it not the landlady who presides over the numerous wants of that peculiar, infatuated creature known by the name of angler ? When he is successful she congratulates him, and when he is unsuccessful, as he generally is, she condoles with him, and comforts him with a good dinner. If he gets over his waders and gets a bad cold, she brings him a treacle posset and tucks him up, and is not happy until the poor creature is once more paddling in the water after the manner of a little five-year-old at the seaside with spade and bucket.

Longtown is well named, for it has one long street with short ones branching out of it. The river is spanned by a handsome bridge, and beneath the bridge is a deep rocky pool in which salmon love to recline on their passage up the river. About three miles off is the mansion of Netherby, the country seat of Sir Richard Graham, Bart., standing in a well-wooded park. The country is very slightly undulating. To the south there is a charming view of the English Lake Mountains. About three-quarters of a mile from the village in an easterly direction is the somewhat quaint parish church of Arthuret, built of red sandstone, with the pretty rectory on the opposite side of the road, enbosomed with foliage. There is a wooded eminence in the rectory grounds, whence there is a splendid view for many miles of a truly charming country with the corn ripe for the harvest, which contrasts so beautifully with the green of the pastures and the varied hue of the woods, and in the far distance the eternal mountains. At the foot of the eminence winds a green lane, which leads to a tiny brook spanned by a tiny bridge. The lovely violet flourishes here and there, for this is not a land of tourists. A sweet calm reigns over all, as I wend my way on a Sabbath morn. By the little bridge lolls a peasant boy who is taking charge of a very fat baby in a perambulator. The church bells sound through the trees, and I retrace my steps.

On Monday the 4th of September I provided myself with a weekly licence to fish, a licence with the honour list on the back, which comprised some of the most respectable inhabitants. I was requested not to employ any of the honourable gentlemen mentioned to assist me. The water was very low,

A LITTLE FIVE-YEAR-OLD (PORT ST. MARY).

and the weather hot and bright. The local hands comforted me with the intimation that I ought to have come a month earlier for herling, or for salmon a month later. It was ever thus. My only excuse is, that I had intended being off earlier, but could not get. By the amended rules of the association, adopted in consequence of the performances of the honourable gentlemen I have referred to, artificial fly only was allowed, as it was no doubt considered by the gentlemen who amended the rules that fish were not so likely to be caught by their tails or back fins with the fly as with Stewart tackle and minnow tackle provided with mammoth hooks and lead enough to sink a sea-line.

Well, on this my first day I duly flogged the river with the intention of catching herling and sea-trout, but I never got farther than the intention. However, I was excited by lots of salmon rising, and resolved to go in for higher game on the morrow; so on the morrow I encumbered myself with my salmon rod, and had some very fine exercise. I came to the conclusion that the honourable gentlemen were right, and that the Esk salmon did not like to be caught by their mouths. I slept well that night.

On the day following I decided to change my ground and try the Liddel, and make an easy day of it; so I commenced operations a short distance below Riddings Station a little after one o'clock. I was charmed with the water, such a combination of pool, stream, and flat amid beautiful scenery, and I was rewarded with 1 herling and 5 common trout, so I had enough fish for dinner and breakfast. I had asked the landlady if she could not get me some fish for dinner before, but she said that under the new regulations fish could not be had, and that previously the honourable gentlemen could catch fish under all conditions of weather and water.

On the Thursday the weather was windy and cloudy, and there having been rain during the preceding night the water had risen a little. I decided to make a compromise. I would fish below Longtown with a fifteen-foot rod, and go in for everything in the river; result, not a rise. The salmon boiled while I broiled, but declined to be boiled in the pot. No fish to be had for dinner.

A reverend gentleman from Wales put in an appearance. He lived not far from the Conway. I asked him why in the name of fortune he came so far when he was so near the Conway, and he replied that the Conway was not worth fishing. Truly a prophet is without honour in his own country, and the same appears to apply to a river. We elected to fish above the junction of the Esk and Liddel on the Friday, and we commenced operations in the celebrated Willow Pool about ten o'clock, wherein a salmon was on the rise, and we fished away until half-past four, and I captured one common trout which formed our united capture. However, we admired the splendid pools about Canonbie, and saw a few herling sailing about regardless of our lures. There was some thunder, which may have to some extent prejudiced our sport.

On the Saturday, considering that there was little use in trying for herling, I wended my way down the river below Longtown with my salmon rod. In Wilkin's Pool there was a salmon on the rise in a rapid glide under the far bank, and as I could not reach the fish from the low side on which I was, I crossed the river. Wilkin's Pool is a magnificent one, but the local hands say that there has never been a salmon caught therein with the fly; all the more reason that the spell should be removed. At the head of the pool there is a glorious rush of water which swirls under the higher bank, and in the swirl salmon often lie. I placed my fly beautifully and there was a mighty pull; I was in him. The murder was soon out. I drew him to the top of the water, and, Great Scott! he was but a villain of a chub, which was so impertinent as to attempt to appropriate my lovely "Jock Scott." The rascal weighed 2 lb. 4 oz. Afterwards I rose several herling. I fished until late at night, but only killed one herling. The custom of the local hands is to fish Wilkin's Pool every night in considerable force, and the average catch appeared to be about one herling to three anglers; there was therefore not much inducement to fish in the dark.

Monday was my last day, and a fine hot day it was. The question was, what to do? the main river was clearly unproductive. I decided to take the 8.29 train to Penton, and fish down the Liddel to Riddings. About Penton the scenery is beautiful. Penton Lynns is the most interesting part of the river. The river is closed in by high rocks with numerous trees, and some of the pools look awful in their unknown depth, and the river bounds over a rocky bed. Everything looks like fish, but, alas, a burning sun overhead, and water low and clear; wind there was none. I tried large flies, and I tried small flies; I even tried a hair cast, but it was all the same—nothing but parr could I catch. I had not a touch from either trout or herling. However, I could not but enjoy the lovely scenery, the woods overhanging the rippling river. A heron bore me company almost the whole day. How tame the bird was! As I approached he would fly about three hundred yards down the river and then alight, and so on. He had not the fear of a Jerry Emmott before his eyes.

Thus ended my excursion to the Border river in 1893. Moral: Don't go there unless weather and water are in order, and unless you are certain that herling are about. Don't swallow all the sporting papers say about the sport. Some years ago I took up my quarters for a few days with a friend at a hotel on the banks of the Eden. The sport was wretched, and I only caught about four trout a day. The sporting papers flattered our performances. A paragraph appeared to the effect that "some gentlemen staying at the Nuftot Arms had excellent sport." We were the only anglers there that week.

In 1896 the run of sea-trout and herling commenced abnormally early in the Esk. In the middle of July large catches were made, and the veteran Colonel Wyberg did wonders among the herling. The Colonel's headquarters are at "Mary's" little inn at Metal Bridge. Mary knows how to make her guests comfortable. Excited by the glowing reports of fabulous catches, I located myself at the Graham Arms, Longtown, on the 6th of August. I found that there had been a general amnesty of the convicts: the gentlemen had promised to be good, and not to do it again. The harmony of Longtown was once more restored.

The corporation or some such body had made arrangements to sound a steam-buzzer at six o'clock in the morning to awaken sleepy anglers, and the landlord of the Graham Arms kept a cock warranted to crow at daybreak, and to awake the most sleepy of anglers. What lungs that cock had!

The reverend the Rector of Arthuret had died, and his son

reigned in his stead. The Baronet had gained immortal renown by having captured 56 salmon in one season, all in two pools. Minnow and worm were allowed until the 15th of September, but the quantity of lead and size of hooks were limited. Great events had therefore happened since my former visit to Longtown.

It was not long before I was informed by the knowing one that I had come at the wrong time. There had been a nice fresh about ten days before, but the water had run down to very low again, and there was nothing doing. I commenced to fish on the day of my arrival at half-past four. I hooked a nice sea-trout with the fly in the narrow gut at the head of Wilkin's Pool, but we soon parted company. Legend says that the pool is so named because a man of that name was so fond of it, that he either got drowned in it or drowned himself in it—it is all the same thing now, however the event happened. I rose several herling with the fly, and as the fly was clearly not attractive I tried the up-stream worm, with which I killed a chub of 1 lb. 14 oz. in Wilkin's Pool, and that was my sole capture, although I fished until half-past eight o'clock. On my way back to mine inn I met a procession of locals wending their way to Wilkin's Pool; their sport was not encouraging, as the maximum catch consisted of 2 herling.

On the following day I decided to give the up-stream worm a good try, but I only hooked 2 herling with it, which got off. With worm I caught 3 brown trout, and with fly 1. I fished at night without any result. There were considerable numbers of salmon and grilse sporting in the pools, and they preferred to remain there. Even a bunch of worms would not tempt them.

The next day, Saturday, I fished both worm and fly, and had only a few short rises with fly. This day brought an accession of anglers : the veteran Major, his friend, and the friend's sister, and a Mr. Andrew, who proved to be the Piscator Major of the party, as like the apostles he toiled all night. I speculated as to whether he might not claim direct apostolic succession. He had the privilege of fishing in Sir Richard Graham's reserved waters, and was not subject to the eleven o'clock rule. The association water could not be fished after eleven o'clock at night. Mr. Andrew's best kill was 20 herling and sea - trout, got between 9 P.M. and 7 A.M. ; but on several nights he only got 6 or 7.

The pleasant company made up for the bad sport. We learned to exist on hope, and we continued hoping. We discussed the question as to what the herling really is. The Major, who originally hailed from Galway, opined that the herling is identical with the Irish white trout, and ascends the river for domestic reasons. Another angler speculated as to the probability of their being young salmon. We always ended where we began, in doubt and uncertainty.

On Monday we all went a-fishing, and the Major actually managed to capture 4 herling. The friend and I felt small in consequence. The friend distinguished himself by his proficiency in catching chub, like the angler in Wilkin's Pool one night who killed 7 very fine chub, while his neighbour on the right at the same time killed 7 very fine herling—rather hard lines. I had to be satisfied with 2 small yellow trout. On our arrival at the inn, we were of course much gratified when the landlady showed us 10 fine herling which had been caught by Mr. Wilson at Metal Bridge, during the ebb of the tide. This gave us a new idea to speculate upon. Metal Bridge at the turn of the tide was the thing, and to Metal Bridge we would go on the morrow and see if we could not do a good thing; and down the river we fished. The weather was bright and hot, and the water so low. On the way down the Major killed one herling. We met Mr. Mason, a local angler, whose creel was graced with the presence of one herling.

The Major's friend and I distinguished ourselves by killing a chub or two. On arriving at Metal Bridge the tide was flowing, and fishing would be impracticable for about an hour, so we betook ourselves to Mary's for lunch. The veteran Colonel Wyberg was in evidence, also several other anglers; and what an array of rods there was leaning against the wall at the back of the house, varying from ten feet and a half to sixteen feet, showing the different ideas of the rod necessary to slay a little herling with. But in one respect there was a concensus of opinion, and that was in the fineness of the fly cast and the smallness of the flies, the flies being about the size of ordinary trout flies.

On the tide being well on the ebb, we all made for the river. The Major signified his intention of commencing with a Devon minnow before the water cleared, and I followed suit with the natural minnow. With our respective lures we each killed 2 chub, and had a pull from a herling, and that was all we could do with minnow. Shortly I encountered the Colonel and asked his advice as to where I had better try for herling. "Well," he said, "whatever you do, do not fish behind those fellows yonder (they were up to their waists); they are just wading where they ought to be fishing, on a nice gravel bed, where the fish would be feeding if they would feed anywhere. They are spoiling the sport of everybody.

As there has been a very high tide," he said, "I advise you to go up. I am going in." This is just what men in wading-trousers often do; they wade where they ought to fish, and are a nuisance.

On the way up, I encountered the Major resting by the side of a splendid pool, tired out with wielding his sixteen-foot rod. He had risen one herling at the foot of the pool, and I rose one about the same place. I proceeded about half a mile up to a lovely flat where I soon hooked and landed a herling, and hooked three more which got off; and I had rises from several other fish, and I ended by catching what I think may be styled a tidal trout of seven ounces. It was then time to join the conveyance which was to take us back to Longtown. The Major had not caught any more and his friend was clean. The Major and a smart boy who acted in the capacity of a "looker-on" beguiled the drive by playing at a game by virtue of which they claimed to be owners of all the gates, houses, stacks, and game which came into our view. The game was quite too much for my limited capacity.

On the next day I decided to worm the Liddel for herling, and I had hopes that I might delude a sea-trout. As I was too idle to go by the morning train, I did not commence fishing until about one o'clock, and about that time rain began to fall, and it blew half a gale up the river. My first was a small trout and then the parr nuisance began, and what a lot of worms they deprived me of. Oh, the time I spent taking the wretched parr off the hooks.

Above the railway bridge there is a very nice rather shallow pool. Under one of the arches I had a pull from a good fish, and thereabouts killed two fair trout. On the other side there was a fringe of willows, just the place for something good. I threw right under the willows, and was soon fast in a good fish. He rushed down the stream and made the reel spin. Then came the inevitable wind-up, and, alas, it was a chub of 1 lb. 10 oz. In the end I wound up at six o'clock with only 7 trout, after having had a most uncomfortable time of it, what with the rain and the wind. The Major and his friend had toiled all day in the main river and taken nothing.

The next day, which was to be my last, opened with a furious gale from the north-west, accompanied by a driving rain which cleared off about eleven o'clock. I equipped myself with a fifteen-foot rod made of mahou wood. There was a little fresh water in the river, but not much. I observed in the pool at the lane end a salmon and grilse rising. I tried them in vain with salmon flies, but they would not take. In a short time the top piece of my rod snapped and I returned to the inn to get another rod: the consequence of which was, that I did not fairly commence fishing until nearly one o'clock. I again tried the same pool, but with the same result. I then changed to herling flies and carefully fished a beautiful flat a short distance below the pool, out of which I managed to take 3 herling and several chub, which latter were duly knocked on the head and left on the bank. I shortly arrived at Wilkin's famous pool, and as several salmon were moving I was again tempted to try a salmon cast to no purpose. I then resumed my herling cast, and soon captured herling No. 4, and hooked several others which got off. Chub were strongly in evidence, and about 10 of them were left on the bank.

I had the perseverance to fish until half-past eight o'clock, but did not meet with any reward. The veteran Major fished until ten o'clock for 2 herling, and his friend until the same hour, but a few chub were his only reward. Night fishing was so unproductive during my visit, that it was not worth while to undergo the discomfort of it. I mean fishing until the regulation hour, eleven o'clock.

One evening our good landlady condoled with us on our bad sport, and she said, "There were two gentlemen here from Wales for three weeks, and they never got anything longer than your finger. I really felt quite sorry for them."

The following incident shows how tales originate. On the morning of my departure, when I was at breakfast, Mr. Andrew came in and said, "What is this that I have been hearing about you? They say you had your rod broken by a large salmon yesterday, and that you caught 14 herling." I laughed and told him the incident about the broken rod, and that the number of herling was 4 instead of 14. During my visit I did not hear of any angler getting even a rise from a salmon, and it was not for the want of trying for them.

Should the angler located in the lower portion of the Esk find the sport with the seagoing salmonidæ unproductive, he has no other resource, as the common trout is decidedly scarce. If the number of the common trout could be increased, it would be an undoubted boon to the angler. The question arises in one's mind, as to why trout are so numerous in the lower reaches of the Cumberland Eden, when they are so scarce in the lower reaches of the Esk. Is it because sea-trout are much more numerous in the Esk and devour the common trout?

Chub appear to be getting very numerous: if only the sea-trout would take a fancy to them, the angler would derive considerable benefit, and often be saved a pang of disappointment when a big chub is mistaken for a lusty sea-trout.

CHAPTER XXIII

THE YORKSHIRE ANGLERS' ASSOCIATION

Well, my loving scholar, and I am well pleased to know that you are so well pleased with my direction and discourse.—PISCATOR.

THE Yorkshire Anglers' Association owes its origin to the late Mr. Thomas Evan Pritt, who was a native of Preston, in which city he was born late in the forties. Mr. Pritt was from his youth engaged in the business of banking, and at the time of his premature death he was the manager of the Leeds Joint Stock Bank, Limited. He was an ardent fisherman from his boyhood, and about the year 1883 he became a member of the Kilnsey Angling Club. In the year 1884 he conceived the idea of forming a great association of Yorkshire anglers, whose object was to be a combination of fishing and sociability. He was ably assisted by some well-known Yorkshire anglers, and for a commencement he got up a big dinner.

On the 5th of November 1884 a grand dinner of Yorkshire anglers took place at the Queen's Hotel, Leeds, at which Mr. Pritt presided, and on his right and left were Major Middleton, Mr. Edward Middleton, the Rev. E. S. Gough, Mr. W. H. Watson, Mr. C. Pebody (the able editor of the *Yorkshire Post*),

Mr. W. Hirst, Mr. Henry Cadman, Mr. Benjamin Hirst, Dr. Parke, Mr. G. H. Richards, and Dr. Drake. There were about seventy gentlemen present. Mr. Pritt made an admirable and characteristic speech in proposing the toast of the evening, "The Yorkshire Anglers," which is well worthy of a permanent record, and especially so now, when Mr. Pritt's

EAMONT BRIDGE.

genial voice cannot again be heard. He was in the very best form that night, and I am indebted to the *Yorkshire Post* for the following extract of his speech.

This company is of somewhat mixed capabilities. There are men present who are equal to killing a 20 lb. salmon with a light rod and a single strand of gut no thicker than a hair. There are others who could not do it in a week with a clothes-prop and a cart-rope. (Laughter.) Within the limits of this wide difference lie the secrets of angling. These secrets are not learned in a day. "Angling is somewhat like poetry," said the great Father Izaak

Walton, "man is to be born so": and he penned no truer words. The art of angling is as old as the hills. One could scarcely imagine how Noah got on without a fishing-rod, considering the exceptional nature of the weather and circumstances in which he lived. (Laughter.) Of no sport in existence has so much been sung, and written, and said from the time of the prophet Isaiah down to these degenerate days in which the modern Yankee libeller has dared to say, "The angler goeth forth in the morning and cometh back in the evening with the smell of whisky upon him, but the truth is not in him." Ancient as the art of angling is, man has not yet overcome all its difficulties. It may indeed be questioned whether we are much more advanced in the details of fly-fishing than were the ancient Romans, who angled with midge-flies upon bronze hooks several sizes smaller than modern skill professes to be equal to. But if man has not progressed in his knowledge of the ways of fish, the fish have acquired a greater knowledge of the arts of man, and the spread of education in these latter days would seem to have affected even the finny tribe ; and we can find fishermen who are willing to confess privately that the fish are not such fools as they used to be. (Laughter.)

The reasons for this are twofold. The railway has brought the town to the river-side, and where formerly we encountered one angler we may now find a score. The trout have not failed to notice this. The man with a pole has become a familiar object to his vision ; his ways, his tricks, his aims are all known. And in their increasing knowledge in this direction the fish have been aided, and the angler correspondingly retarded, by the present system of drainage, which carries the water off the land into the rivers much more quickly than formerly, so that where in old days a fresh would last a week, it is now good for little more than two days. But the effect does not stop there altogether. The water is taken as quickly as possible off the land and finds its way into the river through pipes. Thirty years ago it percolated slowly through the earth, picking up what I may call microscopic nutritious food for the fish as it went, and improving them both in size and quality. But we must be content with things as they are. The difficulty in catching fish will never deter the true angler.

He finds plenty of sport if he has no fish, and he is happy in that his amusement teaches him the virtue of patience and the necessity of bearing disappointed hopes contentedly. You will remember a never-to-be-forgotten satire of John Leech's in *Punch* many years ago.

There was a row of twelve anglers within twelve yards' space fishing in the Serpentine among swans, ducks, rowing-boats, dogs, toy-boats, flying-sticks, stones, and all manner of disturbances. Time, said the wag, Saturday P.M. *Passer-by.* "Had ever a bite, Jim?" "No," said Jim; "I only comed here last Wednesday." (Laughter.) Jim was a true sportsman; he knew that to be attractive, sport of any kind must be either difficult or dangerous; the one obstacle begot perseverance, and the other caution, and both are good qualities. In angling, a very little fish will bring a man to his proper level. (Hear, hear.)

Next to an ambitious youth struggling lovingly with a reluctant moustache, there is no more pathetic sight than a six-foot man vainly endeavouring to inveigle a three-ounce trout. All the glorious strength and intellect of manhood vanish before the cuteness and determination of that little fish. He plays the game better than the biped, and therefore wins it.

But it is not alone the sport there is in catching fish which constitutes the charms of angling. There is born and bred in every one a love of nature more or less predominant, and angling of all other sports affords opportunities for the gratification of this pure pleasure which places it above all other recreations. Therein alone may man combine his admiration of nature in her simplest and most impressive phases with his instinctive desire to kill something—for that propensity is universal. Man is only a refined beast of prey. Every sport or game in which he indulges has for its object the assertion of his own superiority. The very housemaid exemplified this when she came down upon the innocent black beetle with the crack which blotted him out for ever. The art of angling therefore comprises something more than the mere pleasure of killing fish: it is still the contemplative man's recreation, for wherever we are reared, wherever we are trained, whether our lot be cast in dingy cities or away on the rolling main—in those thoughtful moments which come sometimes upon us all, it may be in the old-fashioned peace of a Sunday afternoon, the mind will wander off to the valleys and the hills, to the clear skies and flying clouds, and memory babbles almost unconsciously of green fields made musical by the murmuring of a river and the songs of many birds. (Applause.) This is the sport which is the excuse for our gathering to-night.

My toast is that of "The Yorkshire Anglers." Yorkshire is pre-eminently an angler's county. Its broad expanse is intersected by some of the loveliest valleys and rivers in the land. Whether in the moorlands or on the wide plain of York, there is work for the angler, and wander and wander where they will, southward to the valleys of the Wye or the Derwent, westward to the Dee, or northward to the Tweed, they will come back if they are Yorkshiremen and join me in the honest boast, that for all the joys that angling can afford "there is no place like home." But the fish of the Yorkshire streams are like the men of the valleys, they are not to be caught with the first bait we can lay hold of to set before them. The tyro must serve a long apprenticeship on any Yorkshire river if he would hope to fill his creel. My own personal experience leads me to sum up in the words "Fish fine and keep low." (Applause.) Having no personal claim to be considered a first-rate angler, I will not attempt to teach this company of practical fishermen their art; but I may be pardoned for reminding you that it is not so easy to keep out of sight as it may appear. Owing to the refraction of the rays of light the direct line of vision becomes broken on reaching the water, and a fish lying under a moderately high bank often has one eye upon the angler when by no possibility can the angler see the fish. I will venture a remark upon one other point of great importance—"Watch the becks." (Applause.) There is too much reason to fear that when the breeding fish ascend the becks and the water gets low, many of the best and largest fish in the higher gathering-grounds of the rivers fall victims to the farmer's boy or other local hands who are uninfluenced by consideration of law, or sport, or any question of the flavour of unseasonable fish. The becks up which the trout run out of Loch Leven are watched day and night all through the winter, and therein to a certain extent is to be attributed the continual excellence of the fishing. Many men living in the neighbourhood of Yorkshire trout and grayling streams have long been convinced that the becks are extensively poached during the breeding season, but the difficulty in the way of stopping it is to detect the offenders. This can only be done by constant watching, and that in its turn is a question of funds.

The toast embraces a very wide body of men, for angling is not the sport of the wealthy alone, but of the toilworn workmen from the lathe, and the loom, and the mine. The angler's kit is a light one, and most of the pleasures of the sport are as accessible to the poor man as to the wealthiest at this table. In Sheffield alone there are nearly 300 members of fishing clubs and associations composed entirely of working-men. Do not let us who are round this hospitable board, all of us fly-fishers, forget our humble brethren of the cork and the quill. (Hear, hear.) The toast embraces us all. With some experience of anglers in different parts of the country, I do not hesitate to say that some of the best practical fishermen in Britain are to be found in the Yorkshire dales, and it is the health of these men more than our own that we drink. Therefore I call upon you, anglers and scoffers all, to join me in honouring the toast of "Yorkshire Anglers here and elsewhere." (Applause.)

Most of the leading trout-fishing clubs in the county were well represented, and Mr. Henry Cadman and Mr. Reffitt were selected to reply to the chairman's toast on behalf of the Kilnsey Angling Club; and Mr. Cadman, at the request of Mr. Pritt, urged the advisability of forming a Yorkshire Anglers' Association.

The main idea then was to form an association of existing Yorkshire trout-fishing clubs, and as a matter of fact a considerable number of the first members of the Yorkshire Anglers Association consisted of members of Yorkshire trout-fishing clubs, but an actual union of clubs was never accomplished. It was not until June 1885 that the Association was formed.

On the 16th of June a meeting of anglers was held at the Great Northern Hotel, Leeds, at which Major Middleton presided, and it was unanimously resolved to form the Yorkshire Anglers' Association.

The first regular meeting of the members of the Association was held at the Great Northern Hotel on the 7th of July, Mr. Henry Cadman in the chair, when Sir Reginald Graham, Bart., was elected as the first president, and Mr. Pritt as the honorary secretary, with an *ex officio* seat on the council; and the following gentlemen were elected as the first members of the council: J. W. Addyman, J. V. Burrows, Henry Cadman, Rev. E. Spencer Gough, Dr. Horsefall, Ben Hirst, William Illingworth, Major Middleton, Edward Middleton, R. M. Pratt, Professor Ransome, and W. H. Watson.

The rules commence by stating:—

1. That this association shall be known as the "Yorkshire Anglers' Association."
2. That it shall have for its purposes:—(a) The encouragement of the higher branches of the art of angling; (b) the promotion of breeding, and the preservation of fish; (c) the rental of suitable streams and ponds; and (d) the provision of opportunities for members to meet together socially for the exchange of ideas and experiences.
3. That it shall be composed only of anglers, or those interested in angling and the preservation and cultivation of fish.
4. That it shall be governed by a council of eight members, with a president, two vice-presidents, and an honorary secretary as *ex officio* members.

About this time and for some years Mr. Pritt was the angling editor of the *Yorkshire Post*. He was responsible for the celebrated angling column, in which he ventilated his wit and extraordinary tales of angling and funny subjects in general in an inimitable manner. It at times appeared as though the mantle of Christopher North had fallen upon him, instilled by the *Noctes*. During the autumn and winter months the Association held monthly meetings, at which Pritt was always the life and soul. His ready wit and humour will long live in the memory of the original members of the Association; and he was always in fine form at the great annual dinner. It was Pritt who kept the fun going, he who got out those artistic menus, illustrated by views of places dear to anglers, such as Brougham Bridge, Frenchfield Farm, The Hut, and Kilnsey Crag. It was by the exertions of Pritt that the Association gained their valuable fishing rights.

In matters piscatorial he was an advanced liberal, much in advance of the rank conservatism of angling clubs in general. He was a staunch upholder of the rights of women. He made a great effort for ladies to be eligible as members of the Yorkshire Anglers' Association, and in this he was supported by Mr. Henry Cadman as seconder, and some other members; but the woman-haters, as poor Pritt expressed it, were in the ascendant, and the motion was lost.

Pritt had a dog of uncertain breed called Tulip, and how he did love that dog! They were constant companions by the river-side, the dog with the stumpy tail watching his master landing the trout, and wagging his stump of a tail and barking with delight as each trout was landed. And Tulip was a perfect treasure in a literary sense, as when the fishing was dull Tulip was marched into the angling column by way of a forlorn hope. The "one-eyed perch" of Malham Tarn did duty in the same manner.

Then Pritt was so popular that he had numerous friends

who would make up the gap when Tulip and the one-eyed perch were done up; so under Pritt's generalship the column always did its duty. The scoffers are supposed to entertain the view that all anglers are addicted to romance, and a noted piscatorial journal, the *Fishing Gazette*, is responsible for the publication of the following anent our dear old friend Pritt, written by some one who wanted to be thought very funny. It must be premised that a celebrated angler had laid it down that he knew a good angler by the coot, coot, coot of his rod, and Mr. Pritt in his capacity of "Looker-on" had expressed his inability to do the cooting, and his assertion was joined issue upon in the following manner :—

I would warn all the innocents that although "Looker-on" is pretty honest and truthful — considering he is an angler — his credibility is not reliable when he yarns about his own performances as an angler. I do not say a word as to his credibility in his private or business relations, but simply in his capacity as an angler; he then, to put it mildly, tells yarns. My credibility is of course always to be depended upon, and especially so when I write about Mr. Pritt the "Looker-on." I would here suggest that he should obtain the royal licence to change his name to "Down-looker," which would be singularly appropriate.

Now he tells a regular "whopper" when he says—with regard to that delightful music, the coot, coot of the rod—"I can't do it myself," from which I am at liberty to infer that he can only do it by deputy. Now for the proof, followed by the inevitable argument. I solemnly state, on my veracity as an angler, that during Easter week, not many years ago, I was fishing a certain dub, pool, run, or stream in the Wharfe which I call the Round Bend, but which some anglers call the Sneck Bend, when my solitude was disturbed by the appearance of the "Angling Column," in the shape of Mr. Pritt and his usual attendant with the knob on his tail. A staff some sixteen feet in height, taken from a forest, headed the column, which was planked by a weaver's beam; the attendant with the tail brought up the rear. Under such circumstances I thought it prudent to retreat from the Round Bend without having made a capture. I then heard something; it was the column getting into action. Coot, coot, coot, coot raged over the bend; the trout took the challenge and the battle became furious, and very soon there were five victims on the grass. The attendant wagged his tail, and I made good my retreat to mine inn, of course feeling smaller than usual.

Argument.—If the column did not make the coot, the attendant did it, and that was the dog, that wonderful dog which, when the master cannot get the line out far enough, carries it out for him in his mouth. What can a really honest angler like I am do against the "man and the dog"?

Mr. Pritt made a characteristic reply, which the curious may read with advantage in the pages of the *Fishing Gazette*, and he paid a happy compliment to the writer of the letter which we have given in detail. He wrote: "His word cannot for a moment be doubted, inasmuch as he appeals to us 'on his veracity as an angler,' and we all know what a solemn thing that is, though the late Josh Billings did say, 'The man who can swop horses or ketch fish and not lie about 'em, is just as pious as any man ever got to be in this world.'" Pritt appears to have been a great admirer of Mr. Joseph Billings, whoever that worthy may have been. Mr. Pritt attributed his success on the day referred to, to his fishing with much larger flies than those generally used at Kilnsey, the water being heavy.

For the season of 1886 the Association secured the Nunwick Hall water on the Cumberland Eden, which is a length of nearly a mile. This water is about a mile below Langwathby Bridge, and there was the advantage that the intervening water below the bridge was free. The Nunwick Hall water commenced at an excellent salmon pool, on which there was a boat. Several members of the Association had excellent sport on the Nunwick Hall water, but unfortunately the Association only retained the water for one season, as in the following season it was let to Mr. Horrocks of Eden Brow, notwithstanding that the Association offered an increased rent. However, the Association was so fortunate as to obtain Lord Hothfield's water on the Eamont and Lowther, which extends on the Westmorland side from the Weir Pool above Brougham Bridge and a small portion at the foot of the Lowther, to a deep pool about two miles down the river, overhung by a wood with very steep sides.

Lord Hothfield's fishing is on the Westmorland side only, with the exception of a short length in close proximity to Brougham Mill, wherein is the famous Castle Stream which flows near the ruins of Brougham Castle, which does not belong to Lord Brougham and Vaux, but to Lord Hothfield. Brougham Hall, the mansion of Lord Brougham, is situated about half a mile off on an elevation overlooking the Lowther. The country is well wooded and the scenery is really charming. A short distance off there is Penrith Beacon with the neighbouring hills clothed with trees of the pine tribe. On the west the Lake Mountains tower, and on the east the Pennine range, culminating in Cross Fell, which is often crowned with snow until even the month of June, the summit being clear of snow, beneath which lies the white crown.

The angler can admire the surrounding beauteous scenery; indeed he enjoys the pastime of the contemplative man in pleasant places. He is in pleasant places far from the cares and worry of life, alone with nature, and as he looks on the venerable ruins of Brougham Castle he speculates on the time when the castle was full of life, when lords and ladies assembled in the courtyard prepared for the chase, the hawks on their perches, and on the ground the dogs eager for the start. From this peaceful scene his thoughts may wander to something very different. He is in the Border land. The courtyard is full of armed warriors who are preparing to resist a

FRENCHFIELD.

raid of the wild Scots who are once more on the war-path. In '45 Prince Charlie and his followers were about: perhaps they encamped on Frenchfield Farm, now the headquarters of the Yorkshire Anglers' Association !

Frenchfield farmhouse is situated about a quarter of a mile from the river on the Cumberland side. It nestles at the foot of an abrupt rise studded with tall trees in which there is a small rookery. Frenchfield Meadow, by which the Eamont wends its way, has become classic ground from the excellent sport frequently obtained there,—for it is now called Paley's Walk, in commemoration of the mighty deeds done there by a renowned Lancastrian angler who walked that meadow for a day and more. Likewise lower down the river we have Robson's Rock, so called to perpetuate the mighty deeds of a distinguished Yorkshire angler who loved the place so well that, not content with fishing over it, he sat on it, at least so said the immortal Pritt. Here stands the fishing hut built by the keeper Raine, whence in the late autumn the salmon can be watched on the Redds.

It was in the month of April 1888 that I first met Mr. Pritt at Frenchfield Farm. I travelled by the Settle and Carlisle Railway. Snow lay in immense quantities on the elevated ground; some ravines *en route* were literally full of snow. It looked as though there must be a lot of snow-broth in the river, and my hopes fell as to the chances of sport. The river contained a good volume of clear water, and on the 6th I killed twenty-four trout with fly, the killing flies being purple snipe, March brown, orange woodcock (outside the wing), blue dun, and Greenwell's Glory.

On the following day Mr. and Mrs. Pritt arrived, and we had the feast of reason and the flow of soul. Mr. Pritt was much pleased when I told him of my pannier of twenty-four trout, because the impression had got about that the fishing was not worth much, and there had been no such pannier made before. It was decided to make the Agony Column, I mean the Angling Column, of the *Yorkshire Post* sing the praises of Eamont, and under Pritt's artistic touch it did. The song was sung which thenceforth in the spring months brought the "man with the pole" (Pritt) in crowds to Eamont's banks, and the Armstrongs of Frenchfield reaped their spring corn.

On Sunday morning Pritt and I walked down the river banks, and what a delightful walk we had. It was a lovely spring day, though the snow lay deep on the mountains, but what is so delightful as contrast? We christened the various pools and flats of our own sweet will—Weir Pool, Castle Stream, Bridge Pool, Deadman's Rock, Frenchfield Flat, Frenchfield Dub, Helvellyn Stream, One Tree Stream, Red Scar Pool, Wood Stream, Below Scar Pool, Whinfell Dub, and Red Cliff Pool. We did not then christen Robson's Rock. What delightful talks we had in the evenings! How we discussed fish and fishing! How delightful it was to listen to Pritt's yarns! Now that he is gone, the memory lingers over the past, and recalls that stalwart form which will haunt the banks of Eamont no more. It was during this visit that Pritt made his celebrated baskets of trout, which never have been perhaps equalled since. In about twelve days' fishing he killed nearly 300 trout. He furnished me with an exact record, which I did not preserve. I returned home on the Tuesday after his arrival, so that I was not present when his principal captures were made.

In the same year the Association took the fishing rights in the higher portion of the Aire, from a little above Bell Busk Mill to Airton. In the year 1891 the Association considerably added to their fishing rights in the Eamont and Lowther by taking the Carlton Hall water from Major Cowper. This water extends on both sides of the Eamont from Eamont Bridge to Frenchfield Meadow on the north bank, and to the weir on the south bank, a distance of about three-quarters of a mile, and on the north bank of the Lowther from the road to Ullswater to the weir. The other bank of the Lowther belongs to Lord Brougham. In 1895 Mr. Pritt commenced negotiations with Sir Richard Musgrave, Bart., for the acquisition of the Eden Hall portion of the Eamont. Mr. Pritt died in September of the same year, and the negotiations were completed by Mr. F. W. Branson, the new honorary secretary of the Association, shortly afterwards. The Eden Hall water of the Eamont extends from the Honey Pot water, attached to the Crown Hotel, Penrith, to the junction of the Eamont with the Eden on the north bank. The Association therefore have now almost the whole of the Eamont from Eamont Bridge to the Eden. In 1897 they acquired the Winderwath water on the Eden, which extends for about two miles below Temple Sowerby Bridge. The water in the Aire was given up about the year 1894.

In concluding this short history of the Yorkshire Anglers' Association, I must again make a short reference to Mr. Pritt. As an acknowledgment of his valuable services as honorary secretary, the members of the Association, at one of the annual dinners not very long before his death, presented him with some valuable plate. Mr. Pritt was most affected in returning thanks, and the speech he then made was one of his best.

On one occasion he read before a crowded audience of members of the Association and their friends a paper entitled "The By-paths of Angling," which was very much applauded and has not been published. He was instrumental in the close time for trout fishing in Yorkshire being extended to the 16th of March. He was one of the founders of the Northern Anglers' Association, and its first president. He was a member of the London Fly-Fishers' Club, and he frequently attended their annual dinners, and whenever he did he treated the company to one of his characteristic speeches, which were always fully appreciated. He was the author of *Yorkshire Trout Flies*, the name of which was afterwards changed to *North*

Country Flies, also of the *Book of the Grayling;* and his last work, *An Angler's Basket*, was published after his death under the superintendence of the Rev. C. P. Roberts, M.A., of Longsight Rectory.

The Association have taken Eden Hall lake from Sir Richard Musgrave, and stocked it with Rainbow trout; also several miles of fishing in the Costa, which contains grayling and other fish.

Having now given the history of the Yorkshire Anglers' Association, we will in the next three chapters enjoy a few days' fishing, in retrospect, in some of the waters of the Association.

CHAPTER XXIV

THE EDEN, LANGWATHBY

> The shepherd swains shall dance and sing
> For thy delight each May morning.
> MILKMAID'S *Song*.

THE river Eden may be classed as one of the largest rivers in England. Trout abound throughout the whole length of the river, and the lower reaches are at certain seasons frequented by salmon, sea-trout, and herling. Until Carlisle is reached the river is practically unpolluted, hence the abundance of trout life. The Eden down to its junction with the Eamont is comparatively a small river, but from the junction it is a truly noble river, the volume of water being during ordinary seasons magnificent.

Langwathby is a pretty village situated on the east bank of the Eden about a mile and a half below the junction with the Eamont. About a mile up the river is Eden Hall, the seat of Sir Richard Musgrave, Bart. The river is spanned by a handsome bridge. There is a typical village green, and near by stand two little inns, the Shepherd and the Fish. Fronting on the green is Laburnum House, where Mr. and Mrs. Oliphant welcome the wandering angler and make him comfortable. During the time the Yorkshire Anglers' Association had the Nunwick Hall fishing, Laburnum House was well patronised by members of the Association. For about a mile below the bridge on the east bank the river is open to all comers. The water is a very pretty one, but is very much fished by local men.

We then come to the Nunwick Hall water, part of which is on one side of the river and part on the other. A little lower down there is a splendid pool, which is a good cast for salmon, and here a boat is kept. On a good day the angler may fill his pannier from this pool alone, and as the pool is very wide the boat is a great convenience. A few hundred yards below the pool two brooks of good size which flow from the Pennine range make their contribution to the river, and a little lower down there is a length where the fish love to sport, and a man who has once fished it under favourable conditions will long to do it again and again.

My time came in the bonny month of May 1886. Winter had lingered into May that year, but Wednesday the 19th was a lovely May day, though heavy snowdrifts still lingered on the Pennine range low down the sides. As I wended my way down a grassy lane, the cuckoo's song was heard anon, and I passed a maiden fair, who with knitting in her hand was tending some red cows feeding on the grassy way. I thought of Izaak Walton and the red cow's milk, of the milkmaid's song and the mother's warning. As the maiden did not favour me with a song, I was soon at the Boat Pool, which I fished without success. I intended to cross the river by the boat, but the boat was on the other side, so fortunately—as it turned out—I could not cross the river.

There was a good clear fly-water, just about right. I

carefully fished the Boat Pool—result, only a few faint rises—
and thence down to the first brook. The field the other
side of the brook was not included in the Nunwick Hall
water, and there I came upon an angler who was in the act
of landing a nice trout. He said that he was doing very
badly, and I had not a fish and it was twelve o'clock. I
shortly arrived at the smittle place: for about fifty yards or
so a fringe of willows on my side whereby rather a strong
stream flows, then for about sixty yards a combination of
flat and pool, the water deepening gradually from my side on
which the bank was low, the other bank being rather high;
below this length is a rapid for about sixty yards flowing
into a long deep pool, where the river takes a sudden turn.

To the experienced angler it was apparent that the flat
formed an admirable feeding ground. I was fishing with a
hair cast to which were attached three flies, the tail fly being
a purple snipe (dark), the first dropper dark woodcock (a
small feather from the outside of a woodcock wing hackled on
an orange silk body, with a little hare-lug underneath the
fibres), and the third dropper orange partridge. The water
flowed something like oil, smooth and fairly fast; the weather
was cloud and sunshine, with an occasional catspaw on the
water. From the nature of the water it appeared more
suitable for fishing down than fishing up.

It was nearly one o'clock. I commenced near the bottom of the willows from the bank, and at my second cast
hooked and landed a trout, and when I got to the bottom of
the flat I had about 11. I then retraced my steps, and wading
a few yards out again fished the flat down, and creeled about
10 more. Having had a few minutes' rest I waded outside
the willows, and a third time fished the flat down, being

farther out than before, in fact as far as my waders would permit, and on regaining the bank I turned out my creel and counted 33 trout. It was then about four o'clock. For about half the time the trout mainly took the purple snipe, and the latter half the dark woodcock. As I had to trudge about two miles in waders, I made for my quarters, and as my trout weighed 10 lb. 1 oz., I had had enough of it when I arrived there, and I slaked my thirst with brown ale from the Shepherd.

As I was returning home the next day I was obliged to make rather a short day of it. The fickle goddess had changed her humour · a cold east wind blew from the snow-clad fells, accompanied by cold rain. It was such a contrast to the previous day. I sped for the Boat Pool, and, behold, the gardener-boatman was there. He paddled me about and I soon creeled 6 trout, but for some reason or other I missed many rises, so different to the previous day when the trout meant it. When I had exhausted the Boat Pool I trudged through the cold rain to the scene of the previous day's slaughter, and there captured 11 trout. I pricked and hooked many fish; they got off in a most aggravating manner, and as a usual consequence with me, I lost three flies in fish. I had not lost one the day before.

After putting down all the fish in the Willow Flat I retraced my steps to the Boat Pool, and captured 5 more from the bank, making 22 in all, which weighed 7 lb. 5 oz. I caught two at a time twice. The killing flies were somewhat mixed: purple snipe, orange partridge, orange dark woodcock, yellow snipe, and orange curlew. If I had not missed so many fish I should have made a record basket.

I was again at Langwathby in the following October.

The weather was too wet for good sport with the fly on most days, but on the 9th I was favoured by the elements. It was a lovely autumn morning as I made my way at once to the famed Willow Flat. There were no longer snowdrifts on the Pennine range. The foliage was gay with the tints of autumn. The sandpiper had flown away to his winter quarters, but the swallows still lingered. I commenced at the flat about eleven o'clock, and by about three I had 24 trout to my credit, all caught in the flat. I wound up at the Boat Pool where I caught one more, and as by half-past four the rise had ceased, I gave up for the day. The 25 trout weighed 6 lb. 4 oz.; the average therefore was less than those caught in May. In the night the windows of heaven were again opened and the rain descended, and on the morrow the river was in flood.

The 15th was my last day in the Willow Flat, but the water was much too heavy for the fly; however, I killed 4 there with the fly and 6 elsewhere. Thus ended my acquaintance with the Nunwick Hall water, and I often think of that first day in the flat below the willows.

After 1887 I did not again fish in the Eden until the month of October 1897. As has appeared in a previous chapter, the Yorkshire Anglers' Association took in the latter year the fishing on the Winderwath estate, which extends from Temple Sowerby Bridge for about two miles down the river on the west bank, and also includes the brickworks field on the east bank. The fishing is truly delightful, and in addition to trout there are grayling.

A few years ago a gentleman placed some grayling in the river at Warcop, which is about ten miles higher up the river, and grayling are now numerous in the neighbourhood of

Temple Sowerby, another proof of the fact that grayling are inclined to drop down a river.

I fished the Winderwath water on the 6th of October in company with Dr. Richardson and his brother. The Doctor killed 8 grayling and 2 trout, his brother 3 grayling and 2 trout, and I 7 trout and 1 grayling. I fished a little lower down than the others did, and we all fished with fly. The trout were dark and out of condition with few exceptions, both in the Eden and Eamont, and I came to the conclusion that trout fishing in both rivers ought to cease on the 1st of October. Both rivers are considered somewhat early rivers, so that there does not appear any reason why the close time should have been curtailed.

During the last twenty years I have captured 258 trout in the Eden, 241 of which were taken with fly, 9 with minnow, and 8 with worm, and the total weight was 71 lb. 10 oz.— rather larger than four to the pound, and the largest trout weighed 10 oz.

CHAPTER XXV

THE EAMONT

Then let's meet here, for here are fresh sheets that smell of lavender, and I am sure we cannot expect better meat or better usage in any place.
—CORIDON.

THE river Eamont is the overflow of Ullswater; its watershed is very great in consequence, and as the rainfall is so excessive in the Lake District, save in times of exceptional drought, the flow of water is considerable. After a heavy rainfall the river is in good condition for many days, long after such streams as the Wharfe and Ure have sunk to small dimensions; hence, at any rate in the spring, the water is generally in good condition for the artificial fly. Melting snow on the mountains does not appear to be prejudicial to the rise of fly, inasmuch as the snow-water is mingled with the warmer waters of the lake, out of which it issues with a fair temperature.

There is a marked difference in the lake and the Eamont trout, the former being gray without red spots, and rather elongated, and the latter having the general appearance of river trout with red spots. Trout go down the Eamont from the lake to spawn, and it is not uncommon to capture lake trout in the river above Brougham Mill, and such trout are generally pink fleshed. The Eamont trout are not so pretty in their markings as the Eden trout; they present a somewhat darker appearance. Mr. Pritt (at any rate at one time) formed the opinion that the Eamont trout attain their best condition in early spring, because in the winter they regale themselves with salmon-spawn, and that as the season advanced they gradually lost their condition; but inasmuch as there are in most seasons swarms of March browns in April and part of May, and abundance of creepers and stonefly in their seasons, and minnows are strongly in evidence by May, there appears to be no reason for Mr. Pritt's proposition, and I do not agree with his deduction as to the fact from my own experience.

As a matter of fact more salmon spawn in the Lowther than the Eamont, and the weir in connection with Brougham Mill is the cause. The weir is formed at the junction of the two rivers: in order to ascend the Eamont the salmon must leap over the weir; there is not the slightest impediment to the ascent of the salmon up the Lowther. There is no doubt that the salmon can jump over the weir in a very moderate fresh, but they have never been seen to do so, and there is not the slightest use in fishing for salmon in the Eamont above the weir.

Nevertheless parr are numerous above the weir, and George Raine the keeper opines that they ascend the weir; but this supposition seems utterly untenable, as parr are naturally inclined to drop downwards. Parr are much more numerous in the Lowther. The keeper has come to his peculiar conclusion because he never has seen a salmon above the weir. The probability is that they get over the weir late in the season after the commencement of the close time, which is from 16th November. It would rather appear that salmon do not usually ascend the Lowther until after the close of the fishing season. I have only seen one salmon in the Lowther, and I caught that fish in the deep rocky pool about 200 yards from Lowther foot; but of the salmon we shall have more to

WEIR POOL.

say hereafter, our object now being to discuss Eamont trout.

The trout are very capricious, and the angler must not expect to fill his creel on all apparently favourable conditions. The state of his creel will be very much dependent on the part of the river he happens to be at when the rise of the day comes on. On days when several men are out their takes often vary very much, even from 4 to 25—of course I am not comparing the sport of a novice with that of a good hand.

There are certain places where a man may capture upwards of a dozen fish in only a few yards of water, which will be described later on. Speaking generally as to the productiveness of the river, if the angler can capture from 10 to 15 trout with fly in a fair day's fishing he may well be satisfied. Mr. Denby's capture of 40 trout in the Eden Hall length has so far beaten the record. In early spring it is advisable to use flies dressed on No. 2 or 3 hooks (Kendal size) unless the water be exceptionally low.

It is instructive to be on the river banks before a strong hatch of March browns come down : there is hardly a rise on the water, when all at once trout pop up all over as the flies come down, and the river seems alive with fish; but while the mad rise is on not many fish find their way to the creel. It is the same when swarms of the iron-blue dun (dark watchet) come down later on; the greater the rise, the more infrequent the captures. The Eamont has a very great advantage, inasmuch as it may be fished advantageously from the bank when the water is anything like in order, and for the most part the banks are green sward. It is therefore well adapted for persons who do not like to wade. An early spring day's fishing in the neighbourhood of Frenchfield will now be described.

It was the 8th of April 1895. Some snow had fallen during the preceding night, and the mountains were covered with snow. There was a big fly-water and consequently no occasion to be encumbered with waders. It was just the water for Frenchfield Wood stream and dub. After a rough stream for about a hundred yards a long dub is formed, the north bank of which is a plantation on sharply rising ground; hence the refraction of heat is considerable, and when other parts of the river are chilled by a cold northerly wind, the pool is in shelter and the air feels comparatively warm.

The other bank is grass land with a bush here and there. About ten o'clock I made direct for this place. My cast was composed as follows: tail fly, winter brown made in the manner invented or improved upon by Mr. Bradshaw (a small feather from the inside of a woodcock's wing hackled on a body of bronze peacock harl); head, orange silk; first dropper, a blue dun or water-hen bloa (a small feather from the inside of a water-hen's wing hackled on a body of water-rat's fur ribbed with gold thread; head, yellow silk); and for the second dropper a purple dark snipe. All the flies did their duty, and the order of merit commenced at the tail fly which was most certainly the favourite. The hooks were No. 3 (Kendal size). As I expected, I had some nice sport in the dub, and ere long I captured 13 trout there, and 5 elsewhere, making 18 trout, weight, 5 lb. 3 oz.—rather below the average, and as my best trout only weighed 7 oz., the good trout were apparently not on the fly.

On the following three days the weather was fine and windy, the wind being from N.W. by W., and I only scored 19 trout. The weather on the fourth day was quite different; it was dull with a gentle wind from S.E. by E. The water had considerably fined down, and was in nice order for the Castle Stream, which runs almost under the shade of the ruins of Brougham Castle. This stream gradually deepens from the north or Brougham Mill side to the castle side, and as there are large stones on the castle side, it is good holding ground for trout, and trout come up to feed from the pool under Brougham Bridge. However, I only made three captures in the Castle Stream, and I then crossed by the bridge, and proceeded to the Weir Pool, out of which the Castle Stream flows. As its name indicates, there is a weir across the Eamont for Brougham Mill, over which the waters flow with a roar and form the Weir Pool, and at the head of the Weir Pool the Lowther comes in.

The pool is deep with a fine broad gradually shallowing tail. I fished the pool partly across and partly up, and the

BROUGHAM CASTLE.

fish were taking best near the edges of the shelving shore, so that the cast was frequently about straight up stream; and fishing thus I soon extracted 9 trout from the pool, which made 12 in all so far, and I had only fished two places.

Having decided to give the Lowther a try, I crossed that river and arrived at a deep rocky pool, the south bank of which is a high red rock with trees in places. The north bank, otherwise the bank on Major Cowper's side, is low and con venient to fish from. I extracted 5 trout from this pool, which I have named the Red Pool, and I was singularly unfortunate in hooking several good fish and losing them. I thence fished most of Major Cowper's portion of the Lowther, and killed 5 more fish. In due time I crossed Eamont Bridge, and fished from the north bank of the Eamont through Carlton Hall Park, but only captured 3 more trout, making 25 in all, weight 7 lb. 1 oz. My best fish weighed 8 oz. I had been unfortunate with the larger fish.

There were three anglers at Frenchfield besides myself — Mr. R., Mr. O., and Mr. T., all good fishermen—and we discussed the reasons why and wherefore our sport varied so considerably. Mr. R. had taken 4, Mr. T. 13, and Mr. O. 21, and as usual the killing flies of each man did not correspond with those of the others. My flies had graduated from winter brown to yellow snipe, purple snipe, and gold thread water-hen. During this April trip I fished on eight days and killed 94 trout, weight 28 lb. 11 oz., and the captures graduated from 25 to 4.

The next visit in the same year was from the 27th of April to the 1st of May, four days, during which I killed 61 trout, weight 19 lb. 4 oz. On the last day I killed 11 trout in Frenchfield Wood pool. On this visit the female March brown was the favourite fly.

During the year following, I fished the Eamont the end of March and the beginning of April. I provided myself well with the winter brown made as before stated, but the trout would have none of it. The March brown did the running. The sport was moderate—50 trout in four days, 15 lb. 9 oz. These instances of early spring fishing in the Eamont may suffice. It must be borne in mind that the river is very well

PALEY'S WALK.

flogged, consequently the education of *Salmo fario* progresses in proportion. Now for a few instances of late spring fishing.

On the 10th of May 1889, I was in Frenchfield Meadow (Paley's Walk) by Eamont side. It was a charming May morning. Snow still lingered under the summit of Cross Fell, and there were streaks of snow on the Lake Mountains. The weather was slightly showery; there was a nice water with just a tinge of colour in it. It verily appeared a day for good things.

I began at nine o'clock in Paley's Walk. Paley's Walk is a section of the river which extends from Brougham Mill weir to the fence which separates the Lowther and Carlton Hall estates, about half a mile by the windings of the river, and this is perhaps about the best length in the upper water of the Association; thence the angler has in view Carlton Hall with high trees in the background darkened with rooks' nests on the north bank, a green park in front of the Hall studded with noble trees, then across the river Brougham Castle, and a little west Brougham Hall almost hidden by the May foliage. The birds most in evidence are sea-gulls and rooks. The sea-gulls have come so far to feast on the smolts on their journey to the sea; there they are seen anon dashing into the shallows after their prey. The swallows are about, too, hawking for their prey. The angler is doing likewise, but as his *modus operandi* is based on fraudulent lines, he has to consider what line of fraud to adopt; but inasmuch as it is not a flood water, the angler must confine himself to the fly of art.

At this time of the year it becomes of paramount importance to pay attention to the flies which are about. It is at this time that the yellow dun of May puts in an appearance; the time has therefore come to look out for the swarms of

iron-blue dun. When the yellow dun is on, I do not know a
better rendering of it than the following: a light gray feather
from the back of a hooded crow hackled on a body of yellow
silk, and a little mole's fur under the fibres of the hackle;
and in default a feather from the inside of a starling or young
grouse's wing. About the same time the yellow partridge
becomes a good fly, the hackle being a little lighter in shade

BROUGHAM BRIDGE.

than the one used for the orange partridge, and in all probability the trout take or mistake the yellow partridge for the
yellow dun.

I commenced with a cast of three flies, tail yellow dun,
first dropper orange partridge, and second dropper hare-lug
with gold thread, which is made as follows: wings, feather
from a starling's quill; body, fur from the grizzled part of a
hare's ear ribbed with gold thread, and legs, fibres of fur

pulled out. Up to noon the fish rose fairly well, the yellow dun being the favourite, but the other flies did their duty. Then all of a sudden the fish began popping up all over. Great swarms of the iron-blue dun were sailing down the river, and at the same time my flies became useless; the trout totally ignored them, although just before the swarms came down the yellow dun had been doing well. So down with the yellow and up with the blue. I rigged up a cast of two flies, iron-blue and purple dark snipe. The iron-blue was formed thus: wings, two tips from feathers from the tomtit's tail; head, orange; body, blue mole's fur ribbed with orange silk; legs, honey-dun hackle. Made hacklewise, the best feather is a small feather from the back of a merlin, but there are several feathers which will answer the purpose, such as a feather from the breast of a lapwing; and when the ironblue is on, Stewart's black spider is certain to account for some fish. Thus armed with the iron-blue and the purple snipe, I caught a fish now and then and missed many rises, as I usually do when fishing with No. 0 hooks.

I fished only in Paley's Walk, the Castle Stream, the Bridge Pool, Frenchfield Stream opposite the Dead Man's Rock, and the Weir Pool, all within half a mile from Frenchfield Farm. About three o'clock the rise ceased, and I had to conclude the day with seventeen trout; but there were good things in store that night.

Mr. Pritt and two of his boon Lancashire companions arrived, and there was the feast of reason and the flow of soul. Pritt was in fine form, and incited by the lively boys he brought with him, we had some roaring fun. One yarn followed another, each yarn must in its turn be improved upon; but the first part of the evening was passed in the eternal subject of flies, what cast must be rigged up for the morrow—but for no purpose, for that night the heavens were opened and there was a great rain. Pritt opined that Noah must have had a good time of it in the ark, when there was a good all-round water for forty days.

Druidale (loquitur). Wilt thou, O Pritt, our great master, give the reason why after a good fresh we anglers frequently have good sport, and in long-continued drought bad?

Mr. Pritt. You had better give your ideas, Druidale; you are a past-master in our noble art, and your years exceed mine.

Druidale. Well, *mes amis*, you may have my ideas for what they are worth. In a drought of considerable duration the beds of our streams teem with minute atoms of life, and upon these atoms the trout feed. If you examine the moss on the stones, you will find thousands of minute things about half an inch long, which somewhat resemble tiny eels. Caddis and little shell-fish cling to the stones and rocks. At this time, although it may be the height of the worm season, trout take worm or minnow badly. A good fresh washes many of these minute atoms away. During the fresh the trout have a high time of it among the floating atoms, also on the worms which come down. But there is soon an end of this feast, and by the time the water has fined down the fish are again hungry, and as most of the food has been washed away, they fall victims to the seductions of the angler. Now, my boys, can you prove that I am wrong?

Mr. Pritt. There may be a good deal in what you say, friend Druidale; I am not prepared to prove the contrary. When trout's tails are up we all know that there is no use in our lines being down.

Mr. W. By the way, Pritt, the time has come when we ought to admit ladies as members of the Yorkshire Anglers' Association. Don't you think so?

Mr. Pritt. I do indeed. Do not we all love the fair sex? They share all our sorrows: why should not they share all our joys? And is not fishing our greatest joy? Is it not called the gentle art, and if it be so, why should not the gentle sex share it with us? This would be a charming river for the fair ones to fish; the banks are so firm and dry, they need not wet their pretty little feet. I'll propose that ladies be admitted at the next annual meeting.

Druidale. And I will second you with pleasure. In order that our fair friends may enjoy the pleasures of wading, should they be so inclined, we must devise some rational costume for them. How charming they would look in short skirts just below the knee—only just—and knickerbockers!

Mr. Pritt. My dear Druidale, what a charming picture you are drawing. Won't it be jolly? they can make afternoon tea for us at the hut.

Mr. W. Has it ever occurred to you how portly middle-aged ladies would look in knickerbockers? Think of the apparition of Mrs. Wellingtonea in waders.

Mr. Pritt. My dear boy, who wants to go fishing with his grandmother or his mother-in-law?

Druidale. I wonder what idiot invented the term mother-in-law, seeing that it cannot be denied that the mother of a man's wife is neither his lawful nor natural mother, for strictly a man's mother-in-law would be his own natural mother.

The mother-in-law question is abruptly terminated by the entry of Miss Armstrong with a jug of water and biscuits, who retires wishing us good-night, for it is late—a little past eight o'clock.

Mr. W. Here is the water, but where is the whisky? (How good we all feel—there is not a flask of whisky among the party.)

Druidale. I suppose Pritt keeps all the Keighley cold tea for the angling column. How is the one-eyed perch in Malham Tarn getting on, Pritt, he has not appeared in the column lately?

Mr. Pritt. Now, none of your chaff, friend Druidale. If I had Tulip here he would go for you.

Mr. W. (yawning). Tell us a good story, Pritt, or I shall go to sleep.

Mr. Pritt. What is to your taste, boys, fish or fishy?

Mr. W. Let us have some fish, we may not catch any to-morrow.

Mr. Pritt then related in his inimitable manner the story of the parson and the keeper, which is told in a former chapter.

Mr. Pritt. Yes, that parson is an authority as to what may be said under such trying circumstances. One Sunday afternoon a parson caught me in the act of making flies. I said I feared he would think me very wicked. "Nothing of the sort," said he; "I would make flies on Sunday myself if I could."

Then we have some more tales—some fish and some fishy— and at a quarter to ten o'clock we paddled upstairs to bed, to dream of the fly which will take on the morrow.

Eight o'clock and breakfast—ham and eggs and tea. (Why do most fishermen take tea and not coffee to breakfast?) Enter Raine the keeper at the fag-end of breakfast—at whatever time that meal may be—and says that it has

THE ISLAND STREAM.

rained all night, and that there is a flood, a regular worm-water. A wag remarked *sotto voce*, "There's always Raine at Frenchfield." The other fellows sentenced Raine to one hour's hard labour to dig worms. As they were going to worm, I, from a spirit of contradiction, resolved to minnow. I requisitioned Raine for all the minnows he had, which made a magnificent total of 10, and I had a white Devon to fall back upon.

I commenced operations in the Weir Pool. There was a big yellow worm-water and no mistake. There appeared to be no chance with minnow, but it is the unexpected which happens. I soon used all my 10 minnows and only killed 5 trout with them; I then killed 5 with the Devon, making 10 trout in the Weir Pool. Having pricked them all down, I crossed the river and proceeded to the Bridge Pool. It was in fine condition for the minnow. This pool is but a short one; after a few yards it subsides into a smooth gliding shallow, a beautiful draw for the minnow, and here I caught 6 trout with the Devon, one of which was a beauty of 17 oz., and the next in size 12 oz. I had now 16 trout, 6 lb. 4 oz. Afterwards I tried Frenchfield Stream and Flat, but without success. I do not know how it is, but I never find the minnow succeed thereabouts, although it looks likely for spinning a minnow. Pritt caught 16 with worm, and Mr. W. 10. I expected that they would have killed more, but the fish cannot have been well on the worm.

Again we had a merry evening at the farm, enlivened by the wit of Pritt. Poor fellow, he was in fine form in those days. He appeared to have many years in store. The next day was Sunday, and we had a pleasant walk in the meadows, and watched the everlasting river rolling on its course, seeing a trout pop up here and there.

On Monday the 13th there was a good fly-water, and I managed to creel 27 trout with the yellow dun, blue dun, and orange partridge. The weather was alternate cloud and sunshine, with a breeze from the north-east.

On Tuesday the water had very much fined down, and as I had decided to return home by an early train, I commenced in Paley's Walk in good time—eight o'clock. The trout, however, did not come on the rise until about nine o'clock, and then they meant business. Though the sun was bright, I killed 11 in Paley's Walk, chiefly about the milldam, 3 in the Castle Stream, and 6 in the Bridge Pool, making 20 trout by eleven o'clock, and then I wound up. Raine begged me to fish the day out; it would be a record day, he said, but I said I had caught enough. In my four days I had creeled 80 trout, which weighed a little over 23 lb. Thus ended a very pleasant little fishing trip. Pritt and his friends had departed on the previous day.

We will now sample the Eamont a little later on in the season. It is the leafy month of June 1892, when the trout begin to take the fly at night. It was the 17th. The weather during the day had been cold, with rain and hail showers and some thunder. I began fishing in Paley's Walk at a quarter past eight o'clock in the evening, and fished till ten. I killed 10 trout on the black spider, orange partridge, red partridge, and yellow dun, but from the number of rises I had I ought to have done better.

On the following day the water was in good order, but the elements were disagreeable, there being heavy rain and hail showers with thunder at times. I began at the famed Dead Man's Rock, a little below Brougham Bridge. The rock is on the south bank, a few yards from the bank. Immediately below the rock is a hole of fearful depth, at least twenty feet. In a few yards from the rock there is a rather shallow stream which extends to the Frenchfield side, and on this shallow the trout feed. A little below the rock, impending over the deep water, there is a long ridge of gravel bed. I waded out to the rock, which was covered with water, and from that position killed 14 trout from the shallow stream and the gravel ridge. When the water is rather low, the best plan is to commence about thirty yards below the rock, wade on the ridge and fish up.

Fishing here and there to the pool below Red Scar, I concluded the day with 30 trout, which ran a little below the average, as they only weighed 8 lb. The killing flies were orange partridge, yellow dun, and black spider. I am inclined to think that trout take the orange partridge for the red spinner. Mr. L., a celebrated minnow-fisher, and his amiable lady, also their son, who was following in his father's footsteps, were at Frenchfield, so that we made up a pleasant party. Mr. L. narrated an adventure with a bull, which Mrs. L. had on Coquetside. The bull actually got her between his horns against the wall, and if it had not been for timely aid, it would have been serious for Mrs. L. Mr. L. is a believer in the finest of tackle for the clear-water minnow. He uses the Ariel tackle, the hooks being No. 0, and either drawn gut or the very finest undrawn, and he pins his faith on a stiff rod at least fourteen feet in length.

On Sunday there were again heavy showers with thunder, and I accompanied Mrs. Armstrong, our kind hostess, to the parish church of Penrith, with its red sandstone walls and squat square tower, relieved here and there with luxuriant ivy. Alas, Mrs. Armstrong, hale though she appeared, has since passed to the majority. How often I have seen her wending her way on Sundays to the old parish church, a bright example to all of us. Often she used to come in when I was alone in the evening, to have a crack with me, as she expressed it in her Northumbrian dialect, and talk about her milch cows and the farm in general. She was always cheerful, and never growled about the bad times as many farmers are wont to do. She was up with her daughters at five o'clock in the morning, helping to despatch the milk-cart to Penrith. She was always pleased to hear of our good sport, especially when a big salmon was weighed in the kitchen, and she condoled with us when the sport was bad. We all felt Frenchfield like home, for we always received a warm welcome there.

On Monday the 20th, alas, there was a heavy worm-water—much to my disappointment, as I wished to give the trout a fair try with the fly in the month of June, and to L.'s gratification, as he wished for a heavy slaughter with the worm or the minnow. Contrary to my usual custom I was only provided with a light split cane rod of eleven feet, very unsuitable for worm or minnow. As Mr. L. with his long pole established himself in Paley's Walk, I took possession of the Weir Pool in which I killed 21 trout with the worm.

Being then rather tired of the monotony of the worm in a flood, I went to the Bridge Pool for a try with the minnow, with which I there killed 7 trout and missed many runs—I think in consequence of my rod being so light—and I had the mortification of missing several beauties. I wound up at four o'clock with 28 trout, weight 10 lb. 7 oz. Mr. L. at the same time, ably assisted by Mrs. L., who is accomplished in the manipulation of the landing-net, had creeled 50 trout in

Paley's Walk, and they joined me at dinner, after which I returned home. Mr. L., however, was again on the war-path in the evening, and somewhat increased the total of his slaughter. Is man ever satisfied? Thus in two days and an evening I basketed 68 trout, weight 21 lb. 10 oz., and returned home quite satisfied.

But the angler must not for a moment suppose that such

CROWN HOTEL, EAMONT BRIDGE.

fair creels of trout are the common thing on the Eamont, and I will proceed to give illustrations. The spring of 1893 was an early one, but unfortunately the rainfall in March and April was next to nothing. The water was in fair order until about the commencement of the season, then when the angler hoped for warm showers he was doomed to disappointment.

On the 22nd of March I put up at the Crown Hotel,

Eamont Bridge, about a mile and a half from Penrith, on the Ullswater road. Eamont Bridge is an interesting little village, the greater part of which stands on a fork formed by the rivers Eamont and Lowther, which run very near one another for about three-quarters of a mile. The little village is extremely well provided with public-houses, there being about four. The ancient mounds are interesting to the antiquarian, and it would appear that in days in the far past large assemblies of people were held there for the same or similar reasons which even now draw the people of Manxland to Tynwald Hill. A short distance from the village is the entrance to Lowther Park and Lowther Castle, the principal seat of the Earl of Lonsdale, and near by a handsome bridge over the Lowther.

The windows of the Crown Hotel command a pretty view of Brougham Hall, standing on a wooded eminence above the river. Lord Brougham is extremely popular with the farmers in the district; he bears the reputation of being an excellent practical farmer, and his shorthorns are famous. Visitors at the Crown may fish in Lord Brougham's portion of the Lowther, and Lord Lonsdale is very generous in giving permission for his portion of the Lowther below Garden Bridge, a distance of at least two miles. Eamont Bridge, therefore, is a very convenient place for members of the Yorkshire Anglers' Association to put up at. Fishing down one river as far as Brougham mill-dam, the angler can fish up the other river back to his quarters.

At the inn I was pleased to meet with, on my arrival, Mr. William Exley and Mr. Harold Salt, a grandson of the late Sir Titus Salt, Bart. Mr. Salt, who is a good musician, delighted us in the evenings with songs and some brilliant performances on the piano. Mr. Exley had had good sport on the day of my arrival—23 trout of more than the average size. The weather had been dull. That night there was a very sharp frost, and the meadows were white with hoarfrost until ten o'clock. The sun shone all day from a cloudless sky, and it felt quite hot. There was hardly a fly on the water. About twelve o'clock a short rise came on, and I killed 6 nice trout on the yellow snipe and winter brown, but before two o'clock the rise was totally over. The weather next day was just the same, and I had to be satisfied with 2 trout.

On the third day I decided to change the scene, so I drove about three miles down the river and began at Whinfell Dub. This is an excellent reach under favourable conditions, and a man might well pass a whole day there and the stream at the head of it. About the best portion is where the water commences to get shallow, and thence right down until the water glides into the broad rough stream below. The weather continued the same steely bright, but I managed to kill 5 trout in the dub, and although I fished up to Frenchfield, I only creeled 2 more. In my three days I only killed 15 trout, weight 5 lb. As April advanced the river got lower and lower, and the day temperature in the shade averaged about 68° and there was literally no fly on the water.

On the 20th I fished with fly and creeper, but only caught one trout with fly. While fishing with creeper I caught nothing but parr. The following day I killed one trout with fly—the parr again worried my creepers—and the third day I scored a blank. Thus I actually killed 2 trout in three days, at the very best time of the year. I saw three mature stone-flies. Fishing with the fly was useless, and the parr would not allow the trout a chance with the creeper. The up-stream minnow would probably have been deadly, but it could not be fished until the 6th of June.

What a wretched season 1893 was! In July I inveigled my esteemed friend Mr. Charles Anderton to accompany me to Frenchfield, under delusive promises of no end of sport with worm and minnow. He swallowed the bait, and we hoped that the trout would do the same, but Jove was preparing his thunderbolts for our confusion; there were fire, hailstones, and rain in the land during the four days we were there.

Saturday the 8th was a day to be remembered. The weather was excessively close and hot. There were skirmishing outbursts until about three o'clock, and then Cross Fell was enveloped in indigo-blue, and an incessant roll of distant thunder was heard. The elements looked so awful that I beat a retreat to Frenchfield before the advancing disturbance. I was soon joined by my good friend. Appalling darkness came on and a mighty hurricane. Branches of trees were blown through the air, and the house was shaken; for half an hour the lightning flashed incessantly, and the thunder and wind roared and crashed, and rain mingled with large hailstones fell in torrents; and after the storm there was a great calm, and the air was so cool and sweet. A walk in Carlton Park showed the immense fury of the tempest: trees torn up by the roots, to which tons of earth clung—some trees snapped off in the middle. The vortex of the storm appeared to have followed the river upwards. There were storms on three successive days, the extent of our visit. The two days and one evening produced the magnificent total of ten trout. Could we have stayed a little longer after the vengeance of

Jove had been appeased, we should probably have done great things, but it is ever so. The man with plenty of leisure gathers the eggs.

When the water is in fairly normal condition, there is often good sport with fly during summer evenings and nights, but real night fishing is not often practised. On one occasion Mr. W., incited by his friend Mr. T., resolved to make a night

RED SCAR STREAM.

of it. He commenced with small fly at nine o'clock, and when it got as dark as it would get he put up the lustard, then when day dawned he laboured with the up stream worm until six o'clock—result, an excellent appetite and a determination not to do it again.

From 1887 to 1897 inclusive (I did not fish in 1894 for trout) the result of my fishing was—

Fly.	Worm.	Stone-fly.	Minnow.	Total.	Weight.
706	65	9	43	823	244 lb. 14 oz.

The flies with which the trout were caught were purple snipe, yellow snipe, yellow dun, blue partridge, light and dark March brown, yellow woodcock, Greenwell's Glory, orange dark woodcock, blue dun, woodcock March brown, orange partridge, black spider, iron-blue dun, hare-lug, winter brown, Broughton Point, yellow partridge, brown owl.

CHAPTER XXVI

SALMON FISHING IN THE EAMONT

First you shall observe that usually he stays not long in a place, as trouts will, but covets still to go nearer the spring-head.—PISCATOR.

THERE is little use in trying for salmon in the Eamont until the month of October, when the floods in a normal season enable the fish to get over Armathwaite Weir in the Eden. If the floods are late the salmon are late, and occasionally it happens that the salmon do not arrive in the Eamont until the end of the season, the 15th of November. Although there may be plenty of fish in the river, the sport is very uncertain, and if a man can average one fish in three days, he need be satisfied. If the water is high the fish are on the run, and will not take anything. The best time is when the water is of a medium height; then they become somewhat settled in the pools, and are inclined to toy with the fly.

The following extracts from my diary illustrate the uncertainty of the sport:—

19th October 1893.—Fished from the Weir Pool to One Tree Stream, from 3 to 5.30, and had not a rise; good clear water.

20th.—Commenced in the Red Pool near the bottom of the

Lowther. This pool is under a red rock, and the stream swirls thereunder and then comes round with an eddy. I cast from the low side into the swirl and let the fly come down until it came back with the eddy. After several casts, when the fly reached the slack water, there was a splash. I instinctively struck, the line tightened, and I was fast in a lively fish; after some play I succeeded in gaffing the fish, which turned out to be a cock fish of 8 lb. He was caught with a small Popham.

I then fished as far as the Red Cliff Pool in the Eamont, and did not rise a fish. Three more men were out and did not rise a fish.

21st.—Fished from the Weir Pool to the bottom of the Association waters; no rise.

23rd.—The same; no rise. Mr. Lupton killed an 8 lb. hen fish in the Red Scar Pool, on a small Jock Scott.

9th November.—Fished from 3 to 5.15; did not see a salmon.

10th.—Began at Red Cliff Pool in the Lowther, and fished to Whinfell Dub; saw several salmon rise. Weather cloud and sunshine, gusty north-east wind.

11th.—My last day this season. Fished all the water without a rise, then on returning up the river, I decided to try the Red Scar Pool again. This is a rather long shallow pool headed by a rough stream, which in the end slackens under the far bank, above which there is a high red cliff. This is a favourite lie for the fish. I began at the top and fished to the very tail, which terminates in a rough stream. At the last possible cast there was a tug, and I was fast. Raine, the keeper, soon gaffed the fish, which was a hen of 8 lb. It was then past three o'clock. The wasp did the business.

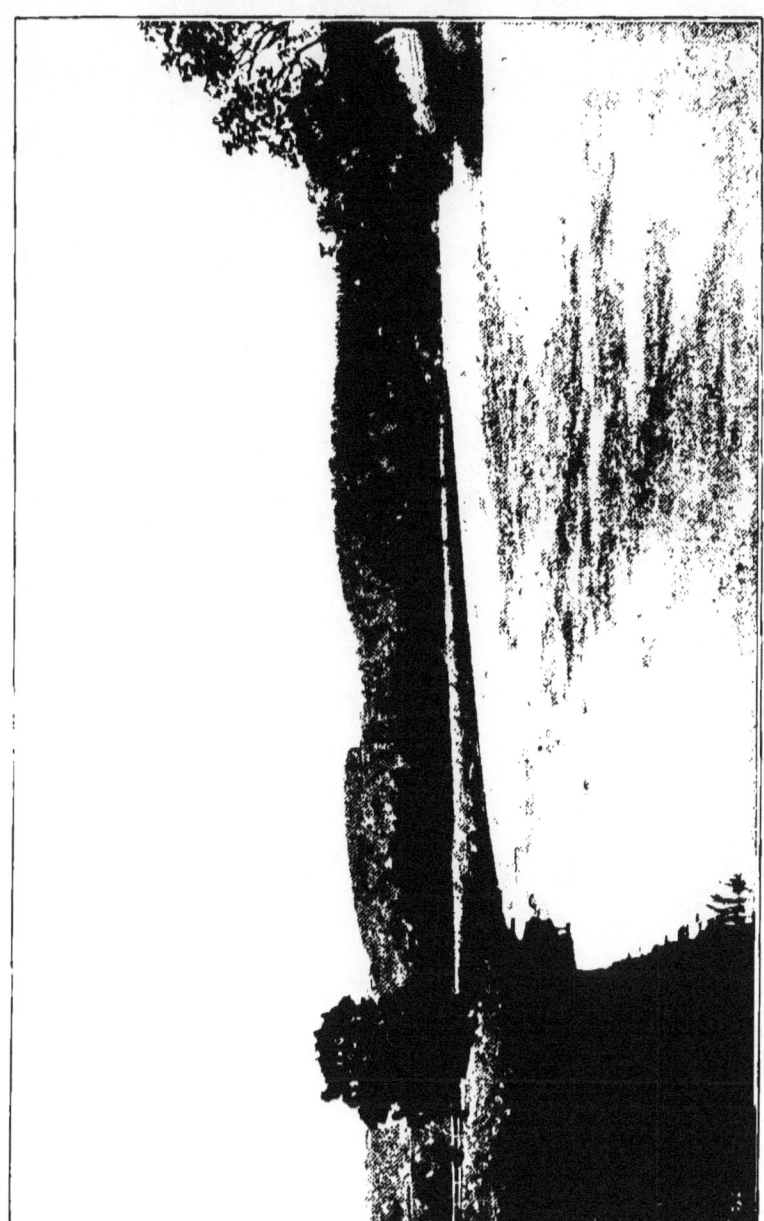

ROBSON'S ROCK.

In 1894 not a salmon was caught, the floods came too late. In 1895 there was considerable execution done. On the 4th of November I journeyed to Frenchfield. I fished from three to five, but did not see any signs of fish. The water was decidedly low—too much so, it appeared to me, for sport, but the unexpected happens.

Tuesday, 5th.—There had been a sharp frost during the night, and there was a dense fog until half-past nine o'clock, and after that the weather was cloudy, with occasional gleams of sunshine. It was a lovely day for November, but the water was low and clear. I did not trouble to send for the keeper. I commenced at the Red Pool in the Lowther, but the water was far too low for it. I then fished the Weir Pool, although the keeper always said it was no good; then the Castle Stream, which bears the same character, but half-way down there was a welcome tug, and I was fast. I was on the Castle side; Brougham Bridge was only about thirty yards below me, and if the fish got below the arches, I could not follow him. Close by, out of the current, there is a sort of bay formed for watering cattle. I must lead the fish into the bay and keep him there; this I succeeded in doing, and I soon gaffed a nice cock fish which weighed $8\frac{1}{2}$ lb. He had taken a medium Jock Scott. I then fished to the Red Scar Pool without anything happening. About the middle of the pool, just above where a stone projects into the stream, I was again fast, and after some good play which made me hot and my back ache, I gaffed a 10 lb. cock salmon.

I was glad to sit down to lunch and enjoy a smoke. In about half an hour I was again at it, and after a few casts hooked a fish near the same place. I soon saw that he was something big. It was not long before he sprang out of the water and revealed his size—upwards of 20 lb. He rushed up the pool, then down, lashed the water with his tail, now and then making great jumps. How I longed for the keeper to gaff him. Three-quarters of an hour passed, and the fight still continued. At length he appeared to give in, and was inclined to roll on his side. I wound up line and

RED SCAR.

was preparing for the gaff, when all of a sudden he gave a mighty plunge, and all was over; he had broken my cast at the top loop-knot and appropriated my medium Jock Scott. So the day ended. Mental note: seek up the keeper next time. At night rain fell.

On Wednesday the weather was very windy with slight showers, and there was about a foot of fresh water down. The water was so full of fallen leaves that at almost every cast a leaf was hooked, and I had not a rise.

Thursday was a lovely day, such a contrast to the previous day. The keeper and I walked down to the Udford length—we had just taken the water from Sir Richard Musgrave. After a beautiful walk of about two miles across the fields, frequently flushing coveys of partridges and a few pheasants, and rousing a few hares, we came to a bank with a stile over it. "Now," said the keeper, "we ought to sit down here, smoke a pipe and admire the view." The view is beautiful, in a sort of ravine below us the river with well-wooded surroundings both up and down. Many of the trees were still covered with leaves bearing autumnal tints of varied hue. There were also the browning bracken, the hawthorn, mountain-ash, and wild-rose laden with red berries. These contrasted with the dark Scotch fir. On the east the Pennine range. On the west the Lake Mountains. As we smoked our pipes in the bright sunshine, swarms of flies fluttered about, as though it were a summer day. All was peaceful and serene.

The water was just in nice order; there were rims of rising trout here and there, but I never saw or felt a salmon until I had fished about a mile down. In the Island Pool or Flat a salmon rose right across the river, but about ten yards beyond the extent of my cast. After a little casting in the direction of the fish, he rose again only about three yards beyond the cast; the next cast, and almost at once the welcome tug. After some nice play, during which the fish sprang several times out of the water, Raine gaffed a nice 12 lb. hen fish. I did not get another rise. In the evening I was joined by my friend Mr. J. Sutcliffe Jennings, who was anxious to obtain distinction amongst the salmon. I have no doubt that he would ensure distinction if shooting salmon were allowed, as he is a crack shot from a tomtit to a driven snipe.

On the 8th I began at the Weir Pool and Mr. Jennings at Frenchfield Dub, and we fished down to Whinfell Dub. We saw several fish move, but never a tug did we get. I caught two trout. I believe I could have filled a creel with small fly, they were rising so.

On Saturday, our last day, I determined to give the Lowther a good try, and I did, but it was no use. I did not see a sign of a fish. I finished the day below Brougham Bridge on the Frenchfield side, and there was friend Jennings opposite. There were several large fish rising, and sometimes they were close to our flies, but it was no good; the fish were clearly on the run for domestic purposes.

The autumn of 1896 was very good for salmon; the freshes in October brought up plenty of fish. I arrived at Frenchfield on the 2nd of November. I fished for about two hours on the arrival day below Frenchfield Wood on the Frenchfield side, and had one pull in One Tree Stream.

On Tuesday I commenced in the Castle Stream with medium silver gray; the water was in nice order, quite clear, but plenty of it. I fished with the same fly to Red Cliff Pool, and had my first touch, a faint one, there. It then occurred to me that my fly might be too small, so I put up a silver gray a good deal larger. I retraced my steps to the long stream above, which I had just fished very carefully. In a few casts I was fast in a fish; and as it was an awkward place to gaff a fish in, I pulled him about 100 yards down to the Red Scar, and there gaffed a 10 lb. hen fish.

I then went down to Robson's Rock, intending to lunch in the hut. I got to the hut at ten minutes to two o'clock, and thought I would just have a cast in the pool before lunch, and I did so. After a very few casts I was fast in a good fish.

The bank on which I stood bristled with woodwork to keep up the bank; should a fish once get under the bank it would be all up with him —I mean the angler. I at once decided upon the exact place in which to gaff the fish. However, the fish did not show any inclination to come near my side; he spent most of his time in a slack stream outside a strong

THE HUT.

stream. He made several bolts down, several up, and some to the other side. So time passed; an hour had gone, and the fish in the same position; an hour and a half had gone. I pulled him down a few yards, then I made him tack up to the fatal spot, but no, off he went for the last time; one more tack up and he lay on his side, then the gaff, and, hurrah! a good 14 lb. cock fish, after an hour and three-quarters' play. It was then close on four o'clock, and I had not tasted since breakfast; to the hut and lunch, and then I had to carry

24 lb. of fish to Frenchfield, nearly two miles. The weather was fine and frosty.

On the next day, Wednesday, Mr. Henry Bradshaw was also fishing, and Raine knocked about between us. There had been about eight degrees of frost the previous night, and it froze nearly all day; but the sun was out, so it was very pleasant. I began at Frenchfield Dub, and fished down to Red Scar without a rise; there I found Mr. Bradshaw at it. Raine accompanied me to Robson's Rock and there waited for some time in expectation of something happening, but nothing did just then, so I had a smoke in the hut, and Raine trotted off in hopes that Mr. Bradshaw might have got into difficulties. My smoke having concluded I would have another try before lunch. I saw a salmon rise right across the river; to reach him I had to throw straight across, and it was a long cast. Almost at the time of alighting the line stuck; I gave a pull down and I was fast. It was then half-past one o'clock. The fish was much inclined to remain on the other side. In about half an hour Bradshaw and Raine came on the scene, but the fight still lasted. Mr. Bradshaw was very kind; he offered me whisky and much good advice. "Give it him hard," he said, but I would not be hurried. At the end of an hour and twenty-five minutes Raine gaffed for me a 14 lb. cock fish.

After I had refreshed it was time to retrace our steps, so we walked up together. As we were passing along the stream above Red Scar we saw a fish rise, and Bradshaw went for him, having Raine in reserve. I paddled up to Frenchfield Dub; before commencing the attack I sat down to rest. After a few casts I was fast in a nice fish. There was no strong current to contend with, and after about fifteen minutes' play I gaffed a 14 lb. hen fish, and just as I was hauling her out, Mr. Bradshaw and the keeper came up. After a few more casts I had a great pull, and he was off. What luck!

It is all luck, or accident, fishing for salmon. Mr. Bradshaw had fished all day without success. Both the fish fell to a medium silver gray. On Thursday there was an intense frost. I wasted a lot of time in the Lowther, then went down the Eamont, and when I reached the Red Scar I found Bradshaw in distress, and the reserve had not come up. I gave him a lot of advice. I sat down and munched my sandwich, washed down with cold tea—real cold tea, not K.C.T.

On receiving a command from the General Commanding-in-Chief, I waded out to the front, but the enemy thought fit to retreat, so I returned to the bank to my cold tea and a pipe. After some time the enemy again came to the front, and I was ordered by the Commander-in-Chief to advance at the point of the gaff, which I did, and after some smart manœuvring directed by the Commander in person, the enemy was defeated at the point of the gaff. "What a beauty he is," said the Commander, as he viewed the fish on the grass. "He is indeed," I said; "in the very pink of condition." He was a cock of some eighteen pounds or so in weight. I went down to Robson's Rock, but it was no good; the day began, continued, and ended in nothing.

On Friday Mr. Bradshaw loafed on his laurels. I fished to redeem mine, but it was not to be. I had one rise in Red Scar, and another in Robson's Rock. The frost was intense. As I returned to the farm my line froze to the rod, and my waders were stiff with ice. Frost remained on the windows all day, and on the morrow it rained as I returned home. I was well content. In four days I had killed 4 salmon, weight 52 lb., and one may easily go farther and fare worse.

Mr. Bradshaw greatly distinguished himself, either after or before my departure, or some time or other. Rumour said that in Frenchfield Dub he rose three salmon in three casts, but only landed one of them, the reserve not having come to the front in time to be of service. However, he covered himself with immortal honour; he had ten salmon to his credit. Now he has only to kill an eagle, a stag, and a seal to earn "Ye Hunter's Badge" (*The Moor and the Loch*, Colquhoun).

AT FRENCHFIELD, OCTOBER 1897.

CHAPTER XXVII

WALES—THE WNION, THE ARTRO, LYNN OGWEN

Bless me, what mountains are here? Are we not in Wales?—VIATOR.

THE month of May 1891. *La Grippe* had been raging, and my eldest son and I had been amongst the invalids. Change of air we must have, to restore our debilitated frames. An excursion to Dolgelly and Barmouth was decided upon. After the manner of anglers I had convinced myself that walking about in waders was the only restorative. So onward we sped along the vale of Dee, past beautiful Llangollen, with the river foaming between the rocks and shaded by the youthful green of the overhanging woods; then on past Bala Lake with the coots sitting on the water regardless of the snorts of our iron steed. On and on we go past the Berwyn Mountains, and after leaving the watershed of the Dee we descend the vale of the Wnion from about its source: how likely the river looked as it rushed through rocks with a whirl, and then meandered through rich green meadows so quietly as if it had never frothed and foamed over the boulders.

It was the first hot day of the season, and we felt quite baked on our journey. Little did we think that intense frost and snow were being got ready for us, the bonny month of

May though it was. We put up at that most comfortable hotel The Golden Lion, my good wife, my son, and myself. How hot it was far into the night—the valley was like an oven! We longed to scale Cader Idris to enjoy the cool air on the top. How grand the mountain looked, with its well-defined jagged outline against the blue sky! On the morrow the sun shone from a cloudless sky; it was hotter than ever. We could only crawl about, we all felt done up with the heat. I just managed to crawl about a mile down the river to see how it looked, and it did look most tempting—a nice water of a pale ale colour.

I interviewed a fishmonger near the bridge, who was entrusted with the sale of licences to fish. He did not give me much encouragement; he said I had come too late for the trout, and too early for the sewin or sea-trout. Alas, it was ever thus! I never go to any strange place at the right time. However, I procured a licence for the following day, and hoped for the best.

In the afternoon we proceeded by rail to Barmouth along the lovely estuary of the Mawddach. It was low water, and we saw some shell-ducks on the sands. The old mansion of Arthog Hall, which is now a sporting hotel, with shooting and fishing attached, looked very pretty among the trees. The estuary is crossed by a wooden bridge, and we are soon at Barmouth. From our apartments we had a charming view of the estuary and the Cader Idris range, also of the steep woods which clothe the sides of the estuary.

On the following day the weather was much cooler. I proceeded by train to Dolgelly, and soon donned my restorative waders, and wended my way down the river, as I intended to fish up and commence from the junction of the

Mawddach and Wnion. When I had got out of the shelter
of the woods to where the river was open I met such an icy
blast from the north-west that I was glad to seek the shelter
of the woods. Oh, how cold it was just round the bend, and
how cosy the other side of it. However, the water was in
very nice order, and the formation of the river all that could
be desired, a very perfection of a trout stream. There appeared to be no reason why it should not contain fine trout;
but the angler should never expect to find trout numerous in
any small stream infested by the voracious sea-trout at certain
seasons of the year. There can be no doubt that sea-trout
and salmon devour all the trout they can get hold of, by
which means the trout are well kept down. I soon discovered
that the trout were small and certainly not numerous. I
fished from ten o'clock to half-past two and captured eleven
trout, the largest of which weighed seven ounces, and the rest
were much smaller.

On the following morning, Friday, the 15th of May, the
mountains were covered with snow, and presented a most
picturesque appearance—such a contrast to the green woods.
The weather was bitterly cold, worthy of the month of
January. On several occasions snow fell on the mountains,
and a little fell even in the valley.

Having been informed that there was good fishing in the
river Artro, which flows into the sea near Pensarn Station, I
decided to try it. Accordingly on Saturday I proceeded by
rail to Pensarn, whence I walked to the village of Llanbedr,
about a mile from the station, and I ascertained at the post
office that the water was divided into two sections. From
Aberartro Bridge to the sea the charge for the season was
£1 : 1s., and no short-time permits were granted. Above

Aberartro Bridge weekly permits were granted, and I was informed that in the lower section there was fair sea-trout fishing after July. As there was then no chance of sea-trout, I decided to fish above the bridge. At the bridge two streams unite and form the main Artro river. I had to walk at least a mile to Aberantro Bridge. At this point the banks of both streams are densely wooded. I decided to fish in the larger stream of the two. The streams were very low, and owing to the bitterly cold weather there was an almost total absence of fly.

Not knowing the river, I lost much time fishing in a dense gloomy wood for about half a mile, above which the valley was open and more likely for trout. I fished from about half-past eleven to a quarter to four o'clock and only captured three very wee trout, and I came to the conclusion that the stream was more suitable for worm than fly, so on Tuesday the 19th I again proceeded to the Artro provided with a bag of worms. I commenced at eleven o'clock with worm, with which I contrived to lure one trout, but not another bite could I get; so I changed to fly, and with fly killed ten trout. They were all very small, and I came to the conclusion that the Artro was not worth fishing.

As I had to walk at least two miles from the station before I commenced to fish, much time was taken up in walking. However, the scenery is very pretty and repaid me for my trouble. The weather was certainly very unfavourable for sport; water dead low, and the weather very bright and cold. I had not one condition in my favour. The lower portion of the river may be worthy of notice after July, during a run of sea-trout, but I am pretty sure that the trout fisher must be content with an average of about eight to the pound or less.

On the 21st I again betook myself to the Wnion, and again fished the water below Dolgelly, commencing at eleven o'clock and winding up at half-past four. The water was low and clear. Weather, cloud and sunshine. I managed to capture eighteen trout with fly, the best of which weighed five ounces. I tried up-stream worm, but I could not get even a bite.

On the 23rd I decided to try the Wnion above Dolgelly, and I commenced about eleven o'clock and wound up at five with twenty trout all caught with fly. The river is a beautiful combination of pools and streams which apparently ought to contain good trout, and the scenery is most charming. The best trout only weighed a quarter of a pound, and I did not see any good trout in the river. I returned many very small trout to their native element. However, it was very delightful to wander about in the green meadows, and gaze on mighty Cader Idris with its jagged sky-line, and derive benefit from the pure bracing air. How often it appears that small trout are associated with grand romantic surroundings, and the mighty ones with tame scenery. It is thus that the angler has his compensation. If the trout be small he can feast his eyes on the everlasting hills and crags, and appreciate his own littleness amid the mighty works of nature; he can speculate on the infinity of time and space, on the ages which have passed since the earth was without form and void, and when stillness reigned over the face of the waters.

I shall ever remember how beautiful Cader Idris looked on the evening of Wednesday the 20th of May. For several hours in the afternoon the mountain was obscured by a heavy snow-storm. As the sun was about setting, the snow-clouds lifted, and the rays of the setting sun shone on the top of the mountain, making the newly fallen snow look pink, with many gradations of gorgeous colouring as the sun got lower and lower and finally sank in the western sea, until in the end the snow formed, as it were, a spotless white robe over the mountain.

On Whitsunday we ascended the craggy height behind Barmouth, whence we had a splendid view of the estuary of the Mawddach, which presented the appearance of a beautiful lake surrounded by overhanging woods and crags, with Cader Idris looking over all, at times hidden by passing snow-showers. This view is well named the Panorama, and a lovely one it is.

Lynn Ogwen

Lynn Ogwen is a celebrated trouting lake about four miles from Capel Curig. The late Mr. Henry Gleadhall of Kilnsey fame made some famous baskets of trout with the wren-tail, much to the edification of the natives. Being in Wales in August 1888, my friend Mr. Charles Anderton and I decided to have a day on the lake. I made some wren-tails for the occasion, and in order to ensure success I purchased some certain local killers at a shop in Capel Curig. Of course they were large. I provided myself with two rods, one of fifteen feet for the local flies, and the other of ten and a half feet for my own small flies on hair. It was the 21st of August. The weather was showery with a considerable quantity of wind, just the sort of a day for big flies. About half-past ten we embarked in a small boat. I commenced with the long rod and the large flies, but could not raise a fish. After some time I tried the short rod with small flies attached to a drawn-gut cast, and among them the wren-tail. With this cast I caught two trout, but neither of them on the wren-tail. I then put up a hair cast, the flies attached being black spider, red spinner, and yellow water-hen (blue dun), and therewith killed seven more trout, making only nine in all. From time to time I tried the large flies, but they were utterly useless. I also tried a Devon minnow, but to no purpose. The trout weighed 2 lb. 4 oz., or just a quarter of a pound on the average. The trout were very yellow and well fed, and cut up pink when cooked, and their flavour was excellent.

I was informed that April and May were the best months. The lake is very much fished, and no doubt as the season advances the trout get more and more shy.

CHAPTER XXVIII

THE NIDD

Well, scholar, you must endure worse luck some time, or you will never make a good angler.—PISCATOR.

THE river Nidd takes its source between the mountains of Great Whernside and Little Whernside, and flows between the rivers Ure and Wharfe. The upper part of Nidderdale has been called the Switzerland of Yorkshire from its romantic beauty. Until Pateley Bridge is reached all or most of the fishing rights are in private hands, Mr. Yorke of Bewerly Hall being the principal proprietor. Below Pateley Bridge both the middle-class angler and the working-man may, to a considerable extent, enjoy the sport of fishing, either by leave from the proprietors or farmers, or by being members of one of the angling clubs. Harrogate may be styled the key to Nidderdale, because the angler may, by means of the Nidderdale railway, have easy access to all portions of the river between Ripley and Pateley Bridge. Harrogate is so fortunate as to possess two angling clubs, the Harrogate Conservative Angling Association and the Harrogate Angling Association—the difference between which, a witty mayor of Harrogate at one of the annual dinners of one of the associa-

BIRSTWITH WEIR, NIDD.

tions is reported to have stated, consisted, he opined, in the object of the former association being the conservation or preservation of fish, and that of the latter their destruction.

Captain Greenwood of Swarcliffe, Birstwith, is the proprietor of most of the river between Darley Beck and about three-quarters of a mile below Hampsthwaite Bridge; and through his liberality members of the Harrogate Conservative Angling Association may fish in the water below Hampsthwaite Bridge, which is a very pretty water indeed. Captain Greenwood reserves his water between Darley Beck and New Bridge for himself and his personal friends; and he permits a limited number of general friends to fish below New Bridge. Captain Greenwood is a good type of an English country gentleman, and while fond of sport himself he likes others also to enjoy it. His residence is charmingly situated on an eminence, from which there is a beautiful view down the river for some miles. The principal fish in this part of the Nidd are trout and grayling.

The members of the Harrogate Conservative Angling Association may fish in the Nidd between some distance above Dacre and a short distance above Darley Beck. As the banks are high and the bed of the river much encumbered with large stones, the fishing is somewhat arduous. Below Hampsthwaite Bridge the fishing is very pleasant, and although one may not in the course of five or six hours' fishing capture more than half-a-dozen fish, the man of moderate views as to the quantum that constitutes sport may fully enjoy himself rod in hand.

Captain Greenwood very wisely allows fishing with the artificial fly only, in his waters. In the other waters of the club the members may fish with any lawful lure they please, and maggot is a favourite bait in the summer. So far as my

T

experience goes the trout do not take the clear-water worm well, and I have not yet descended to the maggot or wasp grub. I have never succeeded in killing more than ten trout in a day with the fly in the Nidd, and I believe that really good baskets are very exceptional. There is no doubt that there are some good fish, but the average size appears to be smaller than that of the Wharfe, as 131 trout captured by me only weighed 36 lb. 8 oz.; but my experience has not been very great.

The Harrogate anglers are keen sportsmen, and some of them hold that the fishing in the Nidd is second to none in the broad country. However, there is nothing like a man being satisfied with that which he hath. There is a deal of luck or something of the kind in fishing. Mr. Henry Gleadhall of Kilnsey fame used to say that the duffer often brought in the best creel. I have been singularly unfortunate in this the Diamond Jubilee year of Her Most Gracious Majesty in my excursions up the Nidderdale; rude Boreas has blown his bellows to my confusion on nearly every occasion—wind, wind, wind. Most anglers at some period of their career are in luck; they are the top-sawyers and get a bit conceited; but the time always comes when they tumble from their high pedestal and find their own level.

In the Diamond Jubilee month of September I had two instances of the manner in which trout persist in picking out a particular fly, in exclusion of the others. It is well known that the red spider is good both for trout and grayling in September. I make it thus: a feather from the outside of a landrail's wing hackled on a body of yellow silk, head bronze peacock harl. On the former day, the 11th of September, my cast was made up as follows: tail fly, red spider; first dropper, watery yellow dun; second dropper, black spider. I captured ten trout, nine on the red spider and one on the yellow dun. On the latter day, the 15th of September, my cast was made up in the same manner, with the exception that the tail fly was a brown owl—ruddy feather from a brown owl hackled on a body of yellow silk, head bronze peacock harl. I soon caught two small trout, which I returned to the water, on the black spider. I then replaced the tail fly with the black spider, and fished with the brown owl as the second dropper, and in the result I killed six trout with the black spider. It was one of my unlucky days. I missed a considerable number of fish. On both days there were about the same flies on the water.

CHAPTER XXIX

TROUT FISHING IN THE ISLE OF MAN—THE SULBY RIVER

> From near the centre, not unlike a house,
> The sloping hills run chiefly north and south.
> *Ellan Vannin,* 1760.

TAKING into consideration the limited area of the Isle of Man, its streams are of fair size. The principal streams have their source in the mountains about the middle of the island, which culminate in Snaefell, 2034 feet above sea-level. The rainfall is very heavy among the mountains, and this accounts for the bountiful volume of the streams of Mona as compared with islands of similar area without ranges of mountains.

The Sulby river is the largest river in the island. It drains the south and west slopes of Snaefell, the north and west slopes of Beinn-y-Phott (1772 feet), and some adjacent mountains. Between Ramsey and Sulby Bridge, about four miles by the road, the river has a very sinuous course and long stretches of calm water. It then becomes a rapid brawling stream, excellent for both fly and worm fishing. The lower part of the river is good for sea-trout in spring and autumn, and there are also salmon. At Lezayre the river receives an important tributary, Glen Auldyn.

Glen Auldyn is a most beautiful vale. The scenery is sweetly pretty from Ramsey to Sulby Bridge. On the left hand or south side as you proceed from Ramsey, there is a steep range of hills much planted. The low land is also extensively planted. Lezayre Church with its ivy-clad walls, standing amid tall trees, has a most picturesque appearance. A little above Sulby Bridge the vale becomes a narrow glen with very

THE ROAD TO ELLAN VANNIN.

steep sides and occasional plantations, and there are numerous deep pools and cascades. The first deep pool of importance is called the "Bull's Pool," where the deep rocky pools may be said to begin. About four miles up the glen from Sulby there is a waterfall in a tributary stream called Thol-ty-Will, the neighbourhood of which is much planted and has been made into a pleasure resort. In the season a good luncheon or dinner can be obtained there, washed down by anything from beer to champagne. The higher portions of the river are described in Chapter IV.

I have fished in the Sulby from time to time since 1859, and the sport has generally been good. I used to walk from the village of Onchan to about the neighbourhood of Thol-ty-Wull, about eight miles, and also walk back in the evening; it was a tiring day and no mistake. I well remember being lost with a friend on the mountains, on a return from a fishing excursion. It was in the month of September. My old friend Ambrose and I started from Onchan about five o'clock in the morning. It was a lovely morning and we much enjoyed the walk by Keppel Gate, which may be said to be the gate of the mountainous region; thence there is heather, varied by bent and rushes. A mile or so forward there are four lane-ends, the one straight on leading to Snaefell, the one to the right to Laxey, and the one to the left to Druidale. We always enjoyed the walk to the fishing ground when we were fresh, and full of anticipation; the return was different, when we were jaded and longed for the rest of home.

We reached the river about eight o'clock, and parted for the day, as was our wont, and arranged to meet at the junction of the Snaefell stream with the main stream at six o'clock—our fishing days were long when we were young. Our sport was good, and we both had good panniers of trout to carry home. At six o'clock we met, and a difference of opinion arose as to our best way home. I insisted that the shortest way was to cross the foot of Beinn-y-Phott, and thus make direct for the four lane-ends. My friend insisted that the safer way was to make for the Snaefell road above us on the left, although it was an extremely steep ascent. As I was the more stupid of the two I prevailed, and we started. I had forgotten the gullies which serrate the slopes of Beinn-y-Phott, which we had to clamber down and up.

Darkness came on, and there was a thick haze which nearly amounted to a fog. We floundered in bogs often up to our knees, and we were lost. How we got to the four lane-ends I do not know, but we did get there, and when we got there we had no idea which was the right road to take. After much discussion we in the end took the wrong one. On and on we wandered, and we heard a dog bark; we followed the direction and came to a cottage, and we were informed that we were at the head of Laxey Glen, and that our best course was to proceed by way of Laxey, Laxey being six miles from Onchan. Between Laxey and Onchan we often had to sit down to rest by the roadside, and I twice fell asleep, and Ambrose had to awake me. In the end we reached Onchan at two o'clock in the morning, after being practically on our legs for about twenty-one hours—the most tiring day that I ever had in the whole course of my life—but we stuck to our precious trout.

As I only commenced to keep a regular fishing diary in the year 1878, I have not a complete record of the trout I captured before that date; but since and including that year, I have fished in the Sulby river on twenty-one days and captured 487 trout, but on at least eight of the days I only fished for a few hours. The largest number captured in one day was fifty, and then I began fishing at seven o'clock in the morning and wound up at a quarter to one. It may be said that trout in the Manx streams take worm well during the whole of the fishing season; the same cannot be said with regard to the fly, but they frequently take fly very freely. The stone-fly does not exist in the Manx streams, neither does the May-fly. There are not any minnows or loaches; there are sticklebacks and miller's-thumbs. Eels are numerous. There are no other freshwater fish except those I have named. There are the migratory salmonidæ. There are no water-ousels, so familiar on our English rivers; sandpipers are numerous in summer. It is more easy to capture a good basket of trout with the worm than with the fly, as the river, speaking generally, and especially when low, is more adapted for the worm up stream. Nevertheless, out of the 487 trout 208 were killed with fly, and generally in low water.

About the year 1884 the Manx Legislature passed an Act of Tynwald for the preservation of the insular freshwater fisheries. A Board of Conservators was appointed, and it became necessary to take out a licence to fish in the rivers of Man. This Act gave great umbrage to many of the farmers, who banded together and resolved that no person who had provided himself with a licence should be allowed to fish. Therefore the unhappy angler found himself in a dilemma; if he did not procure a licence he might be prosecuted, and if he had procured a licence he might be prosecuted for trespass.

On the 7th of September 1887, I had an experience of the temper of the worthy farmers. I arrived at Sulby Bridge about ten o'clock, having decided to commence operations in a pool in which I had killed an exceptionally fine trout the previous year. The day I refer to was the 19th of June 1886. Immediately below Sulby Bridge there is a rather long pool, made by a weir across the river; one side is fringed with willows, the other side is low. There was a strong wind blowing down the river. I was fishing with a horsehair cast, my tail fly being a small black spider. I cast close to the weir, against which wavelets were breaking. I felt something heavy, and found I was into the monarch of the pool. A

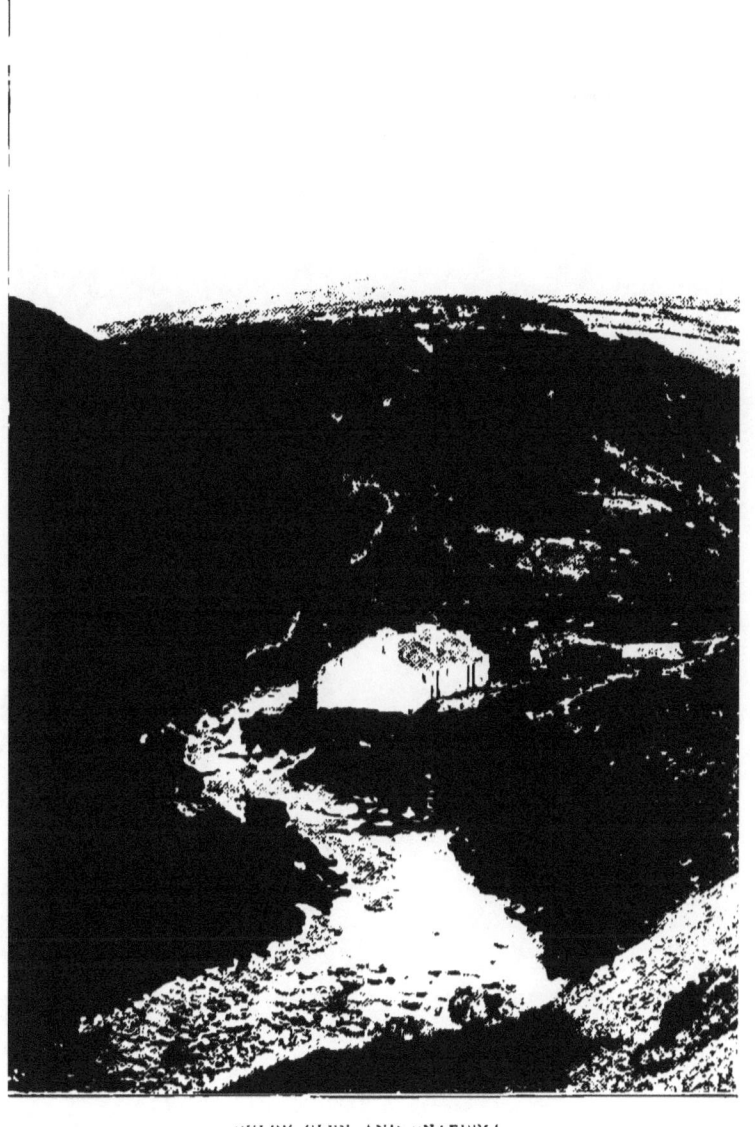

SULBY GLEN AND SNAEFELL.

few yards below was the mill-race, and if he should race down there, there would be a smash, so I pulled him gently up and he came up. He made a desperate rush towards the willows, so I was compelled to pull hard; the run was checked and he sprang high out of the water, and I then saw what a fine fish he was. After some more wild rushes in the direction of the willows, I in the end stranded him on a gravel bed which might have been made for the purpose (I had not a landing-net), and secured my prize, a trout of seventeen ounces in prime condition. I have not caught such a fine trout in Man since, and very likely never shall again. He had taken the black spider.

With recollections of this fish I had just begun to fish the pool in expectation or hopes of something good, when I heard a voice behind, which turned out to be that of Mr. Curphey, farmer and miller.

"Who gave you leave to fish here?"

I turned round and beheld a strong opposing force—a man and two youths armed with sticks, supported by two sheep-dogs—and replied mildly, "I did not know the river was preserved."

"I allow no one to fish here; it is my property," he replied.

"I have often fished here before, and never been stopped."

"It does not matter, I'll not allow you to fish here."

"Do you fish yourself?" I asked.

"No, I don't; I never handled a rod in my life."

"If you kept the fishing for yourself or your friends, there would be some reason in it. But surely I may fish; I've come from the middle of Yorkshire; my fishing can do you no harm."

"The fact is this," he said; "when you get the trout licence abolished you may fish as hard as you like, but until then no one shall fish."

"It is not my fault that your House of Keys made the law; surely I am not responsible for their Acts; I would rather not pay for a licence. However, I suppose I can go down the river; how far does your land extend?"

"There is no use in going down the river, as the next farmer will turn you off if he sees you."

"Well, I must go up, then."

And up I went, and had a mixed day with fly and worm, with which I killed thirty-six trout. Sometimes I confined myself to fly, and my best day with fly alone was thirty-six trout on the 2nd of June 1881.

Between nine and ten o'clock I wended my way from the railway station through the village of Sulby, hemmed in by hills to the south, and proceeded to an old mill, formerly occupied as a starch-mill. Where the mill-stream enters the river there is a splendid pool, shaded on one side by trees, under which the water runs in a smooth glide, just the place for feeding fish to lie awaiting the fly. My cast was a hair one; tail fly, black spider; dropper, orange partridge. I cast right under the trees in the gliding water, and was soon fast into a good fish, and a lively one he was, in the air, and up and down the pool. He might have been a pounder. At last I get him on to a gravel bed, and take him out with my hands, a beauty of half a pound. I account for several more fish in the same pool, but only half the size of the first fish. I then fish up some rapid streams, overhung with trees, and account for some more fish, and on up the lovely glen I wander catching a fish here and there. The weather was bright, and a nice north wind blowing up stream; it was a pleasure to be out on such a day, and admire the ferns and moss growing on the rocks.

But four o'clock comes and we are a good two miles from the station, so we wind up for the day and count our spoils—thirty-six lovely little Manx trout. What a monster the half-pounder looks amongst them all! We hard returned about the same

SULBY GLEN.

number to the water. We wend our way to the Sulby Glen Hotel and get a refreshing tea. The landlord yarns about the huge baskets of trout captured by a wandering Scotch angler, who fished for the wee Manx trout with a rod eighteen feet long, and we are off to the station and catch the train for Douglas. Having described a day with the respectable fly in the Sulby river, we will condescend to the miserable worm.

It was the Jubilee month of June 1887, the Jubilee of Her

Most Gracious Majesty Queen Victoria. My friend Robert and I decided to have a jubilee amongst the trout in the Sulby river, so we arrived at that most comfortable inn the Sulby Glen Hotel on the evening of Monday the 20th of June. We fished with fly in the evening, but for some reason only the wee anes would rise. We rose on the morrow—our Jubilee day—betimes. I despatched Robert about a mile up the river above the place where I intended to commence operations. I commenced in the run above the farthest dam up the river, about a mile from the hotel, at seven o'clock. The weather was intensely hot and cloudless, water dead low. For the first hour the trout came slowly, but after that time well, and trout after trout found their way into my creel. Up and up I fished, often between high rocks with ferns in their crevices, and under dense foliage. How delightful the cool shade amid the dripping rocks after the hot sun! In one beautiful spot especially, a high rock, bedecked here and there with mosses and ferns, quite overhung the stream, and in the dark pool underneath a good trout came to the creel—rather dark though, as trout caught in such places always are. As I emerge from this chasm-like spot, I am dazzled by the glaring sun. How beautiful the gorse looks, a mass of golden yellow!

After another chasm-like place, into which a cascade falls, I arrive at Thol-ty-Wull. I am tired and hot. It is a quarter to one o'clock. I turn out my spoils and count exactly fifty trout, my Jubilee day. I stroll into the pleasure grounds, and regale myself with cold lamb, washed down by a bottle of claret. Oh, what do the Manx fairies think of claret in the heart of Sulby Glen? Alas, where are the fairies now?

While enjoying a smoke under the shady trees, Robert appeared on the scene with a creel of forty trout, and we compared our spoils. Ten of mine were plump herring-sized fish, not bad for little Mona. Robert also had some nice fish. Soon we drive in our landlord's pony-phaeton to the hotel. A cup of tea, and we consign ourselves to the Manx train; for some distance of our journey the mountains of Man on our left, and the deep blue sea low down on our right. At St. Johns we change for Douglas, and Tynwald Hill is soon left far behind. We pass under the wooded rocks of Greeba, and Douglas is soon reached; and so our Jubilee fishing day ended, one of those pleasant days that always linger fondly in our memory.

CHAPTER XXX

THE DOUGLAS RIVER

> Now, Douglas in the centre of our land,
> The best by far we have at our command.
> *Ellan Vannin.*

THE second river in importance in the Isle of Man is the Douglas river, which is formed by the confluence of the rivers Dhoo and Glass. The junction of the two rivers is about three-quarters of a mile from Douglas. The name Dhoo signifies the black river, and the Glass the white river. Almost the whole of the Douglas river, or at any rate the part of it which flows through the Nunnery estate, is the property of Sir J. S. Goldie-Taubman, the Speaker of the House of Keys, and is strictly preserved; and the portion of the Dhoo which passes through the Kirby estate is preserved by Sir W. L. Drinkwater, Her Majesty's First Deemster.

The Dhoo takes its rise in the neighbourhood of Crosby, a pretty village near the rocky slopes of Greeba, about four miles from Douglas, for which distance it is fishable. It passes through a low flat plain, and is consequently somewhat sluggish. It receives tributaries from Greeba and from the somewhat elevated land on the contrary side of the plain.

The trout in the Dhoo are dark coloured, and not nearly so handsome as those in the Glass, and this is accounted for by the peaty nature of the soil through which the Dhoo flows, and from the bogs wherein it rises. In order to fish the Dhoo, the angler should commence at Braddan Bridge and fish up. Between the bridge and the Union Mills there are some good streams and rather deep pools, and should the water be of fair volume, and the fish on, the sport will be good, and he will kill some good fish. There is a good chance of a few half-pound trout, and some chance of even larger fish.

The Union Mills are about a mile above Braddan Bridge. For a short distance above the Union Mills the river is not of much use, as most of the water is taken by the mill-race. Thence to beyond Crosby Station, about two miles, there is some good fishing when there is a good volume of water in the stream. It is advisable to fish with strong tackle, as the river Dhoo, unlike most other Manx streams, is very weedy, and the safest plan frequently is to yank the trout on to the bank at once. The banks of the stream are high in most places, so when the water is low it is difficult to keep out of sight of the trout. It is a much better stream for worm-fishing than for fly-fishing.

I well remember the two best days I ever had in the Dhoo. It was about the end of August or the beginning of September 1872. The rainfall in that year was excessive—the wettest year which I ever recorded. On the first day, I commenced above Braddan Bridge about half-past nine o'clock. The water was of fine volume, but quite clear. I fished with worm up to Union Mills until about twelve o'clock, when I went to Glenlough for lunch, at which time I had 25 trout.

About two o'clock I went out above Union Mills and fished until about half-past five, and creeled exactly 25 more, making 50 for the day. I remained all night at Glenlough.

On the following day, as I was going to return to Douglas, I commenced to fish on the Glenlough estate, and fished down to Braddan Bridge. In climbing up a rather high bank out of the river near the bridge, I fell backwards into the river with such a splash that my head even went under water, and I had to walk to Douglas in a miserable plight. On turning out my basket I counted exactly 50 trout, making 100 for the two days. For the Isle of Man, they were remarkably fine trout, many being herring-sized fish and several more than half a pound. I have never since fished the Dhoo under such favourable conditions. They were all caught with the worm.

We will now ramble up the river Glass. The Glass is in all respects different from the Dhoo. While the Dhoo has a narrow confined bed with high banks, very much resembling a big ditch, the Glass has a broad stony bed with plenty of shore when the water is low, and there are alternately high and low banks so that the angler can always fish from a low shore. It is much more easy to capture trout in the Glass than in the Dhoo. From the confluence of the two rivers to the junction of the East and West Baldwin Streams the Glass is much diverted by mill-dams, the consequence being that much of the bed of the river is in dry seasons almost dried up, therefore the nature of the fishing is not generally so good as it is above the junction.

Proceeding from the Quarter Bridge up the river we go along Port-a-Chee meadow, and soon reach the village of Tromode, where there is a sail-cloth manufactory, in the neighbourhood of which there are some fine deep pools in which there are some good trout, and these pools are very favourable for fly-fishing. About a mile farther, passing through gorsy claddahs, we come to St. George's Bridge, a short distance above which there is a weir, and at the foot a deep pool in which a good trout may sometimes be caught. There is no doubt that sea-trout sometimes get above this weir, as I once caught one in the pool formed by the weir. It happened on this wise.

It was in the month of October 1861. There was a fresh in the river. My friend Ambrose and I had fished with the worm as far as West Baldwin. Towards the end of the day, as we were proceeding down the river homewards, the water began to clear, so I fished the pools down with fly. After getting several rises from good fish, to my surprise I hooked a good fish apparently of about 2 lb. in weight. He fought hard, but after about ten minutes of exciting play I drew him in on a shelving gravel bed and secured him. He was a beautiful fresh-run sea-trout, and weighed 1 lb. 10 oz. He had taken my tail fly, which was made as follows : wing, starling quill; legs, black hackle; body, blue silk ribbed with silver tinsel,—a home-made fly which I called a blue-bottle. It was the largest fish I had ever caught. Mr. Arthur of Port-a-Chee, a veteran angler, was at my father's house on my arrival. Before I exhibited the contents of my basket he said, "I'll be bound that I have caught a bigger trout than you have to-day, Harry."

"I'll be bound that you have not," I replied, and I triumphantly produced the trout.

He said, "You've just beaten me; I've caught one which weighed 1 lb. 6 oz."

He caught his fish more than a mile farther down the river. A worthy man was Mr. Arthur. At that time he occupied Port-a-Chee farm, and preserved a nice stretch of the river, and he was very jealous of any one invading his rights, but he had given me leave to fish as much as I liked.

One day I was at it hauling out the trout, when I heard tremendous roars behind me. I turned round and saw Mr. Arthur, and coolly went on fishing. "Ah, he thinks he has caught a poacher!" thought I. The air resounded with highly seasoned language, and he advanced gesticulating wildly, brandishing a walking-stick. When he saw who it was he laughed and watched me fish, and he gave me a novel lesson in fly-fishing. I missed several trout in succession, and he said I was too sharp with them, that I did not give enough time for them to fasten on the hook. Innocent old Arthur. I have ever thought that being too slow is my fault. The old gentleman insisted on my taking tea with him, and we discussed the whole subject of fly-fishing for trout. He was dead against the worm, as he considered it unsportsmanlike.

A few hundred yards above the pool wherein I caught the sea-trout there is another weir, below which there is also a good pool, and in this pool there is always a chance of a nice fish or two with the fly. Above the weir there is an excellent stream which flows by the side of a plantation, a very good hold for trout, and into this stream there runs a mill-race, or rather mill-tail. We now arrive at the junction of the East and West Baldwin Streams, at which there is a good pool. Hereabouts a stone bridge conducts the road up the East Baldwin valley.

We will first walk up the East Baldwin Stream. For some two miles or so the bed of the stream is gravelly and stony, and the stream forms a happy combination of pool and stream. The vale is sweetly pretty, fairly well wooded, with plenty of the—in Mona—ever-abundant gorse and bramble, intermixed with honeysuckle, here and there wild roses. At the head of the dale there is Beinn-y-Phott with his green slopes and cone-like summit surmounted by a cairn. The mountain looks quite imposing from the vale. As we approach the mountain, the bed of the stream becomes rocky, and there are several cascades, and hereabouts there are some good trout. From the junction of the stream to the source is almost too much for one day's fishing, and especially so if there be a good water. In a nice water the fly may be used with success, but when the water is low and clear recourse must be had to the up-stream worm.

We will now take a walk up West Baldwin Stream, which is rather larger than the other stream. Near the bottom of the stream on the left are a mill and miller's cottage, and as most of the water goes into the mill-race, we must before beginning to fish walk about two hundred yards or so through a meadow, or should the grass be long, make a slight detour on the left and walk on the banks of the mill-race, at the head of which we come to a shallow dam, below which there is rather a deep pool which may be fished with success when there is a fair flow of water over the weir. The stream is somewhat more winding than the East Baldwin Stream. To the left there are gorsy braes, and in front up the river we have a view of Garraghan Mountain, at the base of which lies lovely Injabreck with its fir plantations.

The stream is a nice combination of pool and stream: at a distance of about three-quarters of a mile we reach the picturesque little village of West Baldwin. Here there was in former days a little public-house of old-fashioned Manx type, where good bottled Bass could be obtained by the thirsty angler, kept by one M'Clure, who probably in his day accounted for as many woodcock as any other man on the island, for the glen is famous for woodcock when snow lies on the mountains. At this little village a small stream from the slopes of Greeba and Colden Mountains joins the main stream, and on the banks and braes of this little stream many a cock fell to M'Clure's gun, for he was wont to say that there was no place about like it for the long bills, snipe also in the bogs. What a charming combination of words—cock, snipe, trout!

Should the angler have commenced at St. George's Bridge, he ought to have had about enough of it, but if not, he may wander on, and after passing through a green meadow above the tiny bridge across the river the nature of the stream changes for about half a mile, and it becomes rocky with frequent deep pools and cascades overhung by trees; then the stream resumes its gravelly nature, and in a mile or so, passing through lovely scenery, we arrive at Injabreck Bridge, and hereabouts the stream diverges. The lover of ferns may wander about and gather ferns of several kinds, maidenhair, heart's-tongue, and other kinds to his heart's content; and he may rest under the cool shade of the trees, and be alone with nature, listening to the music of the stream as it ripples over the stones, and the song of the birds. He may hear the raven's croak as he passes overhead, or he may watch the sparrow-hawk hovering over his prey, and in the early summer he may hear the cuckoo's song all the day long, for the cuckoo delights in this secluded vale; and as the shades of evening fall the crake, crake, crake of the landrail in the

long grass, and if he lingers long enough he may watch the
bats flitting under the trees, and the heron flapping to his
evening meal.

The heron is not at all an uncommon object in the Isle of
Man. There are not any heronries; the birds appear to nest
among the rushes in secluded places. Sandpipers, wagtails,
and the fly-catchers are common objects by the streams.
Kingfishers are rare. The hooded crow is common, and
nests either among the rocks or in trees. The sparrow-hawk
and the kestrel are also common, which may be accounted for
by the almost total absence of the gentlemen in plush. Many
times have I fished both the East and West Baldwin Streams,
but my first record was in 1873, when I fished in company
with my brother Charlie. It was on the 1st of September.
It came on to rain in the afternoon, and the trout took like
mad, and we left off with the fish taking. Charlie caught 55,
and I 47. Charlie was a boy for the worm; he did not
believe in the fly, and it was hard to make him leave the
river. At one time I confined myself to the fly, and I used
to consider about 30 a day fair sport with the fly. With
worm it was easy to catch from 40 to 50; it was simply a
question as to how long one cared to fish. I generally began
from about nine to ten o'clock, and as a rule the trout went
off the feed about two o'clock, and few were caught after the
latter hour. My best day in the East Baldwin Stream was 50
trout caught with the worm on the 30th of May 1878, and on
the 2nd of July in the same year I caught with the worm in
the West Baldwin Stream 52 trout. Between 1878 and 1891
inclusive I had seven days' fishing in the East and West Baldwin
Streams, and killed 268 trout.

I had my best day in West Baldwin with the fly on the

4th of September 1891, when I killed 58 trout. There had been a thunderstorm during the previous night. I commenced fishing at St. George's Bridge about ten o'clock. The weather was lovely, alternate cloud and sunshine; the water was big, but quite clear. The trout took keenly until about two o'clock, when they began to slacken, and I ceased fishing at four o'clock at West Baldwin village. The killing flies in order of merit were yellow partridge, yellow snipe, and blue dun, all hackled, and I fished with a hair cast, and up stream. This day's sport shows what may be done in the little Manx streams with the fly when the water is in good order. I fished frequently in the Baldwin streams for many years before 1878, but did not keep any record of the captures save in a very few instances.

CHAPTER XXXI

THE RIVER NEB

And the fair isle shines in beauty,
As in youth it dawned on me,
My own dear Ellan Vannin,
And its green hills by the sea.
Ellan Vannin, by Mrs. E. C. GREEN.

AFTER the Sulby and the Douglas rivers, the river Neb may be classed as the next in importance from a piscatorial point of view, but this is a matter which may be taken exception to by some. If the Foxdale branch of the river were unpolluted, I should be inclined to give the Neb the first rank among the insular rivers; but, alas, the Foxdale branch is so much polluted by the operations at the Foxdale lead-mines that nothing will live in the river from Foxdale to Peel harbour, the consequence being that the only fishing is in the Rhenass branch of the river Neb, which joins the Foxdale Stream about half a mile from St. Johns Station. The best plan is to proceed from St. Johns to the bridge across the river on the Peel road, only a few hundred yards' walk, thence to the junction and fish up to Swiss Cottage, now a hotel, a distance of about three miles, which is quite sufficient for one day, and in that length the angler will generally have no difficulty in creeling from thirty to forty trout with worm or fly, according to the condition of the water. Should the water be in fair volume, the fly will be successful; if low, the deadly up-stream worm. The scenery may fairly be described as beautiful. Below the bridge the vale is open, steep Slieu Whallin to the south, Greeba and Colden Mountains to the east, and Peel

GLEN HELEN.

Hill with its Folly to the west. Above the bridge the valley narrows, and the banks of the river are gorsy.

Near the pretty grounds of Glen Moore, the residence of Mr. Mathews, a mill-race joins the river, a short distance above which there is a deep pool under a high bank on one side, which is a good place for fine trout. In about half a mile we come to Moore's Mill, and above the mill the best fishing commences; thence until the top of Rhenass Waterfall is reached the vale is very narrow with steep sides, in some places planted, in others the gorse and bramble luxuriate. The missel-thrush rejoices in this vale, and the nest is common, also the nest of the magpie, usually built near the top of a tall thin ash tree so slender that no boy dare venture up. About the upper end of Cronkykilly woods there is a pool under a shelving rock, where there is almost certain to be a particularly fine trout on the look-out, but I have always been unlucky there. I get a great tug and he is off.

Proceeding up the vale we come to an old picturesque corn-mill, Quine's Mill. This part of the vale is called Glen Mooar, the word Mooar signifying in Manx "big." A short distance above the mill there is a high weir, and beneath the weir a deep pool which is good for the fly on a windy day. Above the weir there is some very nice fishing, and especially in the neighbourhood of the suspension bridge across the river, which the angler should direct particular attention to. This may conclude the day's sport.

In order to fish in Glen Helen it is necessary to obtain permission at the entrance gates. The fishing is very difficult in consequence of trees, rocks, and huge boulder-stones. Glen Helen is considered to be the prettiest of Mona's glens. The right-hand side of the glen is well wooded, and the other contains a blend of trees, gorse, and heather. From the road which leads direct to the waterfall, beautiful peeps of the river are obtained through breaks in the foliage, as it rushes and bounds over its rocky course, with numerous cascades, and at their foot deep rocky pools in which the water looks blue under the blue sky. The roar of the waterfall can be heard at a considerable distance.

The water-worn rocks are a study, and make the observer

speculate as to what length of time has elapsed since the waterfall was twice as high as it is now, and what length of time will elapse until the rocks will be so much worn that there will be no waterfall. After we admire the waterfall, a winding walk ascending on the left through a larch plantation conducts us to a fence which forms the boundary of the Glen Helen estate. Hereabouts there are two more falls with deep pools, but the scenery is quite changed. The valley is much more open and comparatively free from timber. The air becomes more bracing after the confined glen below, and the region partakes of a mountainous character; we are amid gorse, heather, and bracken. Here one feels the solitude intense, particularly during the season when the glen swarms with tourists, who dance to the music of a brass band. Would that the dancing-platform, band-stands, pagodas, and so-called rustic bridges could be swept away, and the glen restored to its sweet simplicity of forty years ago, when the contemplative man could feel alone with nature in the lovely glen undisturbed by the strains of a band and the noise of the whirling crowds.

And now a word of warning to the angler during the tourist season. Let him so arrange his day's fishing as to be out of the glen by twelve o'clock. After that hour tourists swarm like locusts; some jeer at him and throw stones into the river, and ask if he has seen that big fish jump; others beg him to try and catch that big fish which they have just seen in a pool. He will be safe either above the waterfall or below the hotel. The angler should commence at the bottom of the glen about nine o'clock and fish up to the waterfall, and he may expect to capture about thirty as pretty trout as any in Mona, but he must be prepared for hard work, and know how to switch under trees and avoid getting hung up in the maze of trees and undergrowth on all sides of him.

The last time I fished the glen was on the 27th of May 1878 (alas, how time flies !) when I captured thirty-six trout, the largest of which weighed ten ounces, and a game fish he was, and I really had enough of it. It is a charming place for a boy to roll about in, but when a man has put on weight, oh dear ! oh dear !

I daresay that I am not the only reader of angling works which treat of fishing excursions, who has searched in vain in some works for the result of the fishing ; what sport the author has really had ; whether he has had good sport or not. He describes the beauties of nature, the birds he sees, the flowers, the gambols of the water-rat, and the other common sights by the river-side ; he gives charming extracts from our Father Izaak, and contrives to conceal the results of his excursion from a piscatorial point of view. Now I think that the angling author should tell his readers what he has done in the streams he describes, not merely what has been done or may be done by other anglers. I therefore give my readers the results of my fishing excursions, and they can then judge whether the game is worth the candle or not. Were I silent as to the results, they would be no wiser than they were when they commenced to wade through my meanderings.

My best recorded day in Glen Mooar was on the 7th of August 1880, in company with my friend Joe, when I caught fifty-two trout—thirty with worm and twenty-two with fly. What a jolly day we had ! We began at half-past nine o'clock above Moore's Mill. From about twelve to four o'clock heavy rain fell. After fishing up to Glen Helen Hotel we skipped Glen Helen and passed above the waterfall. The water was coming down thick, and as we did not find the fish on, we retraced our steps, and got on the feed ourselves at the hotel; and what a feed we had!—roast lamb and some more good things, and some really good claret. I do not remember how long we wasted at the hotel, but when we resumed fishing the real sport of the day began. I located myself at the beautiful half run and half pool just above Quine's Dam, and fished with the fly. The water was a little discoloured and the trout were on and no mistake. I threw by the side of a wall on the opposite side and hauled out trout after trout in quick succession. There appeared to be no end of them, and any fly would do. On the way down I tried the pool under the shelving rock, as I knew the big one was there—he had given me the usual big tug in the morning. But no, he was otherwise engaged. It was not to be. Shall I ever get that big trout? I have had a big tug in that place for thirty years and that is all.

The best day which I have had with the fly only was on the 27th of September 1891, when I killed 43 trout. I commenced at Moore's Mill at ten o'clock and fished up to the suspension bridge, where I wound up at three o'clock quite satisfied with my take. There was a good clear water and the trout rose well. The killing flies were orange partridge, blue dun, and yellow dun, all hackled, and I fished with a hair cast.

On the 27th of August in the same year, I commenced fishing at Ballaleece Bridge near St. Johns, at ten o'clock, and wound up at Cronkykilly a little after three with 42 trout, 25 of which were caught with fly and 17 with worm. It rained nearly all the time I was out, and I only put on the worm when the water became too thick for fly. I have only fished on five days in the Neb since, and including the year 1878, the result being 198 trout, 104 of which were captured with worm and 94 with fly.

We will now bid farewell to the bonny Neb, and live in hopes that all the lead in the Foxdale hills will ere long be exhausted, or that the Foxdale Mining Company will mend their ways, and do unto others as they would that others should do unto them; and in conclusion it may be stated that the poisonous water pumped from the mine, and the polluted water from the washing-floors, might easily be conducted to the sea in pipes. What an enormous advantage it would be to Peel, which is now situated at the mouth of a mining sewer, and the riparian proprietors, if the Neb could be restored to its pristine purity! Cattle might again drink of its pure waters, which would once more abound with the salmon and the trout.

CHAPTER XXXII

THE LHEN AND OTHER STREAMS

Some came across the mountain side,
Some many weary miles,
O'er hills and lowland marshy fields,
O'er hedges, gates, and stiles.
Oiel Verree, by WILLIAM KENNISH, R.N.

THE river Lhen is little known to most anglers who fish in the streams of Mona, and it is not easy of access, being about six miles distant from a railway station. This little river rises in the neighbourhood of Ballaugh, and after a course of about four fishable miles falls into the sea near Blue Point. It is very sluggish and very weedy, and not favourable for the minnow or artificial fly; the worm is the most practicable lure, and the only way to fish is to cast the worm between the weeds. The trout are not numerous, but this is compensated for by their good size, which averages about three-quarters of a pound. The banks are rather high, and to a considerable extent flanked with bogs good for snipe.

Consequent on a pressing invitation from Mr. Bernard Brooke of Andreas, who has a farm on the banks of the river, my brother Charlie and I decided to fish the Lhen in the month of June 1896. We chartered a jaunting car in Ramsey, and drove to the river, which we struck at a point about two miles from the sea. We had a beautiful drive. The earth-banks were clothed with honeysuckle, wild roses, and other wild flowers. Some places were blue with forget-me-nots. The *Osmunda regalis* flourishes in the bogs. The country is slightly undulating, and as we drive along there is a magnificent view of Snaefell, North Barrule, and the neighbouring mountains. In the far distance across the sea we see the Cumbrian Mountains, the Mull of Galloway, and the mountains of Mourne. We pass Andreas Church with its peculiar high tower, and wonder who is responsible for its architecture. It somewhat resembles a mill chimney which had been made unusually wide in order to appear unlike a chimney. This is the sanctuary of the Archdeacon of Man, who is rector of Andreas and an *ex-officio* member of the Council of the island, which answers to the British House of Lords, with this difference, that the members of the Council are not hereditary, but are members by virtue of their offices.

We commenced operations about four o'clock in the afternoon, but the fish were not in a taking humour. However, in about half an hour Charlie sang out that he had a bite, then he shouted that he was on and then off, worse luck. A consultation ensued, and I advised Charlie to give him plenty of time should the fish come a third time, which to our surprise he did, and he was well hooked. Then began the tug of war. Our one landing-net was very short, so I took the rod and Charlie scrambled over the wire-fencing with the net to be ready. The fish had got into a mass of weeds, but a gradual pressure brought him slowly out, and Charlie managed to net him, a plump trout of fifteen ounces. I only caught two miserable eels, and at half-past five we wended our way to Mr. Brooke's house, where we had tea.

Mr. Brooke said that the best time to fish was about dusk, and that the Lhen trout would not take red worms, but only white. Charlie had caught his trout with a red worm. We all went out to fish after tea. Miss Florence Brooke, our host's sister, a young lady who delights in taking a rise out of an unfortunate fisherman, warned me that I should not catch a trout in the Lhen because I had caught two eels; but that if I rubbed my hook and cast on the dead trout, the spell might be removed. In the end we all rubbed our hooks and gut on the dead trout for luck and began fishing. Alas, the spell was not removed; I had not a bite. The others were in luck. Charlie grassed two more fish of ten and five ounces respectively, and our host three of the respective weights of fifteen, twelve, and ten ounces. All Charlie's trout were caught with the red worm, and Mr. Brooke's with the white worm. Then over our pipes we discussed the weight of the Lhen trout, and it transpired that Mr. Kelly of Abbeyville had captured the largest recorded trout in the Lhen—which scaled two pounds and thirteen ounces—a few years since. A record kept by Mr. Bernard Brooke shows that the average weight is about ten ounces.

The *modus operandi* is to fish with strong sea-trout gut, so that the trout may be dragged out of the weeds and hauled on to the bank. The Isle of Man Fishery Board had in their wisdom turned into the Lhen 800 trout-fry—what a feed for the big trout! what chance can there be for even one little one to grow to maturity? so thought we all.

But it is time for us to be off, so with a good-night to our good friend Mr. Brooke, who pressed us to have another try

PORT ST. MARY.

soon, we get into our jaunting car and bowl over the road to Ramsey. We had often heard of the big trout of the Lhen, and were well pleased to have had an opportunity of proving the report to be true, and that some good trout may be caught in the little kingdom of Man, if one will only take the trouble to go to the Lhen.

SOME OTHER STREAMS OF MONA

I will not attempt to particularise all the streams of Mona in which trout may be captured; there are numerous little rills, which may be stepped across, where it is necessary to poke the worm in between the grass and brambles as best the angler can. I will content myself and the reader with describing a few streams, as nearly as may be in order of merit.

Silver Burn

This little river, which rises in the slopes of South Barrule (1585 feet) and falls into the sea at Castletown after a run of about five miles, is honoured with the pen of Sir Walter Scott in his *Peveril of the Peak*. How beautifully he leads young Peveril to one of those beautiful streams that descend to the sea from the Kirk Merlagh Mountains. Sir Walter refers to Kirk Malew, which will ever be associated with the name of an eloquent Manx vicar, the Rev. William Gill, who was celebrated as a preacher of no ordinary merit. One wonders how such a man escaped being a bishop.

But young Peveril is not keen on the trout.

> It was maiden fair
> That lured him there.

x

"He chose, indeed," wrote Sir Walter, "with an angler's eye, the most promising casts, where the stream broke sparkling over a stone, affording the wonted shelter to a trout; or where, gliding away from a rippling current to a still eddy, it streamed under the projecting bank, or dashed from the pool of some low cascade." How true to nature the great Sir Walter wrote; only an angler could write thus. He then guides us to Rushen Abbey, the ruins of which still remain. Hereabouts the Rushen Abbey Hotel stands. The stream passes through the grounds, and here the contemplative man may well locate himself amid beautiful scenery, with the somewhat cone-like summit of South Barrule forming a background of heathery mountain with Cronk-ny-Irey-Lhaa on the left. Ballasalla Station is near by.

From Castletown to the Abbey Bridge the country is flat and the ground open. In this portion of the river sea-trout may be caught in the spring and autumn. A short distance above the Abbey Bridge two streams unite, Silver Burn diverging to the left and Awin Ruy to the right to St. Mark's. These streams are typical Manx glens, more or less encumbered with wood and bushes, forming charming solitudes. When there is a fair flow of water fly may be used with advantage, but when the waters are low, as the wandering angler generally finds them, recourse must be had to the up-stream worm.

I fished lovely Silver Burn on the 31st of May 1881 for the first time, when I commenced at Castletown and fished up to Rushen Abbey. The water was dead low and the sun so bright, but between ten and one o'clock I killed twenty-six trout, two of which weighed a quarter of a pound each, and the rest about two ounces. On the same day Robert fished the higher portion of Silver Burn with what he called fly—a scrap of worm being attached to the ordinary fly—and killed about fifty trout, but he made a regular day of it.

I did not fish Silver Burn again until the month of August 1897. I had taken up my quarters with some of my olive-branches, including Bertie, an amateur photographer, at the charming little watering-place of Port St. Mary, a little fishing village on the south coast of Mona's Isle. The mountains of

South Barrule and Cronk-ny-Irey-Lhaa form a rather imposing background, the intervening country being slightly undulating, and partly agricultural and partly pastoral, with plantations here and there. About five miles eastward the ancient castle of Rushen frowns over the fair landscape.

I decided to try Silver Burn above Rushen Abbey. I halted at the Friars Bridge to put up my rod. The Friars Bridge is a most interesting structure; there are two pointed arches, and the bridge was clearly erected for a bridle or pack-horse road. A few yards above the bridge there is a high weir, with a rather deep pool below. The water was very low, and no water was passing over the weir, but at the far corner on the right there was a little trickle of running water. No use trying here with the worm, thought I, but angler-like I take a survey of the pool. Ha! what is that in the trickle in the far corner?—a grand trout and no mistake, of at least ten ounces! It must be a neat cast to lure such a trout in such a tiny trickle. The worm is impelled at the first cast just above the trout, a rush, and *habet;* but, alas, after a little play the hold gave way, and the monarch of the pool was free. Fool, why did you strike so soon? Up I sped, casting the worm wherever practicable, and catching a trout now and then, but it was difficult work getting the worm in under the branches. I wondered if young Peveril wandered so far up the glen, and succeeded in throwing a fly under the hanging branches.

After struggling amid trees for about half a mile I reach a corn-mill with a considerable mill-dam in the middle of which there is a wooded island, then along a gorsy meadow, and I pass under a bridge into a dark plantation in which there are some good pools. A short distance above is a mill in ruins, the mill-race broken down, and all the water flowing over a high weir into a deep pool below. Shortly above this the trees cease, and I am in a regular gill with steep sides clothed with gorse and bramble, the stream forming numerous cascades with deep pools below. The dark cone-like summit of South Barrule appears to guard the secluded glen. The solitude can be felt. The ruined mill below increases the feeling of solitude, as though nature had determined to resume her sway.

I retrace my steps, and as I pass the Friars Pool I see my

friend of the morning in his old position. I ought to try him with a fly, thought I, but I had not much time to catch the train at Ballasalla Station, so I sped my worm as before, but *non habet*; with insulted dignity he swam down and retired under a stone, but his doom was not far distant. Four or five days afterwards I was once more at the Friars Bridge. There had been a little rain and there was a flow of clear water into

the Friars Pool. I soon caught two trout in the low part, and then I attacked the far corner. The line stopped, and I felt that he was on. After a few moments I struck and he was fast, and ere long he was dragged on to the shingle and proved to be a Loch Leven trout of fifteen ounces, the only Loch Leven trout which I ever caught in the Isle of Man. If this little stream were only a little taken care of, and the branches lopped and the many obstructions removed, it would be a charming little river for the artificial fly, but of this subject more anon.

Santon Burn

A short distance north-east of Silver Burn is Santon Burn, which rises in the moorland in the neighbourhood of Granite Mountain and Slieau Chairn, and after a course of about five fishable miles falls into the sea near Cass-ny-Hawin Head. The lower portion near the sea flows through a rocky glen in which there are several cascades with deep pools at their foot, answering well to Sir Walter Scott's description of a Manx glen.

In consequence of the waterfall, which falls down to the sea-shore, the migratory salmonidæ cannot ascend above the shore-pool, but good sport with sea-trout may, when the fates are propitious, be had in this pool; and in the numerous pools above the waterfall good sport may be obtained with fly or worm, and a few really good trout may fairly be expected. Above Santon Bridge the country is open and the stream is easy to fish, but to ensure good sport the water must not be low. It is a great many years since I first fished in Santon Burn, and I do not remember how we got to Santon Bridge, where we began the day's sport, but we fished all the fishable water and then crossed the bogs in the neighbourhood of Slieau Chairn and walked to Onchan village. The water was in good order and I creeled between forty and fifty trout.

The Colby River

As this little river is only about three miles west of Silver Burn it is convenient to mention it here. Colby Station is close to the river, and about a mile and a half from the sea. The greater portion of the river flows through the Kentraugh estate, which belongs to an old Manx family of the name of Gawne. A Gawne of long ago appears to have taken great interest in the cultivation of trout, evidenced by a series of fish-ponds which extend for about a mile from the sea. The fish-ponds have been constructed by placing numerous weirs across the river. Above Colby village we come to a romantic wooded glen, at the upper end of which there is an interesting waterfall. The glen is much favoured by picnic parties. The Gawne family preserve the river up to the head of the glen,

so the angler should commence to fish above that point, and he may fish for two or three miles to the slopes of Cronk-ny-Irey-Lhaa, and then retrace his steps to Colby Station by road. I have only fished this little river on two occasions, and on each I killed about forty trout with the up-stream worm.

Glen Meay River

Glen Meay is the most remarkable of Mona's glens. Between the waterfall and the sea the river flows through a rocky glen, the sides of which are several hundred feet high and present what may truly be called a grand appearance, and the sides are mostly inaccessible. The waterfall, with the rocky glen and wooded surroundings, is one of the sights of

COLBY FALLS.

Mona. Above the waterfall there are Glen Rushen and Glen Dhoo, which are well worthy of exploration.

Until some ten years or so ago the river below Glen Rushen mines was so polluted with lead-washings that nothing could live in the waters, but thanks to the decline of the mining industry, the waters once more abound with trout, and below the waterfall good sport may be had with sea-trout in their season. As Glen Meay is at least four miles from a railway station, in order to enjoy the fishing and explore the glens, rocks, and caves in the neighbourhood, the angler cannot do better than take up his quarters at the Dalby Boarding House, where indeed he may appreciate the charms of solitude.

Glen Mooar and Glen Wyllin, Kirk Michael.

Within easy distance from Kirk Michael Station on the Manx Northern Railway are these two glens, which are very beautiful and abound with trout. Spooyt Vain, a waterfall in the latter glen, is, when in spate, well worthy of a visit, apart from the trout fishing; but the worm must be relied upon as the lure, and two days suffice to test the two streams.

Glen Dhoo, Ballaugh

Glen Dhoo rises amid the mountains of Slieau Dhoo and Slieau Chairn, and Glen Dhoo is one of Mona's most charming glens. From a piscatory point of view it suffers in periods of dry weather to a great extent, as the bed is in many places quite dried up, and one wonders how any trout survive.

The Cornah River

The Cornah river takes its source between the mountains of North Barrule and Clagh Owyre, and after a course of about five miles falls into the sea at Port Cornah. This is one of the most secluded parts of the Isle of Man and somewhat difficult of access, as it is about equidistant from Ramsey and Laxey. The lower portions of the river are good for sea-trout—the best in the island, it is said. The banks of the stream are well wooded, in fact often too much so for the angler's comfort. Ballaglass Waterfall and Glen delight the eye of the angler. The most convenient plan is to drive from Ramsey to Port Cornah, and fish up to where the Douglas and Ramsey road crosses the stream, whence the distance to Ramsey is only about four miles, or the angler may proceed by the electric tramway from Douglas to Laxey, and thence drive to where the road crosses the river.

Glen Roy, Laxey

The electric tramway makes this romantic glen easily accessible. Glen Roy has been described as the Switzerland of Manxland. There is one drawback. Salmon and sea-trout cannot ascend from the sea because of the pollutions of the Laxey Mining Company. Below the washing-floors the water looks like milk, but fortunately they are not far from the sea. In Glen Roy trout are numerous, and the angler may reasonably expect thirty or forty trout as the result of a day's fishing. He may commence in the lower reaches with fly if the water be in order, and as the casting of the fly becomes difficult, owing to the various obstructions, he may put on the deadly worm and fish to the head of the glen, and at the end of his day tramp it to Douglas, should he be so inclined.

THE ISLE OF MAN FRESH-WATER FISHERY ACT

As has before been mentioned, the rivers in the Isle of Man are under the control of a Board of Conservators, and ample time has elapsed to form a judgment as to whether the Fishery Act has had a beneficial effect on the insular freshwater fisheries. Season licences cost 10s. 6d., monthly 5s., and weekly 2s. 6d. The licence is entitled "Licence to kill Salmon and other Fish." The season for salmon is from 9th February to 31st October (both days inclusive), and for trout from 1st March to 31st October; and by By-law No. 4 "No fish shall be killed smaller than five inches in length over all." As the word "fish" is used, it appears clear on the face of the licence that the young of salmon and sea-trout only five inches in length may be killed. These little fish average one ounce in weight.

In my judgment this by-law is calculated to do more harm than if there were no regulation with regard to the size of fish killed. In the absence of any such regulation many anglers would pause before killing a five-inch trout or samlet; but fortified by the regulation, the little fish is without compunction consigned to the creel, and helps to increase the number of dozens at the end of the day's sport.

The Board of Conservators from time to time place yearling trout in the streams, with a view, it may be presumed, of improving the breed of Manx trout; but it appears to be absurd to do this, and authorise the destruction of trout of only an ounce in weight. The better plan would appear to me to let the little trout grow larger, and save the expense of yearling trout. Most of the streams are very favourable for trout in their spawning operations. Tiny runners in which trout may spawn are numerous; nature has provided bountifully for the production of trout. It would appear to be the first duty of a Board of Conservators to employ a sufficient number of watchers to enforce the Act of

Tynwald. So far as I am aware, Mr. Andrew Caley, the Fishery Inspector, is the only person to watch the insular rivers—what can one man do in such an area?

The result is that, so far as the preservation of the rivers is concerned, matters are as they were before the passing of the Act of Tynwald. In my judgment, trout fishing has not improved; the angler pays the tax and does not derive any material benefit. Probably many fish without a licence, knowing that the chance of detection is very remote. What the Isle of Man requires is a strong Angling Association. True, there is an association in Douglas, but it has no fishing rights; it appears to subsist for good fellowship, and for the promotion of the destruction of fish by offering prizes for that purpose.

Although the Board of Conservators are said to have £500 in hand, no steps are taken to restrain the pollution of rivers. So far as can be judged from the state of the river Neb, the Foxdale Mining Company do not even attempt to "settle" the lead-ore washings by means of subsidence. If the Board of Conservators would apply their surplus fund towards the expense of conducting the foul water to the sea in pipes, they would confer a boon on anglers in general and the riparian proprietors in particular; or they might expend their surplus money in lopping trees, removing obstructions, and constructing weirs for the improvement of the rivers where such weirs might be beneficial. But until the resident Manx anglers bestir themselves, the Isle of Man river fisheries will not materially improve; mere legislation cannot effect anything.

AVERAGE WEIGHT OF TROUT IN THE ISLAND

As may be expected from the low standard of a takable trout in the Isle of Man, the general average is small, for the average depends upon the standard. As the trout which I have killed during the last twenty years graduated from 17 oz. to 1 oz., the mean of the extremes would show an average of 8 oz., just in the same manner as the winter mean temperature of a place may be 37 degrees, although there are days when the mean temperature of a winter's day stands at 15 degrees. But as my veracity as an angler is at any rate quite as dear to me as was that of the late Mr. Joseph Billings to him, I cannot let the matter rest here. I daresay that we most of us know very well that if we particularly impress our veracity on people they never will believe our assertions, but if we tell them a right-down thumper they will swallow it; but we must not do it with solemnity, as if we meant it. The result of twenty years' fishing has been 1327 trout, 483 of which were caught with fly and 844 with worm.

The following table shows the order of merit of the Manx streams with regard to the size of trout so far as my experience has been.

	Trout.	lb.	oz.
1. The Dhoo . . .	252	37	5
2. Silver Burn . . .	74	10	1
3. The Sulby River . .	535	65	6
4. The Neb	198	22	7
5. The Glass, East and West Baldwin.	268	28	0
	1327	163	3

With others I have sinned in killing the little five-inch trout. Let us all mend our ways and urge on the legislators of Man to protect the little ones, and so increase the standard of the bonny trout of Mona.

CHAPTER XXXIII

THE DRY FLY

O sir, this is a war where you sometimes win, and must sometime expect to lose.—*Piscator* (COTTON).

SINCE the preceding chapters were written I have read two very interesting works to anglers: *The Book of the Dry Fly*, by Mr. Dewar, and *Angling Holidays*, by Mr. Gedney. It is only within comparatively recent years that the terms "dry-fly fishing" and "wet-fly fishing" have been adopted; and the dry-fly purist or specialist has arrogated to himself a superior position, as though fishing with the dry or surface-floating fly were quite a modern accomplishment, and not probably as old as the art of fly-fishing itself. Like the so-called wet fly, the dry fly is fished either up or down stream, according to the direction of the wind; but when the dry-fly purist fishes down stream, he styles the operation as drifting the fly down over the rising trout. Walton and Cotton did likewise; they turned their back on the wind.

That Walton appreciated the dry or floating fly is proved by his instruction, which I quote: "And when you fish with a fly, if it be possible, let no part of your line touch the water, but your fly only, and be still moving your fly upon the water"—not "in" but "upon" the water. Cotton instructs us how a floating fly should be made, thus: "Leave the wings of an equal length, your fly will never else swim true." By the word "swim" he clearly meant "float," for a thing without life could not swim.

Walton and Cotton used only one fly at a time; the dry-fly purist follows their example. The first Lord Lytton wrote *Eugene Aram* more than sixty years ago, and the passage which I quote conclusively proves that he, Lord Lytton, was intimately acquainted with the mysteries of the dry or floating fly. Writing of the violet fly, which is probably identical with the iron-blue dun: "Now it floated like an unconscious beauty carelessly with the tide." Then the violet fly is changed for the yellow dun—"Softly dropped the yellow dun and swiftly did it glide before the gaze of the latent trout; the yellow dun sails away in affected indifference."

Mr. Dewar quotes freely from *Colonel Hawker's Diary*, and he assumes that presumably because the Colonel fished with two flies, the yellow dun and a red palmer, he did not fish with a floating fly. I have read *Colonel Hawker's Diary*, and I submit that there is not any evidence one way or the other to show whether he dried his fly or not. As the Colonel was an accomplished fisherman, and as Mr. Dewar states that the wet fly is almost useless in the Test, I submit that we must come to the conclusion that the Colonel fished with the floating fly when conditions for that mode of fishing were favourable, that is, in fair weather; and that in stormy weather he fished like we all do—as he could; for be it noted, gentle reader, that fishing with the floating fly is admitted to be a fair-weather amusement.

The modern theorist would fain make out that he fishes

with a dry fly, when the real truth is that the fly is only dry on the first cast; afterwards sufficient moisture is taken off to make the fly float; and some oil their fly and still call it a dry one. The only really new thing is the refined distinction which the modern theorist draws between fishing up with the dry fly and fishing up with the wet fly, when the only appreciable difference is, that the dry-fly man has to spend much time in taking sufficient moisture off his fly to enable it to float, which the wet-fly man has not to do. Mr. Dewar would limit the dry fly to certain streams; whereas all anglers of experience admit that under certain conditions the dry fly may be fished with advantage on all rivers, for there are times when flies are floating down and the trout will not touch the sunk fly.

For the benefit of the uninitiated I must protest against Mr. Dewar's assertion that as a rule the wet-fly fisherman's object is to sink his flies as much as possible, and that as a rule he does not look for the rises. From a perusal of the preceding chapters, the reader will appreciate what a wide divergence there is between his views and mine. Both Mr. Dewar and Mr. Gedney arrogate the first place to the dry-fly purist. But what does Mr. Dewar admit? he, an accomplished dry-fly hand, at page 33 of his work appears to admit that he is not equal to fishing rapid streams up with fly. In my chapter on fly-fishing I have endeavoured to instruct the tyro how to feel fish in a rapid stream.

In truth the dry-fly purist has reduced fishing with the fly to a very simple process; he has only to watch for the rises, and cast over the fish either up or down, as the wind or some other element may permit. The wet-fly fisher endeavours to catch fish whether there is any apparent rise or not, and he has to learn by experience where the fish are likely to be found at the various seasons. He may be compared to a man finding game with the assistance of his dog; while the dry-fly man may be compared to a man who has the game driven over him. Speaking generally as to the rivers in the United Kingdom, if a man would kill a good pannier of trout, he must as a rule rely on the so-called wet fly. I know an accomplished angler who often fishes with the dry fly on the Wharfe for amusement, but he says that he can catch many more trout with the wet. He is a gentleman of ample leisure.

In conclusion let me state that I have the greatest respect and admiration for the dry-fly purist and his art, and would not for a moment detract therefrom. It would give me much pleasure to meet some of our brothers of the dry fly on the banks of Wharfe or Eamont and compare notes, and assure them that all honest anglers love one another, whether they be wet or dry, and that if they cannot always agree, they can agree to differ, and be all numbered among the disciples of our common Father Izaak Walton.

MACMILLAN AND CO.'S PUBLICATIONS.

WILD BEASTS AND THEIR WAYS. Reminiscences of Europe, Asia, Africa, and America. By Sir SAMUEL W. BAKER, Pacha, M.A., F.R.S., F.R.G.S. With Illustrations. New and cheaper Edition. Extra Crown 8vo. 12s. 6d.

SPORTING SKETCHES. By DIANE CHASSERESSE. With Illustrations. Crown 8vo. 3s. 6d.

SKETCHES IN SPORT AND NATURAL HISTORY. By the late GEORGE KINGSLEY, M.D. With Memoir by his SON. Extra Crown 8vo. [*In the Press.*

A SKETCH OF THE NATURAL HISTORY OF AUSTRALIA, with some Notes on Sport. By FREDERICK G. AFLALO, F.Z.S., Author of "Sea Fishing on the English Coast," "Hints and Wrinkles on Sea Fishing." Illustrated by F. SETH. Crown 8vo. 6s.

BIRDCRAFT. A Field Book of Two Hundred Song, Game, and Water Birds. By MABEL OSGOOD WRIGHT. With full-page plates containing 128 birds in the natural colours, and other illustrations. Extra Crown 8vo. 12s. 6d. net.

THE YEW TREES OF GREAT BRITAIN AND IRELAND. By JOHN LOWE, M.D. Edin.; Honorary Physician to His Royal Highness the Prince of Wales; Fellow of the Linnean Society; Fellow of the Botanical Society of Edinburgh, etc. etc. Illustrated. 8vo. 10s. net.

GOLF : A Royal and Ancient Game. By ROBERT CLARK, F.R.S.E., F.S.A. Scot. Second Edition, with many Illustrations. Small 4to. 8s. 6d. net.

THE RULES OF GOLF. Being the St. Andrews' Rules for the Game, Codified and Annotated by Sir NORMAN LOCKYER, K.C.B., F.R.S., and W. RUTHERFORD, Barrister-at-Law, Honorary Secretary, St. George's Golf Club. 32mo. 1s. 6d. ; roan, 2s.

THROUGH JUNGLE AND DESERT. Travels in Eastern Africa. By WILLIAM ASTOR CHANLER, A.M. Harv., F.R.G.S., Hon. Member of the Imperial and Royal Geographical Society of Vienna. With Illustrations from photographs taken by the author, and Maps. Royal 8vo. 21s. net.

A SEASON IN SUTHERLAND. By Sir JOHN E. EDWARDS-Moss, Bart. Crown 8vo. Sewed. 1s. 6d.

MACMILLAN AND CO., LTD., LONDON.

MACMILLAN AND CO.'S PUBLICATIONS.

HIGHWAYS AND BYWAYS IN DEVON AND CORNWALL.
By ARTHUR H. NORWAY. With Illustrations by JOSEPH PENNELL and HUGH THOMSON. Fourth Thousand. Extra Crown 8vo. 6s.

DAILY CHRONICLE.—"So delightful that we would gladly fill columns with extracts were space as elastic as imagination. . . . The text is excellent; the illustrations of it are even better."

SPEAKER.—"Mr. Pennell's exquisite drawings re-create for us our country, not indeed more beautiful than it really is, but more beautiful than ninety-nine in a hundred would ever discover without the artist's eye to help them. . . . Many have written books of their itineraries in the West of England, but Mr. Norway's is the most delectable."

PALL MALL GAZETTE.—"As refreshing and exhilerating as a breeze from the moors in a man-stifled town."

NEW BOOK BY MISS MARY KINGSLEY.

WEST AFRICAN STUDIES. By Miss MARY KINGSLEY. With Illustrations. 8vo. [*Immediately.*

TRAVELS IN WEST AFRICA. Congo Française, Corisco, and Cameroons. By MARY H. KINGSLEY. Illustrated. 8vo. 21s. net. Abridged Edition. Extra Crown 8vo. 7s. 6d.

PALL MALL GAZETTE.—"One of the brightest, cleverest, and most entertaining books of travel that has appeared for a very long time."

ON THE BROADS. By ANNA BOWMAN DODD, Author of "Cathedral Days," etc. With Illustrations by JOSEPH PENNELL. Fcap. 4to. 10s. 6d.

TIMES.—"The visitor from across the Atlantic views the scenery of the Broads with sympathetic and appreciative eyes, and her narrative of her cruise is touched with a native humour of her own. Mr. Pennell's illustrations are very charming in themselves, and are instinct alike with the spirit of the district and the temper of the narrative."

THE LONDON PLEASURE GARDENS OF THE EIGHTEENTH AND NINETEENTH CENTURY. By WARWICK WROTH, F.S.A., of the British Museum, assisted by ARTHUR EDGAR WROTH With 62 Illustrations. 8vo. 15s. net.

SPEAKER.—"It is with regret that we part company with a book that has given us so much pleasure and information. We hope it will meet with the success it deserves, and that every lover of Old London and old times and old prints will add it to his library."

OUR VILLAGE. By MARY RUSSELL MITFORD, with an Introduction by ANNE THACKERAY RITCHIE, and 100 Illustrations by HUGH THOMSON. Crown 8vo. 6s. Also with uncut edges, paper label. 6s. [*Cranford Series.*

SATURDAY REVIEW.—"Mr. Thomson's expressive and humorous art has never been employed with happier results than in this beautiful little book."

MACMILLAN AND CO., LTD., LONDON.

www.ingramcontent.com/pod-product-compliance
Lightning Source LLC
Chambersburg PA
CBHW031428230426
43668CB00007B/476